THE
JESUITS

A STORY OF POWER

Alain Woodrow

**GEOFFREY
CHAPMAN**

Geoffrey Chapman
A Cassell imprint
Wellington House, 125 Strand, London WC2R 0BB
387 Park Avenue South, New York, NY 10016-8810

First published 1995

British Library Cataloguing-in-Publication Data
A catalogue record for this book is available from the British Library.

ISBN 0-225-66738-X

Typeset by Action Typesetting Limited, Northgate Street, Gloucester
Printed and bound in Great Britain by Mackays of Chatham, plc.

Contents

PART III A CHURCH WITHIN THE CHURCH?

Acknowledgements

Apart from the many people, far too numerous to mention by name, whom I consulted in writing this book, I should like to thank three in particular, whose help was indispensable.

Two are Jesuits: Edmond Vandermeersch, a journalist whose specialized knowledge of education in the Society of Jesus was invaluable for the chapter on the closing of the colleges; and Albert Longchamp, editor of the Swiss magazine *L'Echo Illustré*, without whose unfailing support and contribution to the historical survey of the Society my project would not have been possible.

The third is not a Jesuit. It is to Myra that I dedicate this book. She knows why.

A.W.

Preface

On 25 January 1995, the 223 members of the Society of Jesus, assembled in Rome for the 34th General Congregation since 5 January, witnessed a symbolic meeting between past and present. The Society's General, Fr Peter-Hans Kolvenbach, had invited Fr Paolo Dezza – the man chosen by John Paul II as his 'personal delegate' in 1981 to replace Fr Arrupe's vicar general, Fr Vincent O'Keefe, in 'restoring order' after the General's incapacitation through illness – to address a few words to the Congregation. It was a nice gesture of reconciliation, typical of Kolvenbach's diplomacy.

As the 93-year-old, nearly blind, Jesuit groped his way to the front of the *aula*, he stumbled and would have fallen had he not been caught by . . . Fr O'Keefe! The symbol escaped no-one. In his seven-minute speech, Fr Dezza recounted the history of the *aula*, which had seen seven General Congregations, six of which he had taken part in. 'The walls haven't changed', said Dezza, 'although the world has. Don't forget that you are the custodians of tradition!'

On 5 January, John Paul II had received all the delegates individually in the Sala Clementina. He was greeted by Fr Kolvenbach, who insisted in his speech of welcome that 'This Congregation has no desire to act as an autonomous or isolated body; it is totally and unreservedly of the Church, in the Church and for the Church'. The General added that, like Ignatius and his companions, they had come to receive their directions for mission from the Pope.

In reply, the Pope defined two 'specific Jesuit contributions' to the Church's mission: the new evangelization and Christian unity. But, warned John Paul II, the Jesuits should 'avoid every temptation towards individualism, independence or parallelism' and stick to 'fraternal accord and ecclesial harmony'. In serving the universal Church, Jesuits should guard against the temptations of 'provincialism, regionalism or isolationism'. He advised them not to confuse the faithful by 'questionable teachings, publications or speeches clearly at variance with the Church's teaching on faith and morals, or by attitudes that offend communion in the Spirit'. Although the Pope made no mention of the Congregation's agenda – the role of the Jesuit brother or the laity – he stated that the Society's 'basic texts' cannot be altered. The papal encouragements were tempered with cautions.

The 223 delegates – average age 55 years: the majority (75) from Europe, then Latin America (37) and Asia (37) – divided themselves into 16 commissions: 1. Training and studies (15 members); 2. Vocations (12); 3. Co-operation with the laity (15); 4. Revision of the *Constitutions* (12); 5. Theological reflection (15); 6. Interreligious dialogue (9); 7. Inculturation, atheism and new religious movements (17); 8. Media and communication (7); 9. Religious and communal life (14); 10. Collaboration and economic solidarity within the Society (15); 11. Relations with other sectors of the Church, ecumenism (14); 12. Leadership in the Society (9); 13. Jesuit apostolate and discernment (13); 14. The Jesuit brother (13); 15. Justice, the place of women, ecology, violence and racialism (18); 16. The priestly nature of the Society (11).

The Congregation will last under three months. It wishes to avoid publishing a list of decrees. Its main task is to elaborate on the *Constitutions*, in conformity with the new Code of Canon Law, and to redefine the identity and mission of the Society of Jesus. We can expect one major document (on identity and mission), accompanied by considerations on specific topics (such as the role of the Jesuit brother or collaboration with the laity). The challenge consists in remaining vague enough to avoid papal displeasure, but specific enough to give the Society a new impetus, in line with the visionary programmes of the last two Congregations. Fr Kolvenbach has succeeded in fence-mending by recovering the confidence of the Holy See without betraying the Arrupe line – no mean feat! Will the Congregation succeed in treading the same delicate path?

A.W.
Andrésy, February 1995

Introduction

*A saint will always be more useful to the
Church than an army of Jesuits.*

PEDRO ARRUPE
(in an interview with the author in 1972)

The 1994 heatwave hit Rome early. At the end of June, the
Eternal City was already sweltering, shutters were drawn and
the myriad fountains, which are one of the city's crowning
features, drew the tourists like wasps to a picnic. The Jesuit
Curia, a massive and graceless block situated at the top of
the Borgo Santo Spirito, a stone's throw from St Peter's
Basilica, was, because of its fortress-like construction, merci-
fully cool. The new wing, built of flimsier material, is sensibly
air-conditioned. Jesuit efficiency is not incompatible with
poverty.

There I found Fr Mark Raper, an Australian Jesuit chosen by
Fr Peter-Hans Kolvenbach in 1990 to run the Jesuit Refugee
Service (JRS), which had been created by his predecessor, Fr
Pedro Arrupe. He was submerged by the Rwandan crisis. An
Australian nun was sifting through a batch of photographs,
destined for the press, showing the horrific conditions of
the refugees in the neighbouring countries of Zaïre, Burundi
and Uganda. I asked him to define the role of the JRS within
the Society of Jesus. Did Fr Kolvenbach consider it as great a
priority as his predecessor had?

'Absolutely. Cynically I could say we are the victims of our
success: unfortunately we have never been busier. There have
never been so many refugees in the world and, as our work
is highly thought of by the Society and by our supporters,
we are simply overwhelmed by the demand. With regard to

the present crisis, since we are a *refugee* organization, we are not present in Rwanda itself, but based in Kenya, Uganda, Burundi.'

Of the dangers inherent in the work of the JRS, Raper recorded:

'One of the three Rwandan Jesuits killed was Patrick Gahizi SJ, who was working with other religious to help Burundese refugees in Butare. Burundi and Rwanda, whose populations are 70 per cent Catholic, cry out for immediate and effective help and then for deep study and reflection by the Church, at every level. On 25 April, we launched the following appeal: "No sooner had the plane carrying the presidents of Rwanda and Burundi been shot down at Kigali, than mass killing ensued, and tens of thousands have perished. Today, both Rwanda and Burundi appeal to the world to help save lives, support the displaced and negotiate peace."'

The following day (1 July 1994), Raper told me, he was going to Vienna for a Caritas meeting.

'We shall discuss these crimes against humanity and seek to identify their authors. You may wonder why the Church is engaging in "politics". Faith and justice go hand in hand. Cor Unum and Justice and Peace have recently published a document on disarmament, which shows the useful role the Church can play on the political scene.

'As regards the JRS generally, we are expanding in a number of countries and strengthening our infrastructures. Fr Kolvenbach is very supportive; he mentioned our work during the recent African synod [cf. Section 5.4.3 of the Final Document, which is Kolvenbach's personal contribution[1]]. Furthermore, our juridical existence will be reinforced at the forthcoming General Congregation,[2] which will confirm the commitment made at the 32nd General Congregation. Our work is seen as the highest visible profile of the Society's avowed commitment to Justice and Faith.'

The deaths of three African Jesuits in Rwanda, at the Jesuit Centre of Spirituality in Kigali, were announced in Rome on 7 April 1994. Among those murdered were eleven sisters, five secular priests and the three Jesuits: Chrysologue Mahame, aged 67, Patrick Gahizi, aged 48, and Innocent Rutagambwa, aged 46. These are but the latest in a long line of Jesuit martyrs, throughout the ages.[3] As Fr Raper spoke, I was reminded of the last time I had met him, on his arrival in Rome in early January 1990, just two months after the murder of six Jesuits in San Salvador. Fr Alvaro Restrepo, the General Assistant for Latin America, had shown me the photographs of the massacre.

They were difficult to look at. The colour prints revealed six bodies sprawled on the grass, clad only in shorts or pyjama bottoms. The men were impossible to identify since the large-calibre bullets fired at point-blank range had shattered their heads. Blood and brains covered the walls. Fr Restrepo told me the story of these six men, five Spanish and one Salvadorean, who were 'neither Marxist nor violent men, but simply martyrs, murdered for having chosen to help the poor'.

During the night of 15 to 16 November 1989, shortly before dawn and the lifting of the curfew, a commando unit of 30 soldiers of the elite Eighth Atlacatl Battalion burst into the residence of the six Jesuits who ran the Central American José Simeón Canas University (UCA), in San Salvador. The members of this elite corps, trained in the United States to fight the terrorist guerrilla movement the National Freedom Farabundo-Martí Front (FMLN), pulled the men from their beds. They then beat up some of them before dragging them into the garden where they shot them through the head. They also killed two embarrassing witnesses: the cook, Alba Ramos, and her fifteen-year-old daughter, Celina. They tried to cover up their crime by spraying the walls of the house with bullets from Soviet weapons (AK-47 guns), to make it look like an attack by Marxist rebels.

The next day news of the massacre hit the headlines throughout the world. Few, if any, failed to identify the assassins. 'Soldiers kill six priests' was the *Financial Times*'s headline, and the *New York Times* spoke of 'thirty or so men in military uniforms'. The Paris *Figaro* was alone in sticking to the lie of 'unknown armed men'. *The Independent* indulged in black humour, remarking that 'some of the most brilliant brains of the country were scattered around the university campus'.

The chief suspect, Colonel Guillermo Alfredo Benavides, director of a famous military college, was quoted by a witness in January 1990 as warning his men: 'In the present situation it is either them or us. We shall begin by exterminating the leaders of the movement ...' He knew what he was saying. This carnage of a few moments decapitated El Salvador's intelligentsia. Even worse, by aiming at the governing body of the UCA, the extreme Right eliminated some of the men best placed for bringing peace to this violence-ridden country.

The university's 59-year-old rector Ignacio Ellacuria was generally considered to be a born mediator, even by President Alfredo Cristiani. In 1988, he had been called upon more than 400 times to act as arbitrator. This Spanish Basque, who had left his native Vizcaya at the age of eighteen, had spent 40 years in El Salvador, where he was naturalized. Known for the acuity of his political and social analyses, he mixed freely with politicians, diplomats and journalists, and had even served briefly as counsellor to the progressive military–civilian junta which had put an end to General Romero's dictatorship in September 1979.

Since the assassination of Mgr Oscar Romero, Archbishop of San Salvador, by the extreme Right in 1980, Fr Ellacuria knew that his life was in danger. He was on the black list of the death squads, and had already been the object of bomb attacks, along with his fellow Jesuits. The UCA campus had been riddled with machine-gun bullets on several occasions, and yet he had always adopted a moderate position. In the magazine he had founded, *Central American Studies*, he used the language of common sense, addressing himself both to the government elite, to explain that profound reforms were essential to the well-being of the country, and to the political Left and the unions, to convince them that armed struggle was both morally unjustifiable and politically suicidal.

The other victims of the attack were equally peace loving. Ignacio Martin-Baro, the university's vice-rector, at 47 the youngest of the group, had been engaged in psychosocial studies on poverty, violence and religious freedom. Segundo Montes, aged 56, who was interested in the problem of refugees, was director of the Institute of Human Rights. Amando Lopez, aged 53, a theology professor at UCA and rector of the diocesan seminary of San Salvador, had been rector of the University of Managua at the time of the Sandinista revolution. Juan Ramón Moreno, aged 56, master of novices and a theology professor, was the assistant director of the Mgr Romero Centre, which had been destroyed by the same military commando. He too had recently come from Nicaragua, where he had published a magazine of spirituality, *Diakonia*. Finally, Joaquín Lopez y Lopez, known as 'Father Lolo', at 71 the oldest of the group, was the only one to have been born in the country. A founding member of the UCA, he had recently been designated as national director of Fe y Alegría (Faith and Joy), a network of schools for the poor rural communities and urban outcasts.

The well-known theologian Jon Sobrino, another Jesuit professor, who had taught for sixteen years at UCA, had escaped the massacre by mere chance, because he had been visiting Thailand to give a course of lectures on Christology. He received a telephone call at midnight on 16 November from a friend in London. 'Are you sitting down and have you a pencil handy?' asked the friend. 'Ignacio Ellacuria has been assassinated!' It wasn't really a surprise. Since the murder of Mgr Oscar Romero in 1980, Fr Sobrino knew that they were all in constant danger. But when he heard the list of those murdered he couldn't believe his ears. 'After each name, I thought the list was ended', he said.

Why was such a savage attack carried out on unarmed intellectuals, moderate men who had devoted their religious lives to the well-being of their adopted country?

'Since 1980, the university has been the object of a number of attacks. Our house was destroyed in 1983; the computer centre, the library and the printing works have all been attacked. Why? Simply because we preached dialogue, something which is considered here to be treason. The Jesuits thought that they were safe, however, because the house was under military protection. It was for this reason that the cook and her daughter had preferred to stay in our house rather than return home. Ignacio Ellacuria had always worked for peace and dialogue. He had recently had two private conversations with President Cristiani. To our minds, we were working neither for the government, nor for the FMLN, but simply to put an end to the war.

'In 1975 the Jesuits had defined their mission in the contemporary world as the defence of faith and justice. Generally speaking, universities do not take an interest in such goals, but we had transformed ours into a social force for faith and justice. We are prepared to forgive our assassins, as individuals, but we must fight against the structures which allow such massacres – there must be no more killing. It isn't so much the Government that is responsible as those who really run the country: the extreme Right, the oligarchy, the death squads and certain members of the army. The Jesuit Provincial has decided that our work must go on. Neither the Society of Jesus nor the university have been massacred. Of course it will be difficult to replace those who were murdered, but numerous Jesuits throughout the world have volunteered to come and work at the university.'

This unwavering determination to achieve their goals, whatever the odds, explains the quiet force of the Jesuits. As early as 1977, after the assassination of the Jesuit Rutilio Grande by the death squads, UCA's professors had been the object of a campaign of intimidation. A slogan appeared on the walls of the capital: 'Be patriotic, kill a priest!' At the time, the General, Pedro Arrupe, had commented when he heard that the Jesuits had decided to stay in post: 'If you are killed, we will replace you.' A cynical remark? Rather, 'a faith to move mountains'.

In the same spirit, the former Provincial of the British Jesuits, Fr Michael Campbell-Johnston, now director of the Jesuit Development Service in Central America, wrote in *The Tablet* in November 1989:

The six Jesuits assassinated in El Salvador were representative of the other 65 who work in this country, and of all Jesuits everywhere. UCA, which is committed to the fight for social justice, represents a challenge for the powers that be, not only by its teaching but by its publications: *Estudios Centroamericanos* (edited by Ignacio Ellacuria), *Proceso* (a weekly news bulletin) and *Cartas a las Iglésias*, a newsletter edited by Jon Sobrino and addressed to the basic communities. All these publications allow those who are never heard in public to express themselves. That is why they had to be silenced, at any price. The assassination of the six Jesuits is shocking, but hardly surprising. After all, they simply added their names to the 70,000 dead in El Salvador.

Two months after the murder, President Cristiani admitted on television that the army had been responsible for 'this odious crime'. Nine men were accused, on 19 January 1990, of having killed the six Jesuits, their cook and her daughter. Those named included Colonel Guillermo Alfredo Benavides, director of the Military Academy of San Salvador.

But it was only after the United States House of Representatives had in June voted a 50 per cent reduction in military aid to El Salvador (the Senate following in October), and threatened to suppress all aid if the 'Jesuit affair' was not entirely clarified, that the court case was finally brought to the Assizes of San Salvador on 26 December 1991 – two years after the killings. Colonel Benavides and Lieutenant Mendoza were sentenced to 30 years' prison. The other members of the Atlacatl Commando were acquitted.

The example of El Salvador reveals both the weakness and the strength of the Society of Jesus. The weakness is mathematical: faced with ever decreasing numbers, the Jesuits have to redistribute their forces, make difficult apostolic choices and relinquish posts of authority to allow the laymen they have formed to take their place. Thus, the assassination of the Jesuits at UCA destroyed the university's governing body at a single blow. Jon Sobrino speaks of 'an irreparable loss', adding bitterly:

'Things will never be the same at UCA. Ellacuria is no longer there to finish the book we were working on together, Juan Ramón will no longer organize the lecture course on Mgr Romero, Amando won't finish the next number of *The Latin American Review of Theology*, Ignacio will give no more lectures on the psychology of religion, Segundo won't work with the refugees and Lolo is no longer there to speak to us of the hopes of the poor thanks to his Fe y Alegría movement.'

But the strength of the Jesuits lies elsewhere, in their solidarity – numerous volunteers stepped forward to replace the martyrs – in their determination, and above all in the strong influence they have over those they have formed. With almost four million former students throughout the world, the Society is a force to be reckoned with. These former pupils belong to associations whose aim is to maintain bonds of friendship and solidarity between them and to support Jesuit centres of learning worldwide: approximately 1,300 colleges or universities where 10,000 Jesuits teach.

The meeting of the Worldwide Union of former students of Jesuit institutions, held in Versailles in 1986, was attended by 700 delegates from 27 countries. Fr Kolvenbach spoke of this new sharing of work, based on a greater lay participation.

> 'Independently of our decreasing numbers, we conceive of our role differently. The result of a good Jesuit education should be that you no longer need us (...). The Jesuits aren't abandoning you, but they have no intention of directing you. We count on you to bring to fruition, in your lives and in the world, the education we have given you.'

It was an appeal to this 'reserve army', formed of the laity, to assume their responsibilities.[4] Fr Kolvenbach reminded them that 'the teaching apostolate extends beyond the colleges and universities. Today we are called upon to promote justice and to make ours the preferential option for the poor, even at the risk of our own lives and belongings.' This is a far cry from the formation of elites, the work commonly associated with the Jesuits. The 'men in black' were traditionally identified with the strict teachers of the sons of the ruling class.

Fidel Castro, General Jaruzelski, Luis Buñuel and Alfred Hitchcock have this in common: the two Marxist heads of state and the two film directors were all Jesuit-taught. In fact, the list of great men to have studied under the 'good fathers' is long and often unexpected. In England such minds as Sir Arthur Conan Doyle and Paul Johnson, and in Ireland writers like James Joyce and revolutionaries like Patrick Pearse, were formed in Jesuit establishments. The President of the United States, Bill Clinton, studied law at Georgetown University, and in France the list is impressive of thinkers who came from the Jesuit mould: from philosophers and writers –

Descartes, Diderot, Corneille, Molière, Voltaire, Balzac, the Marquis de Sade, Saint-Exupéry – to statesmen and soldiers – Colbert, Condé, Foch, Lyautey, Lattre de Tassigny, Charles de Foucauld, Charles de Gaulle. Racine, in spite of his Jansenist upbringing at Port-Royal, always submitted his writing to the Jesuit grammarian Fr Bouhours, 'for fear of having committed some fault against the French language'.

The black sheep are as significant as the good pupils. A Jesuit training leaves a trace, for better or worse. Some hated their Jesuit pedagogues, but most admired them for their intelligence and their teaching skills even if they disagreed with their doctrine. Castro shows a sneaking admiration for his Jesuit masters, and he has allowed them to teach in Cuba. Alfred Hitchcock, on the other hand, admitted to being terrified by three things: the police, physical punishment and the Jesuits.

Sir Arthur Conan Doyle, the creator of Sherlock Holmes, abandoned his Catholic faith for a vague deism and later took up spiritualism. While at the famous Jesuit public school Stonyhurst he was startled, and shocked, to learn that all non-Catholics would surely go to hell. When he wrote to his mother on the matter, he was relieved by her laconic reply: 'Wear flannel next to your skin, my dear boy, and *never* believe in eternal punishment!' He believed in God but rejected the Church – indeed all churches. 'The evils of religion', he wrote, 'a dozen religions slaughtering each other, have all come from accepting things that can't be proved.'

As for James Joyce, his description of a Jesuit sermon on hellfire by Stephen Daedalus gives some idea of the lasting impression his religious education made on him, having attended Jesuit schools from the age of six-and-a-half to twenty. Louis McRedmond has written:

> The scrupulous authenticity of detail suggests things
> remembered which he had no desire to forget, a sign surely
> that he remembered with affection. He was indeed always
> grateful to the Jesuits and fair to them, yet he caused them
> great embarrassment because of his irreligion, the stridency
> of which only sounded the harsher the more he invoked
> Catholic terminology and concepts. 'His was a Catholic mind
> that rejected superstition and thought it had rejected the Faith'
> (John C. Kelly SJ). This made it understandably difficult for

the Jesuits to appreciate, until distance brought objectivity,
that Joyce was 'an advertisement for the nature and quality
of the traditional Jesuit education, both religious and literary
as well as for that determined realisation of one's own proper
vocation which lies at the heart of the Jesuit ideal of education'
(Peter Costello). He in fact exemplified the proposition that
the Jesuits' encouragement of the pursuit of excellence was
vindicated when former pupils who became rebels proved to be
superlatively effective in their rebellion![5]

And yet today the Jesuits seem to have abandoned their
leading role in education. They leave to others the task of
forming tomorrow's leaders. Through deliberate choice or
necessity, they have given up that 'elitism' which was their
glory and their shame and which aroused the envy that provoked Jean-Paul Sartre to remark: 'Like the Freemasons, the
Jesuits are one of the great occult forces that govern the world.'
There are few religious institutions in the Roman Catholic
Church that have aroused more fascination, during its four
and a half centuries of existence, than the Society of Jesus,
few that have inspired such curiosity and misunderstanding,
such attraction and repulsion.

Were one to play the 'association of ideas' game, the word
'Jesuit' would conjure up a confused mixture of the Reductions of Paraguay, the Indian missions, the 'rites controversy'
in China, the priests' hiding holes in Elizabethan England,
Campion's 'brag', Louis XIV's confessors and the spiritual
counsellors of Catherine the Great's Imperial court . . . There
would be an evocation of casuistry, of Pascal's *Provinciales*, of
the 'probabilist' theological axiom, of the theory of regicide, of
the replacement of the Julian by the Gregorian calendar. One
would quote discoveries in mathematics, astrology, palae-
ontology, remembering that Jesuits have been mountain climbers
and mandarins, that others have studied the topography of the
moon, discovered quinine as an antidote to malaria, invented
the magic lantern or introduced vanilla and the umbrella to
Europe from China. The list is endless.

An article appeared recently in the French daily *Le Figaro*,
entitled 'The Jesuits dream of baptizing the Martians'. It
described the life of the ten Jesuits who compose the staff of
the Vatican's Observatory, founded in the sixteenth century.

In 1935 this was moved from Rome to the Pope's summer residence in Castelgandolfo, and it was recently transferred again, to escape excessive atmospheric pollution, to Tucson, Arizona, where a giant telescope was installed in 1991: the VATT (Vatican Advanced Technology Telescope). The Jesuits have always been fascinated by the stars: Fr Clavius (a Bavarian Jesuit, born Christoph Clau), for example, whose studies in astronomy led to the reform of the Western calendar in 1582, gave his name to one of the largest craters on the moon. Questioned about their activity, Fr George Coyne, the American Jesuit who is the team's technical adviser, replied: 'It would surely be cosmic egocentricity to imagine that we humans are the only intelligent beings in the universe', while his Italian colleague Fr Sabino Maffeo added: 'We cannot know if hypothetical extraterrestrial creatures have sinned and been visited by a Saviour. We must be prepared to evangelize them!'

If one were more interested in the judgements passed by observers on the Society of Jesus than in the acts of its members, the variety would be wide ranging, with a majority of unfavourable comments, no doubt. Polemics apart, it is not purely fortuitous that in all European languages 'jesuitical' means 'clever', 'hypocritical', 'cunning', even 'underhand'. Jesuit historians find this difficult to admit. Joseph Stierli, a Swiss historian of the Society, wrote sanctimoniously: 'The last word on the Society of Jesus belongs to God. He will pronounce it on the Day of Judgement, correcting many hasty judgements pronounced by men.'

Awaiting that last word – not even claiming the penultimate word – this book attempts to explore in what this influence of the Jesuits has consisted, and still consists. What can be said of their relation to political, social and ecclesial power? To answer, we shall have to understand the importance acquired by the Society of Jesus since its creation, and then determine to what extent the Jesuits today still wield any real 'power'.

It will be necessary to seek the facts behind the legends, for if all myths are hard to dispel, that of the Jesuits is particularly tenacious, and filled with contradictions. The Society of Jesus is often described as a disciplined, elitist body, placed unconditionally at the service of the Pope. But it is also accused of being a lair of rebellious snipers. Stress is laid upon the military character of the life and work of Ignatius of Loyola, the first 'General' of the 'Company' of Jesus. But it is rarely asked how this 'army' of religious men, sometimes called the Church's 'light brigade', has evolved into the present socially minded 'peace corps'. As for the famous obedience *perinde ac cadaver* (like a corpse), which Ignatius demanded of his Jesuits, it has disappeared into the mists of legend. But what did he really mean by this apparently blind obedience? Is it compatible with freedom of conscience?

These questions imply others. How is one to explain that the Society of Jesus, which was originally a missionary order known for its great mobility and flexibility, was transformed into a hierarchic and centralized institution, and rapidly burdened with colleges and universities, so that it became a gigantic educating machine? Does the questioning of the Society's teaching vocation, especially since the 32nd General Congregation in 1975, which defined as priorities 'the promotion of faith and justice' and 'the inculturation[6] of Jesuits in the Third World', mark a radical change of orientation in policy or simply result from the decline in numbers? Finally, does the Jesuits' fourth vow of obedience to the Pope make sense today, especially since the postconciliar crisis which led to the opposition of 'white Pope' to 'black Pope'?

All of these questions will have to be answered in the course of our enquiry, based on the long history of the Society founded by Ignatius of Loyola, which will examine the following hypothesis. By diversifying their activities in recent years, especially in the field of the human sciences, the Jesuits have not renounced the influence they were accustomed to exert through their colleges. By adapting to the modern world, they have rather – intentionally or not – taken over new centres of power, even if, more often than not, this 'power' is, paradoxically, a 'counter force'.

In fact, the Society still represents a force to be reckoned with. Its 23,179 members,[7] dispersed throughout the world, continue to fulfil the most diverse tasks. In Rome, Jesuits are in charge of several universities, including the famous Gregorian University, the successor of the Roman College founded by Ignatius himself. There is also the Pontifical Biblical Institute, created by Pius X in 1909, and the Pontifical Institute for Oriental Studies, founded in 1917 by Benedict XV, whose rector Fr Peter-Hans Kolvenbach became the 28th successor of Ignatius of Loyola on 13 September 1983.

The Society continues to supply the Church with eminent writers, thinkers and theologians. Among the most recent, one could mention the British poet Gerard Manley Hopkins, the French palaeontologist and philosopher Pierre Teilhard de Chardin, the American author behind the Vatican Council's Decree on Religious Freedom, John Courtney Murray, the Austrian liturgical expert Josef Jungmann, the German theologians Karl and Hugo Rahner, the French theologian Henri de Lubac and patristic scholar Jean Daniélou, the German ecumenist Augustin Bea, and patristic scholar Alois Grillmeier, the Canadian philosopher Bernard Lonergan, the French writer Michel de Certeau and the Italian former director of Vatican Radio, Roberto Tucci.

Indeed, the media represent an important sphere of activity for the Society, whether it be the press, with specialized magazines in numerous countries, the radio, television or cinema: hundreds of Jesuits are engaged in these fields, including Vatican Radio, which is run by the Jesuits and broadcasts regularly in 40 languages. Vatican Radio was created in 1931 when, during the Fascist regime in Italy, Pius XI wanted an independent voice, a loudspeaker for the papacy. At first the radio did not broadcast in different languages, but it soon became a medium of communication, not to say an instrument of propaganda and support for the Eastern European countries under Communist domination – so successfully that Vatican Radio was frequently jammed.

Programmes are broadcast 24 hours a day, the staff being composed of more than 400 people (of whom 150 are technicians and 210 journalists) belonging to 56 different nationalities, in addition to collaborators in Rome and a network of about 200 correspondents throughout the world, especially for news bulletins, broadcast three times a day in English and French.

The annual budget is 20 million dollars (30 to 40 billion

lire). The money comes mainly from the Vatican, a little from donations. Broadcasting conditions are now good, via the satellite Intelsat. Until 1 January 1993, Vatican Radio was solely dependent on short wave transmission. Whereas before, it was difficult to pick up the signal in certain countries, like China, thanks to the satellite it can reach everyone clearly. In Africa and Latin America, for example, a contract was recently signed to set up two stations to relay Vatican Radio's programmes to these continents.

Other sectors have recently attracted the Jesuits' interest: atomic research; medicine and psychoanalysis; social, cultural and religious development in the Third World; and others. In 1965, Paul VI himself assigned a new task to the Jesuits: 'to oppose atheism'. In order to respond to this request, in the widest sense, that is to study atheism and its causes, West German Jesuits created an Institute of Atheism, where Christian–Marxist meetings were held, and Spanish Jesuits founded a similar one in Madrid, called the Fe y Secularidad (Faith and Secularism) Institute.

But in spite of this intense activity, the Society has not escaped the crisis that the Roman Catholic Church is itself undergoing. On the contrary, it is perhaps hit harder than other religious congregations. The figures speak for themselves. Since 1965, when the Society reached an all-time high with 36,038 members, the number of Jesuits has been in constant decline, with a loss of 800 a year between 1966 and 1973. In 1983, the number had dropped to 26,000; in 1990, to 25,000; and in 1994, to 23,179.

What of the future? According to the news bulletin published in April 1994 by the Jesuit Curia in Rome,

If we assume that the current intake of 600 novices a year will remain stable, that the number who leave will continue to be 1.75 per cent each year and that the number of deaths will gradually increase from 2.1 per cent to 2.3 per cent, a mathematical computation shows that the Society will not reverse its downward trend until it has been reduced to 14,814 members, which will occur in approximately the year 2040! This is not a prediction of what will certainly happen, but a projection. If the trend is to be reversed more quickly, then either the number of vocations must increase, or the percentage of those leaving must decrease.

But arid statistics do not tell the whole story, and the reassuring explanations given by certain Jesuit authorities cannot conceal the depths of the identity crisis that many Jesuits are going through. Fr Kolvenbach considers it to be 'a problem that concerns the whole of religious life', adding 'vocations do not depend on us, but on the Holy Spirit'. For the General, there is a danger of panic and of succumbing to what he calls 'crisis management'. Rather than simply 'filling the gaps', he suggests 'making rational choices by taking individual talents into account'. He explained:

> 'It isn't so much that vocations are down, but that those who
> die are not replaced. There is also the problem of perseverance,
> of the inevitable number of drop-outs. We could accept many
> more novices in Africa, in Asia and in Latin America, but
> we don't wish to lower the standard. We prefer quality to
> quantity.
>   'In the East European countries too the number of
> postulants is high and it is a question of discernment. The
> young candidates are very eager to leave their countries
> for the West. When we decided to open a novitiate in
> Romania, for example, instead of bringing the students
> out of the country, the number of aspirants dropped
> immediately. Lay vocations must also be fostered. For
> example, our Jesuit Refugee Service attracts laymen for
> a year or two. It is false to say that today's youth lacks
> ideals: they simply have different commitments from our
> generation.'

This realistic attitude is similar to that of his predecessor. In 1972, at the height of the postconciliar crisis, Fr Pedro Arrupe told me that he was naturally 'preoccupied' by the situation. 'There have always been Jesuits who have left the Society, especially among the scholastics, before they are ordained. What is more worrying is that their numbers are increasing.' But he added with a smile: 'Numbers are unimportant, you know. A saint will always be more useful to the Church than an army of Jesuits.' This sentiment was echoed by Michel de Certeau, a brilliant French Jesuit who died of cancer in the 1990s, when he told me:

'Whether there are 30,000 Jesuits or ten is immaterial. What
must be avoided is that the Society should become timid
as it dwindles in size. That is a sure sign of death. The
less numerous we are, the more prepared we should be to
take risks.'

And risks were not something that frightened Fr Arrupe.
One of his first decisions after his election in 1965 was to
launch a sociological survey among the Jesuits, to discover
their state of mind, their problems and wishes. His first
priority was to prepare the Society to adapt to the needs of
the age. This decision is unprecedented in the annals of such
an undemocratic institution as the Roman Catholic Church.
It revealed that the malaise experienced by the Jesuits had
an external sociological cause as well as a deeper spiritual
dimension. A crisis of identity, of authority and of obedience
contributed to create a climate of pessimism, leading not only
to a drop in vocations but also to an increase in the numbers
leaving.

At the trough of the wave, in the early 1970s, the Society
recorded each week six arrivals, seven deaths and twenty
departures. In 1969, the expulsion – at the request of Paul
VI – of three Jesuit chaplains, Josef Vrijburg, Huub Oosterhuis
and Ton Van der Stap, accused of defending the marriage of
priests, led to the resignation from the Society of the Dutch
provincial Jan Hermans. Of the well-known Jesuits who left
the Society at this time one could cite Peter Hebblethwaite
and John Harriott in England, and Georges Morel, Jean-Louis
Schlegel and Bruno Ribes in France.

Fr Arrupe, who always showed total loyalty towards the
Holy See, suffered from this crisis of obedience, but he nonetheless carried out – and sometimes anticipated – the reforms
decided by the Council. In fact, the Society of Jesus – or at
least the more advanced of its members, supported by Fr
Arrupe – were ahead not only of the Council but also of the
Holy See and the Roman Curia to such an extent that John
Paul II, irritated, finally asked 'the Church's light cavalry', to
quote Fr Pittau, 'to dismount and to realize that everyone
should advance at the same pace'.

This explains the incipient conflict, which was brewing since
Fr Arrupe's election in 1965, between the 'black Pope' and the

'white Pope', a conflict that came to a head under the present pontificate, which has seen a general tightening of the reins. Paradoxically, the religious order founded by St Ignatius in order to serve the Pope and carry out the 'missions' he wished to entrust to it, is the very one that has the most often come into conflict with the last three occupants of the see of Rome. The election of Pedro Arrupe as 28th General of the Society of Jesus coincided with the end of the Second Vatican Council, two years after the accession to the papacy of Giambattista Montini, under the name of Paul VI, and it wasn't until the forced resignation of Arrupe and the election of his successor, Peter-Hans Kolvenbach, that the Holy See could hope to rectify what it saw as a dangerous situation.

Paul VI, it is true, unhappy about certain progressive tendencies of some of the Society's most eminent members, hadn't hesitated to intervene in the deliberations of the 32nd General Congregation of the order, forcing the Jesuits, for example, to give up their intention of suppressing the three 'categories' of Jesuits (professed priests, priest-coadjutors and brother-coadjutors). It is also true that, during his very brief reign, John Paul I had found the time to prepare a speech, which he was to have delivered the day after his death, in which he would have echoed the misgivings of Paul VI. But, whereas Paul VI and John Paul I merely 'took note of', 'disapproved of' or, at worst, 'warned', John Paul II, with his customary vigour, took action. Having discerned what he termed 'deplorable deficiencies' in the Society, he began by rejecting Fr Arrupe's resignation. Then, when Arrupe suffered a stroke, the Pope replaced the vicar general chosen by him to act 'temporarily' in his stead, and named two 'personal delegates' of his own choosing.

In spite of the resentment felt by many in the Society of this high-handed action, the Jesuits revealed their legendary obedience. To such a degree that the Pope, much impressed, allowed the convocation of a General Congregation to elect Arrupe's successor in September 1983. The task was a delicate one for the Jesuits. They were faced with a determined Pope, who hadn't hesitated to abrogate, albeit temporarily, the Society's internal legislation to impose his views. In order to maintain their power within the Church, the Jesuits had to find a new General whose election would neither represent a challenge to the Pope's authority ('If we make the wrong choice', a European provincial told me, 'we shall end up in a year from now with a Cardinal-Protector'), nor an abdication of the Society's legitimate autonomy.

The designation, at the first round of voting, of Fr Peter-Hans Kolvenbach, aged 54, the second Dutchman in history to occupy the post, was a brilliant choice, politically, not to say a Jesuitical one. They refused to choose either someone favoured by the Pope, such as his delegates Frs Dezza or Pittau, or even someone favoured by Fr Arrupe, like his vicar general Fr Vincent O'Keefe. They cleverly chose someone of a third type: neither Roman nor Third-World-minded but an Orientalist.

In his simple black cassock (most Jesuits prefer civilian dress, with a discreet cross pinned to the lapel), Fr Kolvenbach looks like an Eastern prelate: of medium height, he sports a white goatee beard and wears hornrimmed spectacles. He was born in Druten, near Nijmegen, in Holland, but his twenty years spent in the Lebanon seem to have made him forget his origins: German (by his father) and Italian (by his mother). He has become Orientalized, without losing his Northern sense of humour. After his election, his colleagues who went to his room to congratulate him found the room empty and a note pinned to the door: 'I am at the General's.'

I was received by him most cordially at the end of June 1994. He appeared out of the gloom of the corridor of the fourth floor of the Jesuit headquarters in the Borgo Santo Spirito, and greeted me with an affability that put me at ease and soon made me forget that I was in the presence of the legendary 'black Pope'. After a few kind remarks about an earlier book of mine, he ushered me into a pleasant, if austere, private dining-room, for an informal interview over lunch. The only ornament was a primitive Nativity scene. We were accompanied by Fr Jacques Gellard, his French assistant. The meal was simple but pleasant – soup, roast beef and potatoes, salad, chocolate cake, red wine, coffee and liqueurs (of which neither Jesuit partook). Fr Kolvenbach's proverbial humour was intact. When he mentioned the recent death of the Jesuit philosopher Frederick Copleston, I recounted the story of 'Freddy's' reaction to reports of the alleged 'living Virgin' in Ireland, a statue which was said to move if stared at long enough. He had replied pensively: 'If I stare long enough at my colleagues at Farm Street I too get the distinct impression that they are alive.' After a gleeful smile, the General countered: 'When I was in the Lebanon, we had an aged Oriental patriarch in the house who was only brought out of his room for the Church services; he kept so still during the last five years of his life that no-one knew if he was alive or dead.'

Fr Arrupe's successor seems to possess above all the chief quality prescribed by St Ignatius for this post: 'a perfect union with God our Lord and a great familiarity with him, through prayer, in all his actions'. Fr Kolvenbach is a deeply spiritual man whose austerity of life – he eats little and sleeps even less – is, according to the malicious comment of a friend, 'more Franciscan than Jesuit'. For many years he taught linguistics, German and Armenian, and this polyglot who speaks at least eight languages is a born teacher. After studying in Paris, he earned a reputation as mediator, fostering dialogue and peace in strife-ridden Lebanon. He avoided taking sides and saw to it that the Jesuits worked in different parts of Beirut, refusing to endorse the principle of partition favoured by the Maronite Christians in government. He turned the Jesuit Saint-Joseph University into a haven of peace, where Syrians and Lebanese, Christians and Muslims lived in harmony.

The choice of Fr Kolvenbach was not only astute, it was subtle. As rector of the Pontifical Institute for Oriental Studies, he was engaged in ecumenical relations with the Orthodox churches, especially the Russian Orthodox Church. He has even adopted the Oriental rite. His knowledge of the East could only endear him to John Paul II. But he was also an Arrupe man: it was the latter who had appointed him as provincial of the vice-province of the Middle East, before summoning him to Rome to run the Oriental Institute.

Although he is less outward-looking than his predecessor, less interested in politics, less given to making grand speeches and more tolerant towards the 'laggards', Fr Kolvenbach defends the texts voted by the last General Congregations, in which he participated. According to Fr Henri Madelin, a former French Provincial, 'It was necessary to close the Arrupe era ...in order the better to preserve Arrupe's heritage'.

What is the difference between the two men? It is more a question of temperament than of ideas, of style than of content. Fr Kolvenbach's close collaborators in Rome all agree that he is pursuing the 'Arrupe line', but in a different manner. The former Belgian General Assistant explains it thus:

> 'He is much more diplomatic than his predecessor. This is why he succeeds in dealing with the Curia, whereas Fr Arrupe, newly arrived from Japan and used to plain speaking, was ignorant of the arcane methods and the protocol of the Vatican. Arrupe was a visionary, who had a way with words, whereas Kolvenbach's much lower profile is not a threat to John Paul II's leadership.'

Even Fr Giuseppe Pittau, the Italian Jesuit chosen by the Pope as his 'personal delegate' to take over from Fr Arrupe when he fell ill, admits that the new General hasn't abandoned his predecessor's policies.

> 'On the contrary, he has had to deal with new problems, but his secret is working more closely with the local bishops and the Holy See. The chief virtue of this General is his spirit of pacification. Nothing troubles him. Having lived in Lebanon he is immunized.'

Among his other qualities cited by his staff one could mention 'an aversion to the limelight, with a certain prudence in the written word and a greater freedom in speech', 'an enormous capacity to imbibe information and a phenomenal memory; a deep spirituality and a sense of humour that disarms all criticism', 'the gift of listening to others, whether it is the General Congregation, the source of his authority, or the provinces, whose autonomy he respects', and 'a conciliar theology whereas, paradoxically, Fr Arrupe's was much more traditional'.

After ten years of Generalship, Fr Kolvenbach still enjoys the trust and admiration of his collaborators. I asked the same question in 1994, in Rome and of leading Jesuits throughout the world. Fr José-María de Vera, in charge of the Press Office, replied:

'They have different charisms. Fr Kolvenbach is not glamorous like Fr Arrupe and he is more openly obedient – without being servile – to the papacy. He shows a deep respect for others and a real humanity. It is very impressive. He is especially attentive to marginal Jesuits. He has the gift of serenity and, above all, a superb sense of humour. This is probably due to his Dutch origins. Recently, five or six empty spaces were discovered in the Jesuit archives and when I quipped that they could serve as cells for recalcitrant theologians, Fr Kolvenbach replied instantly: "There aren't nearly enough."'

Fr Edward Yarnold, who teaches theology at Campion Hall, the Jesuit college in Oxford, thinks that Fr Kolvenbach's 'less charismatic leadership is compensated by his enormous grasp of details'. And Fr Henri Madelin, who is now the editor of the French Jesuit magazine *Etudes*, repeated that

'In order to ensure the continuity of Arrupe's policies, it was necessary to choose someone else to safeguard the "Arrupe line", that is, the freedom of our religious acts and the seriousness of our commitments. Kolvenbach has maintained the major elements of this policy, including the 4th Decree (on faith and justice). He has shown a gift for courageous diplomacy. He speaks out fearlessly, but it is difficult for the press to oppose him to the Pope, because of his low profile. He practises the principle of subsidiarity,[8] acting dynamically in Russia, in China, in Asia.'

Fr Gianpaolo Salvini is the editor of the Italian Jesuit magazine *Civiltà cattolica*. According to him,

'The main change is in the amelioration of our relations with the Holy See. There wasn't a war or a rupture between us, simply a misunderstanding: the channels of communication were blocked ... Frs Dezza and Pittau made no fundamental changes, they simply restored confidence between the General and the Curia, especially the "Polish faction" surrounding the Pope. Fr Dezza explained the misunderstanding by the different temperaments of Pedro Arrupe and the various Popes. Paul VI was very roundabout in his criticisms of the Society. He would begin by paying compliments to Arrupe before reproaching him for something, and since Arrupe was an optimist by nature, he missed the point. A proof that all is well now is that Fr Vincent O'Keefe (*persona non grata* with John Paul II) has been invited by Fr Kolvenbach to be a member of the *coetus praevius* (the official preparatory committee) of the General Congregation. This shows the General's confidence in the continuity of the Society's policy. Pedro Arrupe was a charismatic "saint", not a man of government. Fr. Kolvenbach intends to consolidate the "Arrupe line" by means of the General Congregation.'

And what does Fr O'Keefe, now living in New York, himself think?

'Fr Kolvenbach restored mutual and trusting communication with the Holy See, while continuing the line of the last three General Congregations with regard to the mission of the Society today, i.e. the service of faith and the promotion of justice in the name of the Gospel. From his election in 1983 to the present day, he has referred constantly to the person and spiritual legacy of Fr Arrupe.'

Fr Leo O'Donovan, president of Georgetown University in Washington, puts it into historical perspective:

'To compare the two Generals, one must keep in mind the different contexts in which they held office. Fr Arrupe was elected General in May 1965, when not just the Society of Jesus but the Church at large was suffused with the enthusiasm of John XXIII's *aggiornamento*. Fr Kolvenbach was elected in September 1983, five years after the end of Paul VI's pontificate and the beginning of John Paul II's, when the Society and the Church at large were coping with the inevitable conservative reaction both to the new programme of Vatican II and to whatever misinterpretations it may have occasioned. The times were different in 1983.

'In addition, Fr Arrupe was a uniquely charismatic figure, exactly what was needed for promulgating a new vision. By the time of Fr Kolvenbach's election, what was needed was not so much charism – the Society by then had its new programme – as political astuteness in enabling the Society to follow through on the programme. Fr Kolvenbach is just the man for this, and in fact he was elected on the first ballot when the members of the 33rd General Congregation cast their secret votes.'

Bishop Corboy is a retired Jesuit bishop living in Zambia. He also remembers how

'Fr Arrupe was elected at a time, during the Vatican Council, when things were beginning to change rapidly. It was a very difficult period for a General faced with so many problems and an uncertain future. I think he was a man of great vision. He was also very charismatic and therefore, like Pope John XXIII, attracted attention. Fr Kolvenbach seems to prefer to adopt a lower profile and at the same time, coming after Arrupe, seems to have retained the confidence of the Society, which is no easy achievement these days. At present, for many reasons it would seem preferable for a General to listen much and act quietly.'

For Fr Joseph Fitzpatrick too, of the department of sociology and anthropology at Fordham University, in New York:

'Fr Pedro Arrupe was special. No-one would expect Fr Kolvenbach to be like him. Kolvenbach's major achievement has been maintaining the stability of the Society of Jesus throughout the world and of meeting the challenge of the disappearance of Communist Russia and of Communism in general in Eastern Europe. He has also faced the responsibility of the development of the Society in Africa and Asia. I think he will be recognized as having had a remarkably stabilizing effect on the Society throughout the world.'

This opinion is shared by John Padberg, director of the Institute of Jesuit Sources, in St Louis, Missouri:

'It is too early to "sum up" Fr Kolvenbach's term of office. But comparing it so far with the term of Fr Arrupe, I would say – quite briefly and therefore incompletely – that Fr Arrupe's term was one of innovation to meet the current needs of the Church and of the Society of Jesus, whereas Fr Kolvenbach's term has so far been one of consolidation of those changes and of seeing them inserted more fully into the ongoing life of the Society. Just as the Church after Vatican II had an enormous amount of change to digest, so did the Society of Jesus after the 31st and 32nd Congregations.'

Even those who are the most socially and politically engaged agree with this. The former British Provincial, Fr Michael Campbell-Johnston, who now runs the 'Pedro Arrupe Jesuit Development Service' in San Salvador, is a fervent admirer of Fr Arrupe and was with him in Manila just before he suffered his stroke in 1981. Fr Campbell-Johnston remembers that

'In the first interview he gave on being elected General,
Fr Kolvenbach described the main outcome of the 33rd
Congregation as being "a dynamic consolidation of forces".
Consolidation because we returned to the structures of normal
government and strongly reconfirmed the line adopted by
the preceding Congregation and pursued so vigorously by
Fr Arrupe. But also dynamic because "to consolidate does
not mean to become frozen". There must be an openness to
new apostolic and spiritual ventures. While not possessing
the charism or vision of Fr Arrupe, I think Fr Kolvenbach has
followed this agenda admirably. There have been important
new ventures but the emphasis has been on consolidation,
picking up loose ends, rebuilding relations.'

Several people mentioned the importance attached by Fr
Kolvenbach to the *Spiritual Exercises*, which Fr Arrupe rarely
mentioned in public. Fr Arthur Vella, for example, editor in
Rome of the *Review of Ignatian Spirituality*, pointed out that

'Since Fr Kolvenbach's arrival, greater stress has been laid on
spirituality, with a return to the sources of Ignatian spirituality,
namely the *Spiritual Exercises*, Ignatius's autobiography and the
Constitutions. A practical result of this spiritual awakening is
the habit of practising the Exercises in one's daily life, and not
only on retreat.'

Did the last General Congregation – the one that elected Fr
Kolvenbach in 1983 – mark the peak of the Society's period
of self-questioning? It recommended both a return to the
origins – a return to St Ignatius's intuition of the need for
an authentic Christian humanism – and a new departure to
render the Christian message credible once more in our disillu-
sioned world. The task, as defined by the Jesuits, is daunting.
An evaluation of its successful realization by the present General will serve as a test for our hypothesis concerning the
'redeployment' of their forces by the Jesuits.

In September 1990, all the provincials of the Society were summoned to Loyola to open an 'Ignatian Year', celebrating the fifth
centenary of the birth of St Ignatius, and the 450th anniversary of
the creation of the Society. At that meeting, Africa was declared
a 'global priority' and the Jesuits accepted the Pope's request to
're-evangelize' the Eastern European countries.

Four years later, the Jesuits embark upon another soul-searching exercise, which could prove to be another watershed: the 34th General Congregation, held at the beginning of 1995. Two basic sets of themes are under discussion. One *ad extra*: Evangelization in a very new world context and sharing the Jesuits' mission in the Church with the laity; the other *ad intra*: Revision of law (the Constitutions), integrating faith and justice, vocations, formation and internal organization. 'The purpose is not to multiply the already numerous publications on the problems of our time', writes Fr Kolvenbach, 'but to discern the presence of the Lord in what we experience within ourselves and around us.'

I asked the General what he hoped would be achieved by this Congregation. He replied:

'There are two main tasks facing the Society: the renewal of our legislation and the redefinition of our purpose. The review of our internal law will demand a lot of work. The last time we did it was in 1927. There is no natural evolutive process of reform of the Society's juridical system. We have to turn it into a fitting instrument of the service of the Lord, in keeping with modern times. The Society is four and a half centuries old ... St Ignatius allowed for great flexibility, with room for adaptation. He believed in "inculturation" concerning the use of languages.

'As for our *raison d'être*, we must examine the present situation, with its challenges and opportunities. The specific mission of the Society is quite clear: it concerns justice, inculturation and dialogue. Our numbers decline by 1 per cent every year. We must take this into account, weigh up the pros and cons and concentrate on our priorities, avoiding a dispersal of our efforts. The key words are collaboration, co-operation and partnership with other sectors of the Church, other religious orders, lay organizations, and so forth. This is not something that comes easily to Jesuits. Our younger members, in particular, are attached to their independence.

'For a Jesuit, the process of "taking stock and renewal" doesn't have to wait for the calling of a General Congregation. In Ignatian spirituality, what we call discernment means constantly asking the Lord of the vineyard whether the task we are working on at the moment is what God really wants. A General Congregation is needed when the Society as a worldwide body of more than 23,000 Jesuits has to look to the future, on the basis of its past experience and in view of the call of the Church. This is the case at this time. Twenty years ago, the Society decided that the promotion of justice and the option for the poor were integral parts of its proclamation of the faith. The time has come to reflect on our experiences, the happy ones and the less happy ones, so that we can lay out a course of action for moving into the third millennium.'

NOTES

1 In his intervention during the African Synod, in April 1994, Fr Kolvenbach drew attention to 'the shameful and poignant fact of the sheer numbers of African refugees and forcibly displaced people. (...) To the figure of approximately six million refugees one must add all those forcibly displaced from their home territories, i.e. nearly 17.5 million persons. This is more than 50 per cent of the total number of refugees world wide, in a continent which represents only 9 per cent of the global population.'

2 The 34th General Congregation opened on 5 January 1995.

3 Since 1973, 29 Jesuits have died for their faith: Brother Alfredo Lobato, Spanish, 36 years old, killed in El Guéra, Chad on 1 December 1973; Brother Nicolas de Glos, French, 65, stabbed to death in N'Djaména, Chad on 23 May 1976; Father João Bosco Burnier, Brazilian, 59, killed in Ribeirao, Brazil on 12 October 1976; Fr John Conway, Irish, 57, and Fr Christopher Shepherd-Smith, English, 34, shot in Musami, Zimbabwe on 6 February 1977; Fr Rutilio Grande, Salvadorean, 45, gunned down in El Paisnal, El Salvador on 12 March 1977; Fr Desmond Donovan, English, 41, disappeared in Makumbi, Zimbabwe on 15 January 1978; Br Bernard Lisson, German, 69, and Fr Gregor Richert, German, 48, shot in Magondi, Zimbabwe on 27 June 1978; Fr Bernard, English, 53, stabbed to death in Georgetown, Guyana on 14 July 1978; Fr Gerhard Pieper, German, 38, shot in Kangaire, Zimbabwe on 26 December 1978; Fr Francis Louis Martinsek, American, 67, killed in Mokame, India on 24 February 1979; Fr Matthew Mannaparambil, Indian, 42, killed in Burham, India on 7 March 1980; Fr Luis Espinal, Spanish, 48, tortured and killed in La Paz, Bolivia on 22 March 1980; Fr Godofredo Amingal, Filipino, 59, killed in Kibawe, Philippines on 13 April 1981; Fr Carlos Perez Alonso, Spanish, 45, disappeared in Guatemala on 2 August 1981; Fr Francesco Saverio Chu, Chinese, 70, died in a work camp in China on 28 December

1983; Fr Klaus Kluiters, Dutch, 45, taken hostage and killed in the Lebanon on 14 March 1985; Fr Gonçalves Kamtedza, Portuguese, 55, and Fr Silvio Moreira, Portuguese, 44, killed in Mozambique on 30 October 1986; Br Vincente Canas Costa, Portuguese, 48, killed in the Mato Grosso, Brazil on 13 April 1987; Fr André Masse, French, 47, shot in Sidon, Lebanon on 24 September 1987; Fr Sergio Restrepo, Colombian, 50, killed in Tierralta, Colombia on 1 June 1989; Fr Ignacio Ellacuria, Spanish, 59, Fr Amando Lopez, Spanish, 53, Fr Joaquín Lopez y Lopez, Salvadorean, 71, Fr Segundo Montes, Spanish, 56, Fr Juan Ramón Moreno, Spanish, 56, and Fr Ignacio Martin-Baro, Spanish, 47, savagely murdered in San Salvador on 16 November 1989.

4 In the United States, the Jesuits created a voluntary body – the Jesuit Volunteer Corps, an organization which has since spread to Britain – to allow young people who do not wish to enter the Society to support its social action.

5 Louis McRedmond, *To the Greater Glory: A History of the Irish Jesuits* (Gill and Macmillan, 1991).

6 'Inculturation' means the introduction of the Gospel message into a given culture.

7 On 1 January 1994, the Society of Jesus numbered 4,178 scholastics, 2,735 brothers and 16,266 priests, i.e. a total of 23,179 Jesuits.

8 The principle of subsidiarity is that according to which the upper echelons of a hierarchy do not take decisions that can be made by the lower echelons; in other words, it is a principle of maximum delegation of authority.

PART I

FOUR CENTURIES OF BRINKMANSHIP

1

The origins

A CERTAIN LOPEZ

What is this new life that is now beginning?
IGNATIUS OF LOYOLA

I have no intention of rewriting the history of the Jesuits here, but simply of highlighting a few episodes of the Jesuit story in order to demonstrate how the genius of Ignatius of Loyola unfolded, especially when faced with the temptation of power, not without deviation or compromise.

The Society of Jesus was born of the encounter of an extraordinary event and an exceptional man. The event was the Renaissance, that flowering of culture when Europe rediscovered the values of classical and pagan humanism and extended its conquests to the 'new worlds' of the Americas and the Indies, with their fabulous treasures. The man was Ignatius of Loyola, a passionate Basque, as ardent in his quest for human happiness before his conversion as for 'the greater glory of God' after his commitment to the service of the King of Heaven. According to the Jesuit historian Emile Rideau,

> Great saints appear opportunely – from some obscure and unintelligible force – to complete, or at least pursue, a design. The evolution of the Church and the world were crying out for a man – a creator of society – situated at the watershed between the Middle Ages and the new era but capable of reviving the spirit of the Incarnation, at its very source, (. . .). The group founded by Ignatius was to be that of the new humanity, born of the Renaissance, in harmony with it and agreeing with its aims, but also in opposition to it, at open war with everything that was unauthentic and inhuman in the spirit of the Renaissance.[1]

An attraction and admiration for the world of the Renaissance can clearly be found in Ignatius, even after his conversion. This no doubt explains his decision to bring the Gospel to the world without leaving it and also his tendency to use very 'down to earth' means to attain spiritual ends. It is not surprising, then, that the vagaries of history have often encouraged the Society of Jesus to work behind the scenes of power, and sometimes to play an active part in political tragedies. The mistake to avoid – a common one – is to infer from this a thirst for power. It was absent, beyond any shadow of doubt, at the time of the modest beginnings of the Society. And yet this major ambiguity was already stamped on the features of the young squire from Loyola.

On his own admission Ignatius was, until his twenty-sixth year, 'a man given over to the vanities of the world, whose chief delight consisted in martial exercises, with a burning and vain desire to win renown'. This uncompromising self-criticism should not be put down to pious exaggeration. When he dictated his memoirs in 1554 – his *Autobiography* – to the Portuguese Jesuit, Luis Gonçalves da Camara, leaving us precious details of daily life in Rome in the early days of the Society, Ignatius of Loyola had a tumultuous life behind him. He was sufficiently clearsighted to recognize that, until his thirties, there was little prospect of anything but very worldly conquests. Ignatius became a saint. But he had been 'conquered' himself by a hard-fought struggle; his early years did not betoken virtuous intentions.

Loyola is an old Basque family name meaning 'face up to the enemy'. Quite a programme! The ancestral castle of the Loyolas was in fact built to withstand a siege. It was unattractive, its thick walls faced with red bricks, and spacious enough to house a large family. Bertrand of Loyola and his wife Marina Licona had thirteen children, of whom Ignatius was probably the youngest, born between 1491 and 1493, and baptized Inigo Lopez. His older brothers were killed fighting on various battlefields; one in Hungary, two near Naples and a fourth in the Indies. Another, Pedro Lopez, was destined for the clergy, like Inigo, and tonsured at the age of seven. However, according to the customs of that period and place, the clerical state did not automatically commit one to austerity.

Pedro Lopez, rector of the church of St Sebastian in Azpeitia, the Loyolas' neighbouring town, fathered no less than four children.

Orphaned at fourteen, Inigo was sent to the court of Juan Velázquez, the treasurer of the Kingdom of Castile, at Arevalo. Painstaking over his appearance, the young page was well known for his gallant exploits. Juan Polanco, his future secretary in Rome, was to write, no doubt after sharing a few secrets, that the young Inigo was somewhat turbulent and addicted to gambling, the love of women, quarrels and the pleasures of fighting, tastes which one day came close to costing him his life.

In 1515, Inigo was in Loyola. With his brother Pedro he was involved in some unsavoury affair. The nature of the crime is not known, but it is certain that murder was not involved, because the death penalty was not demanded in the formal proceedings brought against the guilty pair. Their deeds were nonetheless 'very serious, having been carried out at night, with deliberate intention and premeditation, as has been shown by the enquiry'. It was also noted that the accused Inigo, in spite of his clerical state, carried arms, wore an open cape and had 'long hair with no sign of a tonsure'. To escape punishment Inigo fled to Pamplona and gave himself up to the ecclesiastical court. He was imprisoned, but only for a very short while. His brother was not sentenced because of 'high-ranking' protection. Inigo went back to his post. But his protector, out of favour and ruined, died in 1518 and Inigo then offered his services to the Duke of Nájera, who was viceroy of Navarre, which Ferdinand the Catholic had taken from the d'Albret family in 1512.

In 1521, Pamplona was under threat from the armies of Francis I, and Inigo was sent to recruit reinforcements from his native region. He returned with a contingent commanded by one of his brothers, Martin. The French troops, led by André de Foix, entered the town without any difficulty: the inhabitants had no desire for war. The commander of the garrison, Miguel de Herrera, was likewise tempted to surrender. For Inigo, however, such a thing was out of the question: honour must be saved. There was no priest in the citadel; as a good Christian and a knight he followed the medieval custom and made his confession to a comrade-in-arms, and he stood firm. But after six hours of heavy artillery bombardment a cannonball fractured Inigo's right leg and damaged his left. With the soul of the resistance out of action, fighting ceased. It was Easter Monday, 20 May 1521. Inigo had acquitted himself brilliantly, but his military career was over. It had lasted less than a single day.

The valiant defender of Pamplona was not neglected by the victors. The French treated him with extreme courtesy and carried him back to the castle at Loyola. The wounded man was then delivered up to the surgeons. His injuries had been roughly tended and the fracture had set badly. An operation was called for – the tibia had to be broken and reset. 'Una carniceria', related Inigo, 'a butchery'. Inigo gritted his teeth and bore the pain. Towards the end of June, however, his condition became really serious. Everyone thought he would die, when suddenly he felt a definite improvement – and regained his pride. As there was an ugly swelling along the scar tissue, he asked the doctors to operate again. His friends protested, and Martin advised against it, but Inigo insisted. Once again he was submitted to torture, but he brushed it aside. This time the operation was a 'success', although it did not spare him the limp that afflicted him until the end of his life.

While lying convalescing, Inigo dreamt. Of love, obviously, and of how he would woo a certain lady, a woman of such high birth, so inaccessible, that he was never to disclose her name – perhaps for fear of being laughed at. Again, honour must be preserved. In the meantime, he needed excitement and asked for books, in particular romances that he had been in the habit of reading. But his sister-in-law could find him only *The Life of Christ*, by Ludolph the Carthusian, and *The Golden Legend*, by Jacobus de Voragine. Since there was nothing better, Inigo started reading and became totally absorbed: sometimes by the exploits of St Francis and St Dominic, sometimes by his own worldly ambitions. He had not been able to save Pamplona, but he could go barefoot to Jerusalem; that would be a worthwhile exploit. What for? Nothing. For the love of God, to imitate the great saints, to give himself a challenge.

The patient asked for writing materials. On 'glossy, lined

paper' he copied passages from his readings. Then he lay
back, to spend hours meditating and weighing up the emo-
tions he was feeling. Inigo became aware that, imperceptibly
but deep inside him, something had radically changed. Sometimes he was afflicted by deep sadness, a staleness that took
away the taste for prayer. Sometimes, on the contrary, he
enjoyed immersing himself in lengthy prayer and savoured
the words of Christ and Our Lady. He was no longer master
of his dreams. He experienced them with fear and a sort of
rapture. Soon he was forced to acknowledge the change in
himself. 'What is this new life that is now beginning?'

Someone else had noticed the change in his behaviour: his
brother Martin. When Inigo went to tell him 'Sire, the Duke
of Nájera, as you know, has learnt that I am better. It would
be good for me to go to Navarrete', Martin was not fooled. He
led him into one of the castle chambers, then another. 'And,
while displaying admiration for him, he set about begging him
not to throw his life away.' Why this wealth of precautions?
Ignatius had, it seems, too great a sense of modesty to reveal
the exact content of the discussion, but his vague intentions
no doubt worried his elder brother greatly. The trial in 1515
had already tarnished the Loyolas' reputation. Did these new
projects not contain a hint of heresy, a whiff of illuminism?
Inigo would then risk affronting the Inquisition. It would be
his ruin. Martin did everything he could to hold him back from
the edge of the abyss.

Inigo paid no attention. At the end of February 1522, he left
Loyola. Richly dressed and armed, attended by two servants
and accompanied by one of his brothers, Inigo rode off on a
mule. He was true to his word: he indeed went to Navarrete,
saw the duke and settled a few debts. Then he dismissed his
followers and, alone at last, set off on an adventure with no
clear idea of where it would lead him. It was not mystical
ecstasy which drove him, nor intellectual certainty, but the
need to test his strength. He sought to accomplish great feats,
to beat records and to undergo every hardship. And again and
again he would tell himself 'St Dominic did that; I also must do
it. St Francis did this; therefore I shall also do it.' Inigo decided
to travel to Jerusalem.

The journey was to be undertaken as a beggar. He had thus

to trade in his clothes and dress as a pilgrim. The famous
abbey at Montserrat was a required stopping-off place on the
way to Barcelona, where he was to embark for Jerusalem, via
Rome and Venice. On 21 March, he arrived at the shrine,
which was looked after by Benedictine monks. He spent three
days in confessing the sins of his whole life. He received abso-
lution, secretly gave away his clothes to a poor penitent, put
on a sackcloth garment and hung up his sword and dagger on
the church railings near the statue of the black Virgin. He spent
the night of 24 March in prayer, either standing or kneeling. At
dawn he received communion and then left. From then on he
had just one passion which he was to mention so often in his
writings: 'to serve Our Lord'.

An overriding passion; the phrase is not too strong, for
it almost led him astray. After the momentous experience
in Montserrat, Inigo went through a period of doubt and
anguish. To serve, yes, but how? He stopped at the foot of the
mountains, at Manresa, where he thought he would stay for a
few days at most. The Dominicans were not afraid to give a cell
to this vagabond. The former defender of Pamplona begged
in the streets, only accepting meat or wine on Sundays. He
let his hair and nails grow in expiation of his earlier sinful
love of elegance. Seven hours a day were spent in prayer.
This did not prevent him from being plagued with scruples,
experiencing incredible disgust and being visited by diabolical
visions. Such excesses ruined his health. The quest for God
led him to become obsessed with suicide. Inigo might well
have become, like thousands of other *alumbrados* or *illuminati*
(the 'enlightened'), a pathetic neurotic.

In his fascinating psychological study of St Ignatius,[2] Dr
William Meissner writes:

> In the case of the pilgrim of Manresa, the difficult psychic
> crisis he endured undoubtedly brought about a regressive
> state, marked by severe suicidal depression, a loss of ego
> boundaries in which the capacity to differentiate self and
> object was undetermined, and acute identity diffusion. As the
> conversion process continued, the resolution allowed for the
> shaping of a new identity, now cast specifically in religious and
> spiritual terms.
>
> From a psychoanalytical perspective, however, the resolution

does not appear complete and the underlying conflicts do
not seem fully resolved and thus continue to exercise their
derivative influence. Supporting this view are the mystical
experiences Inigo describes, including a variety of hallucinations
along with ruminative states, which issued eventually into
internal influences of deep understanding and illumination.
Some of the hallucinatory experiences he ascribed to the
influence of the good spirit, some, like the dragon of the many
eyes, finally to the evil spirit.

After hours of anguish he experienced, by his own account,
intense mystical experiences. Inigo spent nearly a year thus
before the decisive event which was going to direct his
whole life. When going to St Paul's hermitage one day,
along the path above the Cardoner river, Inigo sat down on
the bank. He was dazzled. The transformation was radical, as
the *Autobiography* suggests: 'He understood and knew many
things, things spiritual as well as things of faith and the
profane sciences; and this happened with such a great flash
of illumination that all these things appeared new to him.'
The content of the experience escapes us and the 'objective'
historian is left unsatisfied. Be that as it may, its effects were
permanent. Before his death Ignatius said that it seemed to
him that he had received more at that one time than during
the rest of his life.

The Cardoner illumination – which should not be translated
as a 'vision' – was a complete 'spiritual rebirth'. It made a
different man of him. In his cell in the abbey, Inigo thought
hard about this transformation and wrote down the fruits of
his meditation with an astonishing sureness and sobriety for
a man overwhelmed by the inexpressible. These notes were
never to leave him. Revised and extended, they would become
his little book *The Spiritual Exercises*, the foundation of all Jesuit
spirituality.

However, Inigo stuck to his plan of going to Jerusalem.
Towards the middle of February 1523, he sailed from Barcelona. He had first to go to Rome to receive the Pope's
blessing, according to custom. On 14 July, when he was
about to leave Venice on board the *Negrona*, he was laid
low with such a fever that the doctor forecast a watery
grave for him, but Inigo obstinately went ahead with his

plans. The crossing was an ordeal, but on 4 September, escorted by Turks, the pilgrims arrived at the Holy City. Inigo was captivated by it and wanted to settle there. The Franciscan custodians of the shrines, who were very touchy about their prerogatives, vigorously dissuaded him. He went back to Europe, firmly decided to return as soon as possible to the land where, as he continued to believe for a long time, he had to follow in Christ's footsteps and 'be useful to souls'.

That little phrase, taken from the *Autobiography*, played a large part in the subsequent development of the 'pilgrim', as Inigo called himself. It revealed the apostolic intent of the convert. Inigo felt an obscure need to share his experience, to find men willing to live in poverty like him and to preach the Gospel. On his return to Spain, his decision was made: to be able to 'help souls' it was his duty to 'study for a time'. Hence the vagabond of over thirty returned to the classroom, declaring himself ready to confront the rudiments of Latin grammar. He had faced the dangers of war and sea and was not afraid of a few declensions.

Inigo spent two years in Barcelona, and then enrolled at the University of Alcalá. There he met three young men, whom he inspired with his project to go to Jerusalem, this time as a group. This little band of companions, including a Frenchman, soon drew attention to themselves, especially on account of their distinctive garb – they were known as the 'Grey Habits' – and it was not long before the Inquisition became suspicious. On 19 November 1526, the commission of inquiry sat in the episcopal palace in Alcalá. Inigo, who had been arrested, was given a fairly light sentence: he and his followers were to dress like other clerics. Once released, Inigo left for Salamanca, where he was immediately spotted, suspected of heresy and thrown into irons. He spent 22 days in prison. His notebook, containing *The Spiritual Exercises*, was carefully examined. The verdict at Salamanca confirmed that of Alcalá: there was nothing heretical in those pages or in the companions' teaching. But they were forbidden to discuss theology in public until they had finished another four years' studying. Inigo lost heart: he was forbidden to preach, his apostolic venture was thwarted and the Inquisition was on his heels. His disciples from Alcalá became discouraged and deserted him. He left Spain and went to Paris, where he arrived in February 1528, ready to make a completely new start. He was back at square one.

Paris had not been chosen at random: it had four thousand students, fifty colleges and the best university in the West. There he would be able to get a sound education and would find the companions he needed. Inigo enrolled at Montaigu college. The indomitable Basque was not afraid to confront the harsh discipline railed at by Erasmus, nor to sit on school benches along with ten-year-olds. As he had no money, he lived in an almshouse and had to beg for food, which took up a lot of his time. Too much time. During Lent 1529, he went to Flanders to beg from rich Spanish merchants. In 1530, he went as far as London. Once he had enough money for his keep he was able to attend his lessons more or less normally, first at Montaigu, then at Sainte-Barbe college, from 1 October 1529. From then on he wore the soutane of Parisian clerics, which he would continue to wear until his death.

Inigo was now a paying student and a boarder. He shared a room with Pierre Favre, from Savoy, and a nobleman from Navarre, Francisco de Jassu y Xavier. For the time being, he abandoned his long hours of meditation to give himself over to scholastic logic. In 1532, he passed the baccalauréat and registered at the university. For the first time the name 'Ignatius of Loyola' appeared. On 14 March 1535, Ignatius received the degree of 'Master of the Most Illustrious Faculty of Arts of Paris'. His first goal had been achieved, he could henceforth envisage 'helping souls' without hindrance – a hope that never quite materialized. In Paris, and later even in Rome, Ignatius found he had to obtain certificates from the Inquisition. It is a paradox of history that the person who is considered to be the champion of the Counter-Reformation was, for a large part of his life, suspected of heresy and under the surveillance of the Inquisition.

Although studying hard, Ignatius did not forget his other reason for being in Paris: to gather new companions. He presented the *Exercises* to three Spanish fellow students who, carried away by their enthusiasm, distributed their goods among the poor. The affair caused such a stir in the Spanish colony that Ignatius was threatened with the whip by the head of Sainte-Barbe. This second attempt at forming a group came to nothing. One of the three students entered the Carthusians, another became a rich canon and the third disappeared without trace.

The third bid proved successful, though its beginnings were very uncertain. While there was immediate affinity between Loyola and Favre at Sainte-Barbe college, relations with Francisco were at first quite distant. The older student annoyed the hotheaded Basque with his advice, but after three years' gentle coaxing Ignatius managed to win him over. 'I have heard our great moulder of men say that the toughest clay he had ever worked on', his secretary Polanco was later to report, 'was that of young Francis Xavier in the early days.' His patience was rewarded. Xavier was converted around 1533 and became not only a very close friend but also the apostle of India and Japan, where he left the Christian faith already firmly implanted when he died, exhausted, on 3 December 1552, at the gates of China.

Around Ignatius and Favre, then Xavier, the group grew little by little. First Simon Rodriguez, who arrived in Paris from Portugal in 1527. Then two from Castile, Diego Laynez and Alfonso Salmeron. The former came from a family of Jewish converts and, in 1558, was to become Ignatius's first successor as head of the Society. Salmeron, born in 1515, had already been an inseparable friend of Laynez's when they were in Spain. A seventh recruit – Nicholas Bobadilla – joined the group in 1534. He was to become the most awkward of the early companions and to cause Ignatius the biggest worries, but allowances were constantly made because of his pranks and his impulsive nature.

Initially, all that the seven companions had in common was a certain spirit, imbued with Ignatius's experience and personality. But they adopted a particular lifestyle: evangelical poverty and chastity. They gathered for 'spiritual meetings'. On Sundays they all went to Mass together at the Carthusian monastery. Devout, studious and free, they had no desire to enter a religious order, and still less to found a new one. Nevertheless, they decided at the end of their studies to go to Jerusalem or, failing that, to Rome to put themselves at the Pope's disposal for any other mission he thought fit. Furthermore, they decided to become priests. On the feast of the Assumption their decision became a sacred vow.

In the early morning of 15 August 1534 the companions went to Montmartre. At the top of the hill, whose slopes were then simply open countryside, stood St Peter's Abbey. Halfway up there was a chapel dedicated to St Denis, and it was in its crypt that the group assembled. Pierre Favre, who had been ordained less than a month before, celebrated Mass. When the time came for communion, each person made the vows that would bind them henceforward to the group, a commitment that was only a private gesture, with no official recognition. But the rite had been created. Even today, the Jesuits take their final vows at a usually very simple celebration of the Eucharist, during which they place on the altar, before receiving communion, the signed text of their religious profession:

I, N, do hereby profess (...) and promise poverty, chastity and obedience for ever.

I also promise to devote myself particularly, in accordance with instructions that will be given to me, to teaching the young and the poor.

In addition, I promise a special obedience to the Supreme Pontiff for the missions he will entrust me with.

In these words, still in use today, one can see that beside the solemn promise, and on an equal footing with it, are the famous vow of obedience to the Pope and a promise to teach the young and the poor. The Society has not forgotten in the least Ignatius's first intuition and his attempts, so suspect in the eyes of the Spanish Inquisition, to transmit the faith to the man in the street. As for that 'unconditional' submission to the Pope, let it be noted that its wording includes a vital proviso. The Jesuit puts himself at the service of the Church, leaving the Pope the initiative of entrusting him with specific 'missions'. Apostolic zeal is not tantamount to servility.

The weight of history has put the generous simplicity of the initial project to the test, but the vows of Montmartre, while not to be confused with the act of founding the Society, already included everything that was to charac-

terize the future religious order: communal life, openness
to the world, obedience to the Church and readiness to go
on missions. They represent a bridge between personal generosity and collective ecclesiastical reform. Did they reduce
'mysticism' to the level of 'politics'? The temptation to do
so was to make itself felt before long, and many Jesuits suc-
cumbed to it in the course of history. But the primitive ideal
was above all a mystical intuition, realized in an apostolic
body. In any case, at that crucial period, Ignatius and his
companions were far from being the only ones to feel the
urgent need for 'new blood' in the Church.

At that time, a serious spiritual crisis was brewing up on
all fronts. The Augsburg Confession of 1530 had just defined
the basic tenets of Lutheranism, which was embraced by a
large number of German princes. In January 1533, Henry VIII
broke with Rome; in 1535, he ordered the execution of Thomas
More, who had remained faithful to Catholicism. In 1536, John
Calvin published the first edition of his *Institutes of the Christian
Religion*. A wave of mysticism swept through Spain, bringing
with it the worst excesses of a morbid religion, side by side
with the authentic sanctity of people like John of the Cross and
Teresa of Avila. The 'Placards' affair,[3] in October 1534, threw
Paris into turmoil and was the beginning of a long period of
bloody conflict. In 1535, Francis I published an edict ordering
'the extermination of the Lutheran sect'. During that time in
Rome, Paul III, elected Pope in 1534, was setting up a reform
commission. Since the end of the Lateran Council, in 1517,
innumerable measures had been proposed, indeed approved,
to put right the deplorable state of the Church. Despite admi-
rable attempts at evangelical renewal, the functioning of the
Curia, the system of ecclesiastical benefices, the ignorance of
the clergy, the decadence of convents, the quarrels between
princes and the Church, and the incessant rivalries between
senior members of the clergy – taken all together – paralysed
the pastoral renaissance that could be detected in the Church.
Christendom was breaking up under the pressure.

This was the drama being enacted on the stage where the
neophytes of Montmartre were just making their entrance
with youthful fervour. It was not long before they were confronted with its cruel reality. On 25 March 1535, Ignatius left

his companions to go to Spain and then on to Venice, where he completed his theological studies. The 'Parisians' joined him in Venice on 8 January 1537, together with three new recruits. Ignatius and most of his companions were ordained on 24 June 1537.

All were eager to make the pilgrimage to the Holy Land, but no ship left Venice that year as the seas were not safe. Instead, in accordance with the vow of Montmartre, the ten companions made their way to Rome to put themselves at the Pope's disposal. Before separating, for they travelled in small groups, they discussed what to answer should they be asked who they were: 'Seeing that there was no leader among them, nor any superior other than Jesus Christ, it seemed appropriate to call themselves the Society of Jesus ...'[4]

Once in Rome, the group had to suffer another campaign of slander. Clearly, rumour of heresy travelled as fast as the wind: from Spain and from Paris it had preceded Ignatius. This difficulty dealt with, in November 1538 the companions were received by Paul III and offered themselves to him 'to be sent wherever he thought necessary'. The Pope, who had great need of them, wanted to keep these zealous priests, who were nicknamed 'reformed priests', near him. As their first mission they were to teach the catechism to the children of Rome.

The little group's reputation grew more quickly than expected and spread well beyond the confines of Rome. Charles V wanted them for the Spanish Indies and John III for those of the Portuguese. Candidates came forward. What should be done? The companions had a feeling that their time of easy friendship was drawing to a close and that the group was in danger of breaking up. As was their custom, they got together to discuss the issue. Opinion was divided: 'We differed in regard to feelings and opinions on the subject of what our state should be.' The first question was: should they stay united? And, if so, should the group obey one of its members? The debate lasted from March to June 1539. The decision, not reached easily, was 'yes' on both counts. The companions considered that it was 'more necessary' and that it would 'be better' to promise obedience to one of them in order to safeguard the group's unity. But the name 'Society of Jesus' was maintained.

The deliberation of 1539 was decisive for the future of the 'little society', even if it then numbered only ten men and had no canonical validity until it had been duly approved by the Holy See. While the companions scattered to Siena, Parma, Piacenza, Naples and Brescia, Ignatius set to work to draw up a document defining the Society's characteristics. Thus, it chose to 'help souls' to 'progress in Christian life and doctrine', it also undertook to 'spread the faith by preaching, the *Spiritual Exercises* and works of charity, particularly by bringing Christianity to children and ordinary people'.

This mission was to be carried out

> ... in faithful obedience to our Holy Father Paul III and his successors (...) in such a way that, whatever His Holiness commands us to do for the good of souls and the propagation of the faith, we are to carry out immediately without procrastination or excuse, and as far as it is in our power, whether he send us among the Turks, to the New World, among Lutherans or anyone else, be they believers or infidels.

The scope of the apostolic aims of Ignatius and his first companions was therefore practically limitless. The routes to Jerusalem were closed, but those to the world, both the old and the new, were wide open.

As soon as the Pope had read the five chapters of that 'First Summary of the Institute of the Society of Jesus', he gave it his oral approval. It was a whole year, however, before confirmation came in writing. On 27 September 1540, Paul III promulgated the bull *Regimini militantis*, ratifying the terms and objectives of the document and thereby setting his official signature to the birth certificate of the Society of Jesus.

SENT AMONG INFIDELS

Provided nothing in India prevents my departure, I hope, in this year of 1552, to go to China, for it is possible that a great service to God in that country and in Japan can come of it.
ST FRANCIS XAVIER

Paul III had approved the Society's constitution. They were over the first hurdle. But the new religious order had neither an elected superior – Ignatius was acting only as 'spokesman' – nor a basic charter. The papal bull specified the two tasks that the companions should undertake without delay: elect a 'General' and draw up some Constitutions.

Heavy weather was made of the election. Ignatius challenged his companions' unanimous choice. And yet they had not only voted for him but also justified their choice, sometimes in moving terms. Francis Xavier, already on his way to the Indies, left a sealed letter in Rome. He was voting for Ignatius, he wrote, because 'it is he who has gathered us together, not without great difficulty; and he will again, certainly not without further difficulty, know how to keep us together, govern us and make us go from good to better'. Why did Ignatius refuse the responsibility? Was it a clever ploy to get even more overwhelming approval? This is not very plausible. In any case, Ignatius himself gave as the reason for his refusal his previous wicked behaviour (the proceedings in 1515 had left their mark) and his present faults. A second ballot was therefore necessary, which produced the same result – followed by another refusal.

Diego Laynez lost his temper. If Ignatius insisted on going against the obvious revelation of God's will, he might just as well leave the Society. This tactic, apparently, was the right one. Ignatius started to weaken: could he dare to refuse the will of Him whom he had so sought to serve, love and honour since Manresa, Jerusalem and Montmartre? He asked for a further delay, consulted his confessor – who urged him to accept – spent three days in prayer and drafted his own ballot paper, in which he gave his vote to whomever the majority named. On Easter Tuesday, 19 April 1541, Ignatius of Loyola thus became the Society's 'General', the first Father General of the Jesuits. On 22 March, the six companions present in Rome made their profession of faith in the basilica of St Paul's Outside the Walls.

The new General lived in a rented house near the church of Santa Maria della Strada. That chapel and some of the neighbouring buildings were made over to him and became the Society's headquarters. On that spot today is the church of Gesù, built between 1568 and 1584. In the house next to the church one can still visit the little room from where Ignatius ran the Society and where he stayed until his death in 1556. At the request of Fr Kolvenbach it has recently been restored to its original state of poverty, after years of accretions and embellishments.

The Society today has its headquarters in a cold, anonymous building: 5 Borgo Santo Spirito, just two minutes away from St Peter's Square. From the street outside one can see the forest of telecommunications aerials on the roofs of the Jesuit Curia. Obviously, there was nothing like that in Ignatius's day, yet the Society was already opening up to the demands of a fast-expanding world. Ignatian spirituality, inspired by the concerns of the day, was quick to give Jesuits a taste for activities as varied in their achievements as their geographical settings.

Ten companions offered their services to the Pope in 1539. There were about 1,000 Jesuits when their founder died. Divided into twelve administrative units, called provinces, they were to be found in Paris and Warsaw, in Japan, Brazil, the Congo and Mexico. One could call it, to quote Fr Emile Rideau, 'maximum occupation of territory'.

The extension of the Society has been the product of a combination of intent and necessity. Consider the amazing destiny of Francis Xavier. Gouvea, the principal of Sainte-Barbe college in Paris, had come close to whipping Ignatius for the trouble caused by his excessive pious practices. He had however retained a keen admiration for his former pupil and his disciples, and imparted some of this to the king of Portugal, who in turn asked his ambassador in Rome to investigate the value of these 'reformed priests'. If the ambassador was satisfied, he was to request two of these men for the Indian missions. No sooner said than done. Ignatius could not shirk his obligations, and so he chose Simon Rodriguez, since he was Portuguese, and Nicholas Bobadilla, who was robust and enterprising. As for Francis Xavier, his health left much to be desired and, perhaps, Ignatius was not so keen to part with his most hard-won companion.

Bobadilla, however, was struck down with fever when he was about to leave Rome. Ignatius, himself in bed, called for Francis. The conversation between the two men, at least as reported, is edifying. It is difficult to go further in one's readiness for duty. 'Master Francis', said Ignatius, 'you know that on the Pope's command, two of us must go to the Indies, and also that Master Bobadilla is prevented from going because of illness; the ambassador can wait no longer. It is your venture.' Xavier replied: 'Pues, sus. Heme aquí.' Which can be translated as: 'Perfect. Then I am your man.'

Two days later, on 16 March 1540, Francis left Rome with no hope of return. First to Bologna and Parma, where he planned to make his farewells to Pierre Favre, who had unfortunately just left for Brescia. The two friends were never to see each other again. The ambassador and the Jesuit reached Lisbon about mid-June. Simon Rodriguez was already working hard, while at the same time begging for food. King John III, impressed by the companions' zeal, kept them a further eight months in his capital. Finally only Francis was given permission to make the journey to the Indies; Simon Rodriguez had to remain in Lisbon. He would later become the first superior of the Portuguese Jesuits, in spite of serious mistakes and a stormy relationship with Ignatius.

Francis Xavier set sail on the *Santiago*, a massive galleon, on 7 April 1541. Although he was leaving with the grand-sounding title of Apostolic Nuncio – a visiting card that would in fact give him some authority with the Portuguese settlers – all that he carried with him was a few books and coarse-woven clothing to protect him from the cold of the Cape of Good Hope. One of the king's courtiers advised him to take at least one servant to do his washing for him, for such a task was beneath the dignity of a nuncio. Francis's reply was scathing: 'Sir, it was that dignity that reduced the Church of Rome to its present state; the best way of acquiring real dignity is to wash one's own underwear.' Francis Xavier's apostolic methods were not inspired by the circumlocutions of Parisian scholasticism. It was, rather, a sound feeling for the ills of the Church that made the Jesuit apostolic nuncio's actions reliable and genuine.

The crossing was a nightmare. One line taken from Francis's correspondence is enough to sum up his impressions. He wrote to Ignatius: 'The hardships and problems have been such that, left to myself, I would never, for the whole world, have dared to confront them a single day.' He finally arrived in Goa on 6 May 1542 and immediately set to work. The task was immense, primarily in regard to the Europeans, whose debauchery was a permanent object of scandal. Francis was so appalled that he went so far as to ask for the presence of the Inquisition. But his vocation called him towards the pagans. The year of his arrival he went to live among the Paravas, on the south-eastern coast of India. Within a very short time he had baptized 40,000 natives. Their preparation, as one can well imagine, was extremely rudimentary. Basically, it consisted in learning to recite the most important articles of the Creed. Francis nevertheless trained catechists and called incessantly for extra people from Europe.

'Catechists' is a rather pretentious word here: they were in fact not much more than interpreters. They translated – with great difficulty – the phrases spoken in poor Portuguese by Xavier. Later the Jesuit went amongst the native peoples without even an interpreter: 'You can imagine', he wrote, 'the exhortations that I am able to make, since they do not understand me and I understand them even less (. . .). I baptize the newborn who are brought to me; for that, there is absolutely no need of an interpreter.'

Such a practice of baptizing whole populations, not only *en masse* but also without the 'new converts' understanding even the rudiments of the faith to which they were expected to adhere by baptism, is rightly shocking to our modern way of thinking. It should be remembered, however, that the notion of religious freedom did not exist at that time; and, more to the point, Christian missionaries were convinced, according to the current theology of redemption, that by baptizing the pagans they were rescuing them from the fires of hell.

This readiness for baptism of peoples who were almost complete strangers to Christianity remained an enigma for a long time. There are two possible explanations for his success. Firstly, Catholicism was the religion of the Portuguese settlers and so, by adopting their faith, the local population obtained some sort of protection, however slight, from their brutalities. Secondly, Francis appears to have had an undeniably powerful influence over the natives. Although he did not have a gift for words, he always displayed a very real charity. Forever on the move, most of the time in bare feet and with a tattered cassock, he never turned away the children that crowded around him.

In 1545, Francis set sail for Malacca and Indonesia. His 'method' had been perfected; with the collaboration of the native elite, he prepared a catechism in Malay. In 1546, Simon Rodriguez sent ten Portuguese companions to India, and when Xavier returned to Goa in 1548 he discovered that there were 23 Jesuits in the colony. He was delighted about this, but his mind was already turning towards another project: Japan. While still in Malacca, in December 1547, Francis had got to know a young Japanese man. Their conversations convinced him that there was a genuine opportunity for evangelization in the Empire of the Rising Sun. Francis Xavier knew absolutely nothing of that country nor of its language, but that did not deter him. He left Goa in April 1549 with two missionaries. First stop Malacca, then 3,000 miles of open sea in a battered old tub.

A real shock awaited him. On arrival, he discovered a well-developed civilization with an established religion. He landed in the south of the archipelago, where he was detained by the overlord of the island. He set about learning a little basic Japanese and endeavoured to meet the Buddhist elite, who asked him daunting questions about the relationship between evil and the divinity. They also tested his scientific knowledge. During the winter of 1550–51, Francis went on foot to visit the Mikado, in the hope of converting the highest authority in the land. To get to Miako (now Kyoto) there were 600 miles to cover – another tough venture, with an extremely disappointing result. The town had been half destroyed by civil war; the Mikado had but a shadow of his former power and refused to see Francis.

Fortunately Francis, who had remained a pragmatist, had prepared several valuable gifts: a clock, a musical instrument, an arquebus, glass decanters and some mirrors. In the role of Portuguese ambassador, laden with presents, Xavier cut a fine figure. One of the great feudal lords took him in and, better still, allowed him to preach. Francis no longer carried out mass baptisms. He had understood that the situation in Japan was nothing like that in India or the Malay islands. A small nucleus of Christians was gradually built up: after two years about 2,000 had been baptized, most of them belonging to the nobility. By the end of the century the Church in Japan had some 300,000 members. One of Francis's greatest converts was not in fact a nobleman but a strolling singer, a 'jester', who was so ugly – with a single, half-sunken eye – that children ran away at the sight of him. The man had a lively mind and a warm heart. He was christened Lawrence and later became the first Asian Jesuit.

His mission accomplished, Xavier went back to Goa in January 1552. Almost immediately he wrote to Ignatius: 'Provided nothing in India prevents my departure, I hope, in this year of 1552, to go to China, for it is possible that great service to God, in that country and in Japan, can come of it.' Signed: 'The most exiled of your sons'.

Francis Xavier was aware – and he would not be the last to be – of China's decisive role in the evangelization of the Far East. For him it was the Promised Land. But the country was forbidden territory. The Portuguese did have a trading post at Canton, but the emperor, exasperated by the practices of some of the merchants, had finally banned all Europeans from entering his country. Francis straight away dreamt up a strategy that appears to our eyes singularly 'Jesuitical'. He suggested that the viceroy of India should send an official ambassador to China. One man was particularly well suited to that mission, one of his friends, a certain Diego Pereira, a merchant and ship-owner. Francis would simply accompany his friend. Once on the spot, he would be able to request permission to preach the Gospel. He also promised to ask for the abolition of the laws against foreigners and the liberation of the Portuguese imprisoned in Canton. In short, an excellent arrangement for all concerned.

The deal was settled. Francis's last action in India was to appoint a man after his own heart as superior – Gaspard Barzée, a Flemish Jesuit, who had promised when he joined the Society to 'serve my neighbour whoever he is, the leper and the plague victim, all the patients in hospitals ...'. Francis Xavier went to meet Pereira in Malacca. When the merchant arrived from Singapore in the *Santa Croce* to pick up Francis, the governor, jealous of the merchant's power, had the rudder removed from the vessel. Francis could go to the devil if he wished, but Pereira would not leave so long as he, the governor, Alvaro de Gama, was commander of the seas. He loosed his fury upon the nuncio, calling him a hypocrite and accusing him of having forged his letters of credit. Xavier was reviled by the whole Portuguese colony.

When his jealousy was finally appeased, Alvaro de Gama authorized the *Santa Croce* to sail, without its 'ambassador' of course, but with Francis. Towards the end of the summer they drew alongside the island of Sancian (now Shang-ch'uan Tao), off the Chinese coast, a paradise for smugglers. Francis, obsessed with his desire to get to Canton, was prepared to haggle over his passage with a Chinese trafficker, who agreed to smuggle him to the gates of the city. In November, however, Francis was still waiting. Fever, hunger and cold sapped his strength. From his miserable hut he watched the shore with hope. But it was death that arrived instead. During the night of 2–3 December 1552 he passed away, his face set towards China. He was 46 years old.

Francis Xavier had already been dead for six months when Ignatius, who did not hear the sad news until the autumn of 1555 – although it is said that the rumour had reached Rome by the beginning of that same year – ordered his companion to return to Europe. This decision is surprising. Some have thought that the General, sensing his own death was close, wished to make sure of a successor of the first order in Francis. The reason given in his letter of 28 June 1553, however, was quite different. Ignatius put forward the need to inform the Apostolic See about the Indian missions. He also hoped to 'fire' the king of Portugal with a desire to convert Ethiopia, an evangelization project appaently deeply rooted in Ignatius's mind, though not very clearly defined. And, fearing Francis would argue that his responsibility as Provincial of India kept him overseas, the General had a counter-argument ready: 'If it seems to you that your presence there is important for government, you could just as well govern from Portugal as from Japan or China, if not much better. You have often had to accept longer absences. Add this one to them ...'

The argument was irrefutable. In spite of the extreme slowness and the danger of maritime communication, the

Jesuit General, who was said to watch constantly over his troops, was of the opinion that a superior of India could run his province from a distance. This characteristic of Ignatius of Loyola's has had a great influence on the Society, even to this day. A French Jesuit working in Chile, for example, knows he belongs to a particular community in Paris, where he will always find board and lodging and also ... his colleagues' questions, with a mixture of criticism and praise. Another, in an isolated mission as a member of a research team or a manual worker, may see his provincial superior only once a year. It is possible that he will never meet the General, but he knows that he can be sure of getting a reply to the slightest request, often by return of post.

The brotherly relationship that existed between the first Jesuits, scattered far and wide since the Society's beginnings, continues with modern forms of communication. Institutional ties, especially the vow of obedience, act as a safeguard of basic unity. The Jesuits value that intimate aspect of their order. They will tell you that because they are spiritually united they can be spread out to meet the needs of the Church and the world. The theory is splendid – the apostolic community's geographical centre is only symbolic; the true centre is elsewhere: it is a mentality, a way of life.

Reality, of course, is sometimes less idyllic, and institutional ties go a long way to explain the Society's cohesion – and, some would say, its power. It was the Society's remarkable *esprit de corps*, based on total obedience, that made it an effective and awe-inspiring elite corps, not to say 'strike force', even during the life of its founder. With the rapid growth of numbers, its effectiveness and influence could only grow stronger.

After Francis Xavier's death, the Society quickly found new fields of action in which to serve, in the Ignatian expression, 'under the standard of the Cross'. Whilst the Indian missions were expanding, Ignatius had to satisfy other pressing requests, of a completely different nature. The Pope wanted to reform the Church from within. He needed the companions for that major, and patently urgent, task. The Protestant Reformation had resulted in the establishment of separated Churches. Christian communion had been shattered. A second reform had to be carried out which would be able to preserve the endangered unity. It would be known as the Catholic Reformation or the Counter-Reformation, whose main expression was the Council of Trent.

The idea of a Council had been around for a long time. In 1524, the Emperor Charles V had suggested Trent as a suitable place for a meeting, within the Holy Roman Empire yet also an Italian town. The Emperor's interference in the Church's internal affairs was a sign of the times. We have already seen that the King of Portugal was responsible for Francis Xavier's going to India. The Christian princes at that time were still 'protectors', often oppressive ones, of ecclesiastical life. And, conversely, men of the Church often became advisers or *éminences grises* to princes – a situation that the Jesuits were to use to their advantage. The Reformation became established in Germany: the principle *cujus regio, hujus religio* obliged the people to profess the same faith as their prince. Charles V, firm in that belief, therefore considered he had a role to play in the convening and the progress of the Council, and he did not hesitate in letting it be known, though the war that he was waging against Francis I of France prevented the Council from meeting until the Crépy peace treaty had been signed in 1544.

The Council had been convened three times (1536, 1542 and 1544) by Paul III, before it managed to gather in Trent on 13 December 1545. Only 28 bishops were present at the opening ceremony, among them only one Englishman, one Frenchman and one German, somewhat meagre for an 'ecumenical' Council. A century and a half later Leibniz was to write to Bossuet that Trent had basically been 'a synod for the Italian nation, where others were allowed in only for the form and as a cover-up'. The English Cardinal Reginald Pole, however, was one of the three legates appointed in 1542 to preside. At the end of the Council, on 4 December 1563, there were nevertheless 27 French bishops out of a total of 237.

Though the Council failed to satisfy the Protestants, and its reforms were less comprehensive than many had hoped, it established a solid basis for the renewal of discipline and spiritual life in the Church. A tedious series of ups and downs, as much political as theological, Trent nonetheless marked the beginning of a genuine Catholic reform. This helps to explain Ignatius Loyola's instructions to the three Jesuits that he sent to the Council on the Pope's orders: Diego Laynez, Alfonso Salmeron and Pierre Favre, the last of whom died on 1 August without having been able to obey the pontifical command. The General's text took the form of personal programme: 'As for me, if I have to speak, I shall be slow, thoughtful, and loving, especially if it concerns questions being dealt with, or that might be dealt with, by the Council.'

The Jesuit 'experts' at Trent were not content with good advice and protracted, often trivial, discussions. They preached, heard confessions and visited the poor. There was no question of stirring up quarrels in public. Ignatius's instructions were explicit: 'When preaching, I shall not touch upon any point that separates Protestants from Catholics, but I shall content myself with treating standards of good behaviour and devotions in common practice in the Church.' Everyone they met, children, penitents and the sick, was to be asked to pray for the Council. Finally, one hour every evening was to be given over to 'sharing the results of the day and fixing the objective for the following day'. Ignatius, who wrote this order with his full authority as General, in his conclusion forbade any objections: 'This order is to come into force within five days of your arrival at Trent. Amen.'

At the Council, then, the Jesuit priests, who followed the programme to the letter, attracted the attention of the bishops present by their lifestyle. On a theological level, however, and contrary to a persistent legend, the Jesuits did not determine the course of the Council. Not one of them, for example, took part in the final session, which lasted from January 1562 to December 1563.

Thus, as is clear from reading Ignatius's texts and personal instructions to his subordinates, the Jesuits were not at first seeking to join a crusade against heresy, but were trying instead to make every effort to change the Catholic Church. And if they did have a master plan, one must not, as some have done, look for it in some 'secret instructions'. It is sufficient to refer to the spirit and the letter of the *Spiritual Exercises* by which 'man is enabled to conquer himself and to decide on his way of life with a determination that is free from harmful attachments'.

It was characteristic of the early Society that it made constant reference to the *Exercises* and showed a distrust of contemporary writings and thought. Throughout his life, the founder of the Jesuits mistrusted 'intellectuals', beginning with Erasmus. The companions, like Ignatius, wrote thousands of letters, but no formal work of great literary, philosophical or theological importance came from their pens; practical subjects predominated. Having been himself under suspicion for so long, Ignatius mistrusted original ideas.

At times he became downright intolerant. The Protestants never forgave Ignatius for one particularly outspoken letter to Peter Canisius.

> All heretical books ... found in bookshops and private homes must be burnt or cast out from all parts of the kingdom. A similar treatment should be meted out to all books by heretics, even if the contents are not heretical, such as Melanchthon's works of grammar, rhetoric and dialectic.

For Ignatius it was a question of all or nothing. Though he required his men to listen to, and to love, people, he did not tolerate any 'feebleness' in regard to ideas. It was not yet time for ecumenism.

What, then, should be offered as wholesome reading matter? According to the same letter, it would be useful to have: a catechism for children (Canisius obliged by writing his still-famous 'little catechism'); a book for 'the less-well-educated parish priests and ministers but who are of goodwill'; and finally, on a higher level, a general survey of scholastic theology for educated people or 'those who believe themselves to be so'. Ignatius's distrust of the teaching of the time led him to approach the subject of training candidates for the Society with the greatest caution. Paradoxically, his position on this would in turn determine decisively the subsequent development of the tasks undertaken by the Jesuits.

At the outset, the candidates admitted into the Society were all educated men. Like the first companions, they had achieved academic qualifications. But soon young men who had not finished their studies came forward. They lived with the priests and studied at university. This was how it was in Padua, Valencia and Coimbra (Portugal). It was then that the idea arose of having an institution for Jesuit students, where they could receive the necessary education without having to travel to a university. In 1546, Francis Borgia founded the first college where future Jesuits were taught by Jesuits, in Gandia, Spain. The following year Paul III raised the college to the status of a university.

It was in 1548, in Messina, that students who did not intend to enter the Society were allowed, for the first time, into the circle of 'scholastics' (Jesuit students). This innovation, made with no ulterior motive, was overwhelmingly successful. The colleges soon swallowed up a large proportion of the available workforce. Ignatius himself, who had never expected to create a teaching order, paid particular interest to the work carried out in Sicily. Ten companions were sent there that same year. The General asked other regions to send qualified teachers to the island, to which Simon Rodriguez replied drily that such teachers, if they existed, would be better employed in other universities and in more prestigious places than Messina. A second college was nonetheless founded in Palermo in 1549.

In the Eternal City itself, Ignatius founded the Roman College, which had over 2,000 students by 1584, and which was the predecessor of the present Gregorian University, one of the leading schools for theological training in the Catholic Church. When it opened on 22 March 1551, it bore the simple inscription: 'School for grammar, the humanities and Christian doctrine; non-paying'. Chairs of philosophy and theology were established in 1553, and the following year Paul IV gave the Roman College the right to award academic degrees.

The College was to play a major role after the Council of Trent, particularly under the influence of St Robert Bellarmine as Professor of Theology. While following the example of his contemporaries in thinking that the Church was a 'perfect society', comparable to the Kingdom of France and the Venetian Republic, he differed from them – who exalted the Pope's prerogatives as being quasi-absolute – by formulating the thesis of the Supreme Pontiff's indirect power in temporal affairs. This proposition nearly got his writings put on the *Index librorum prohibitorum*, the catalogue of books banned by the Church, first drawn up in 1564 and not abolished until four centuries later, in 1966. Bellarmine also called for the Pope to consult his brothers in the episcopate before taking decisions concerning the universal Church. Was this the first suggestion of the collegiality highlighted by Vatican II?

The Gregorian University has been involved in all the major debates that have shaken Catholicism from the sixteenth century and has been responsible for forming nearly all the Popes, including Pius IX, Leo XIII, Benedict XV, Pius XI, Pius XII, Paul VI and John Paul I among the more recent ones.

In opening colleges in Messina and Rome, Ignatius did not immediately recognize the scope and consequences of his decision. Perhaps he even remained cautious, in his heart of hearts, in the face of the avalanche of requests that soon poured in. In the draft of the new order's constitution approved in 1540, there is a phrase, abandoned later but indicative of the state of mind of the first companions: 'Neither university nor schools in the Society!' By the founder's death, however, the Society of Jesus was already running 29 colleges. By 1580, there were 144 colleges, as against only 55 houses in the order's 21 provinces. In the space of 44 years the Jesuits had become a fully fledged teaching order.

The change was not imposed on them against their will. Not only was children's education implicitly provided for in the initial project, but in 1551 Ignatius wrote to the Duke of Bavaria: 'Our task is to promote science, theology and religion. We must prepare pupils in the basic subjects, the humanities, philosophy and science.' In other words, the whole range of knowledge. And to do this the Jesuits invented secondary education. From being distrustful of books and learning they were soon to become known – even if to a large extent unjustifiably – as the most 'intellectual' order of the Church and as champions of modern humanism.

This evolution did not take place without causing some upheavals within the Society. Its enormous educational machinery, while ensuring great influence, weighed heavily upon it. It took up the time and energy of most of the workforce, it delayed or prevented the launching of many projects of equal importance, and it caused debts to mount up behind the imposing façades of buildings whose founders had more ambitions than resources. But, above all, the colleges restricted the mobility that, according to Ignatius's wishes, was to characterize the Society. The 'shock troops' had settled into their winter quarters and would find it extremely difficult to get going again.

This problem did not worry Ignatius overmuch; it was the cost of the colleges that really concerned him. And, from 1540, he was occupied with a completely different task – drawing up the *Constitutions* that Paul III had requested. It had been the first companions' intention to write their order's constitution collectively, as they had done in earlier instances, but circumstances, especially their rapid dispersal, prevented them from doing so. Ignatius therefore became the sole architect and submitted all his drafts for approval to the *primi patres* and to those new companions who seemed best able to understand the spirit of the Society. For that reason the *Constitutions* took all the longer to draw up. And the process became even more complicated when Bobadilla, passing through Rome at the beginning of 1551, swept aside all the work with a somewhat thoughtless remark: 'It seems to me that the same thing is repeated several times. It would be a good thing to make a short summary giving the substance of all these rules.'

The first draft was presented to the members convoked in Rome in 1550–51, ten years after the Society's recognition. Besides the notes of Polanco, the faithful secretary, the manuscript contains over 220 corrections and additions in Ignatius's hand. Whole passages were sometimes altered. In 1552, when Ignatius and Polanco started to write a new version of the text, Ignatius continued to seek advice. He added even more rules that betray his painstaking, not to say fastidious, attention to detail. One is surprised to find this man, who was constantly concerned with weighty Church matters, seriously worrying about tiny details of dress and food, domestic duties and behaviour in society. For example, he laid down 'rules for deportment' requiring one to lower one's eyes in conversation.

After returning continually to the drawing board, the work of drafting the *Constitutions* was finally completed in 1553. The text was promulgated in Sicily, Portugal, Spain and Germany by Jerome Nadal, who had entered the Society in 1545 after fiercely resisting Ignatius's 'advances' for a long time. Thus the *Constitutions* could be 'tested' by each region and so, when they were finally confirmed in 1558 at the Jesuits' first General Congregation (general assembly), they appeared as a well-tried rule and not one that had been imposed on the members from above. By then Ignatius had been dead for two years.

Fr André Ravier was correct in stating that Ignatius fathered the Constitutions of the Society of Jesus 'personally, dramatically, and in saintly fashion'.[5] But this legal text, whose style is often laboured and complicated, was also the fruit of experience: of that of a group of men who had staked their lives on the Gospel lived in the Church. The ten chapters that were to shape the image of the future Society also reflected a commitment that had already been put to the test. Francis Xavier in his far-off India lived by the spirit of the *Constitutions* without ever having known the letter of the law.

As is to be expected, the first part of the *Constitutions* deals with the admission of candidates. Perfectly legitimate qualities are required: natural goodness, a peaceful character (*sic*), sound ideas or the ability to acquire them, solid will-power and 'an honest appearance'. To be a gifted speaker would be an advantage, not forgetting 'health and strength to bear the strains of our Institute'. Reasons for dismissal are listed next, as in the case of a subject who is 'absolutely useless, and more likely to hinder the Society than to help it'.

The *Constitutions* then go into details of education and incorporation into the Society. An examination of the subjects to be studied provides an insight into the demands made on Jesuit students. Mention can be made here, for example, of a comment that still holds good, *mutatis mutandis*, in the training of Jesuits today: 'When planning to train people in a college or university for work with the Moors or the Turks, then Arabic or Chaldean is called for; and Indian for work in India; and likewise other languages that might be useful in other countries.'

The sixth part of the *Constitutions* concerns the 'personal life' of those persons admitted or incorporated into the Society. If the order's aim is to travel all over the world 'wherever there is hope of giving greater service to God', then *obedience* is the condition of survival for that 'nomadic' community. The Jesuit's obedience is therefore to be total – at least in principle. He is not only to obey orders without question and carry out every mission to the letter, but he must also model his personal judgement on that of his superior. As one particularly famous article in the *Constitutions* reads:

> Let us think that whoever lives in obedience must let divine
> Providence lead him and guide him, by means of his superior,
> like a corpse [*perinde ac cadaver*], which lets itself be taken
> anywhere and be treated as anyone wants, or like an old man's
> stick, which is used anywhere and for anything that is required
> by the hand holding it.

The mere mention of 'corpselike' obedience has earned the Society more insults, hostility and biting irony than all its political mistakes and daring pastoral ideas put together. Especially as, to complicate matters, the individual's obedience to his superior is closely linked to the whole order's obedience to the Pope.[6] The terms are perfectly clear: the members of the Society 'can be sent to one place or another by order of the Supreme Vicar of Christ Our Saviour, or else by the Society's superiors, who equally represent for them the divine Majesty'. No excuse can be made. And the task set may not be abandoned for the sake of other opportunities, however praiseworthy, to serve God and the Church.

This obedience, in appearance as rigid as a corpse or an old man's walking stick, would no doubt have quickly fossilized individual dynamism and the creativity of the Society as a whole if it had been observed in its strictest sense. In fact, critics least likely to be sympathetic towards the Jesuits must recognize their flexibility, their ability to adapt and their often fierce independence of spirit. Is there a contradiction between these two attitudes? No, because Ignatian obedience is not spiritual browbeating. A form of 'death' is inherent in all obedience, as it is present in the exercise of freedom. And obedience can be lived as a union of two freedoms. Furthermore, since obedience binds the superior himself to the corporate Society, he is unable to play the dictator. He provides and embodies the communal bond. Fr Dominique Bertrand rightly considers that in speaking of Jesuit obedience

the term 'submission' is not suitable; he prefers that of 'a conspiracy to serve the mission'.[7]

Absolute obedience, for the Jesuits, then, does not imply
absolute power on the part of authority. To convince oneself of
this it is enough to read the articles of the *Constitutions* dealing
with the Father General. He is so much a corporate part of
the order that he cannot refuse its election of him. He enjoys
extensive prerogatives but, as the original text stipulates, for
the 'construction' of the Society and not its 'destruction'.
Moreover, and this point is of the greatest importance, the
General is not the sole authority empowered to take decisions involving the future of the Society: when the case arises,
he must call a General Congregation. Although this assembly
does not meet at regular intervals, every three years a meeting
is held of delegates from the whole world, with the responsibility not only of informing the General of the state of the
Society but also, if necessary, of asking him to call a General
Congregation.

Furthermore, the *Constitutions* make provision for a complex
system of elected assistants and advisers who run the Society,
with the General, and limit the absolutism of central authority.
For it remains true that the order is governed according to a
monarchic principle, by the elected members of an aristo-
cracy. A cruel definition of the Society of Jesus by a dis-
abused, but prudently anonymous, Jesuit is the following:
'The most despotic autocracy ever devised, luckily tempered
by the disobedience of its members and the incompetence of
its superiors.'

But, if one can say that monarchic systems of government
are kept in check by the resistance of their subjects, it is certainly not untrue to say that the power of the Jesuit General
is tempered by the appraisal of his subordinates, who can, as
a last resort, remove him from office during a General Congregation. This has never happened. The very existence of
this right shows, however, that if Jesuits obey one of their
members it is with a view to a higher good: the unity and the
greater service of the Society.

Ignatius was not the last to show that the obedience he
demanded was not to be confused with the trampling of
conscience and even less with the crushing of men. Antonio

Araoz, one of his nephews, entered the Society in 1539 and was sent to Spain, where he put all his energy into preaching and making converts. He was brilliant and became the first Provincial of Spain in 1547. But, according to witnesses, he was ruining his health. How was he to be persuaded to slow down? A true militant does not like to be told to be careful. Ignatius knew this and wrote him a few lines reminding him of his own experience. It is necessary to pay attention to food and the amount of sleep, he wrote. And, to convince Araoz of his sincerity on this point, he added: 'I order you in the name of holy obedience to observe what I have said.'

The apostolate should not make too great a demand on the body, and neither should the observance of ascetic rules or devotional excesses. The man who had subjected himself to unreasonable mortifications in Manresa had not forgotten the disastrous consequences of his privations. In Rome, Ignatius repeatedly showed caution with regard to the 'demands' of piety. Among the obstacles to admission to the Society, Ignatius lists 'sinful' habits that one could not hope to 'change greatly'. Immediately afterwards came, side by side: 'thoughtlessness and incompetence' and indiscreet devotions that lead to serious errors and illusions, especially when personal judgement is inflexible.

Some of the Jesuits in the Roman residence wished to make Friday a day of fasting rather than one of mere abstinence. Ignatius would not hear of it. In fact his companion Ribadeneira wrote: 'he takes great care to avoid the introduction of new rites, ceremonies, prayers or customs into the Society without his knowledge.' The same witness noted that, regarding prayer and meditation, Ignatius 'was convinced that it was better to find God in everything one did rather than spend long hours at prayer'.

As for mortification, he preferred practices attacking honours and vainglory – especially for highly esteemed or self-important people – to those affecting the flesh by fasting, physical punishments and hair shirts. This sound attitude could be taken to extremes. In 1545, Ribadeneira was forced by his doctors to give up Lenten observances, which at that time were very harsh. Fearing that he would offend the other members of the household, he complained to Ignatius, who told him to silence his scruples and even threatened to chastise any member of the Society who was scandalized. The General did not flinch from self-criticism on this subject. In order to persuade Francis Borgia – then still Duke of Gandia but secretly professed in the Society – to give up extreme austerity, he admitted: 'I have greatly praised fasting and rigorous abstinence ... For some time I considered it an excellent thing, but I could no longer do it now that I can see that such fasting and abstinence prevents the stomach from behaving normally and even from digesting a little ordinary meat ...'

Ignatius did not scorn bodily needs. What counted was to subordinate the means to the highest end. Today we would talk of a scale of values: one's apostolic work was of greater importance than all other aspects of religious life, rites, prayers, fasting, devotions and even obedience. Ignatius was ready to defend his viewpoint even before the highest authority in the Church: witness the conflict that brought him up against the formidable Paul IV. The incident appears insignificant, but Ignatius felt that the Society and its future were at stake.

On 23 May 1555 Cardinal Giampietro Caraffa was elected Pope. He succeeded Marcellus II, a great friend of Ignatius's who had, however, reigned for only 21 days. The new Pope was of all the cardinals the one from whom Ignatius had most to fear. Caraffa had been one of the founders of the Theatine Congregation and had, on at least two occasions, suggested that Ignatius merge the Society with it. The proposal had been firmly refused. Furthermore Caraffa was a Calabrian, and in Naples he had learnt to hate the Spaniards. It was a delicate situation.

When relations had deteriorated so much that an open conflict between Caraffa and Philip II of Spain had broken out, the fiery pontiff ordered the Jesuits' house to be searched: they were suspected of conspiring with the enemy. Rumour had it they were hiding weapons for the Spanish party and were therefore potential terrorists. Although the episode was humiliating for Ignatius, worse was to come. There was no choral recitation of the Office in Jesuit communities. Changing this principle would weaken the whole structure. But since the Theatines, founded by the Pope, sang the Office, Ignatius found himself forced to accept a compromise. To keep Paul IV happy, Vespers would be sung in the church of Santa Maria della Strada on Sundays and feast days.

This difference of opinion between the Jesuits and the Pope, in spite of the vow of obedience, was only the first in a long series. But Ignatius had shown the way: he chose to give in temporarily rather than to keep up subtle intrigues through stubborn pride. He knew how to bow to circumstances without, however, abandoning his convictions. Blessed with sound judgement and intuition, he subjected his decisions to the principle of 'discernment': were not the pursuit of God's will and the good of the Church above human contingencies, even those produced by the uncertain tempers of Popes?

People close to the General said that a quarter of an hour would have been long enough to persuade him to accept the abolition of his Society. He was not called on to make that supreme sacrifice, but he gave ample proof of his realism. Tradition attributes a maxim to him, which, while not in fact to be found among his writings, perfectly sums up his blind belief in action: do everything as if its success depended entirely on yourself, and rely upon God for everything.

'Relying on God' did not mean doing nothing, and Ignatius, as General, was forever active. In spite of numerous illnesses, which even led him to offer his resignation in 1551 (it was refused), he received endless supplicants, settled disputes, wrote or dictated nearly 7,000 letters; organized and co-ordinated projects; encouraged, comforted and visited people; and, of course, conducted the *Exercises*. He was not always an easy person to get on with and punished even his most faithful followers for trifles. General-elect Diego Laynez said that in 1555 he was so harshly treated by Ignatius that in despair he prayed: 'Lord, what have I done to harm the Society that this saint should act in this way towards me?' And there would have been many more than a thousand members of the Society at the end of Ignatius's life if one included those he had expelled. In any case, it is certain that he went to it with a will. At Whitsun 1555, for some unknown reason, he expelled twelve Jesuit students from the Roman College, at one blow, among them a close relative of the viceroy of Sicily, who was a great protector of the nascent Society.

While the Society now stretched from Rome to Paris, Germany, Portugal, India and Brazil, the old fighter felt his strength declining. Towards mid-June 1556, he handed over a large part of his authority to Juan Polanco and Cristóbal of Madrid. Then, at the beginning of July, he withdrew to a holiday house he had just set up in an Aventine vineyard for the students at the Roman College. On 28 July, feeling extremely ill, he went back to Rome. Two days later, after his midday meal, he called Polanco and announced that he was going to die. Polanco was asked to go and request the Pope's blessing for Ignatius and for all the sick people in the Society. Having seen him in a similar state before, Polanco consulted two doctors and then decided to wait until the next day. That evening Ignatius asked about the progress of negotiations to buy a house. He seemed to be over the crisis. During the night the medical orderly heard him cry out 'My God!', but did not go and have a look at him. By dawn the patient was at death's door, and Polanco rushed to the Pope's palace. When he returned, at about 5.30 am on 31 July 1556, Ignatius was dead.

NOTES

1 Emile Rideau, *Les Ordres religieux actifs* (The active religious orders) (Paris, Flammarion, 1980).
2 W. W. Meissner SJ, MD, *Ignatius of Loyola: The Psychology of a Saint* (Yale University Press, 1992).
3 In the night of 17 to 18 October, notices attacking Catholic doctrine were put up in Paris and Amboise by the Protestant party. Some were even found on the door of the royal chamber.
4 Juan Polanco, quoted by André Ravier in *Ignace de Loyola fonde la Compagnie de Jésus* (Desclée de Brouwer, 1974).
5 Ibid.
6 For a fuller discussion of Jesuit obedience, see Part III, Chapter 2, pp. 252–5.
7 Dominique Bertrand, *Un corps pour l'esprit: Essai sur l'expérience communautaire selon les* Constitutions *de la Compagnie de Jésus* (Paris, 1974), p. 140.

2

The rise and fall of the Jesuits

THE GLORY AND THE CROSS

Your humble servant has perfect knowledge of the celestial sphere, of geography, geometry and arithmetic. He observes the stars with the help of instruments and knows how to read a sundial. His methods are entirely in keeping with ancient Chinese methods.

MATTEO RICCI to the Emperor of China

A saint is not without faults – and Ignatius was no exception. He left the Society a fine heritage: a strong impetus, his spirituality and the *Constitutions*. But he had not prepared his succession. On 4 August 1556, the young Society found itself with two vicars-general: Diego Laynez and Jerome Nadal. Bobadilla, for his part, schemed to introduce collegiate leadership by all the founder members. Even more serious was the fact that Paul IV demanded that the Society's *Constitutions* and all its bulls should be given to him within three days. Lastly, the Jesuits did not know who exactly would take part in the General Congregation. Although there were a thousand members in the order, there were only 42 professed priests, those Jesuits allowed to pronounce their vows of poverty, chastity, obedience and submission to the Pope, and the only ones entitled to hold high office in the Society.

Legal uncertainty and quarrels over precedence risked shattering the newly acquired unity, but the first General Congregation was finally convened for 19 May 1558. On 2 July, the twenty electors who had been able to reach Rome met, under the direction of Cardinal Pacheco, in the room where Ignatius had died. The Cardinal told them that the Pope desired only that the new General should live in Rome. For the rest – and this remark was of the greatest importance for the later history of the Jesuits – the Congregation was to act in complete freedom. He then left the room where the election was to take place.

Diego Laynez got thirteen votes – an absolute majority – and became General. Thus ended a long and dangerous period during which the seat of power was vacant. Division, which had been a serious threat, had been avoided, but the comfort this brought was short-lived. During the following days the Jesuits expressed their attachment to the *Constitutions* drawn up by Ignatius and endorsed the text. But, as they well knew, Paul IV was determined that Divine Office should be sung in Jesuit churches and did not want to hear of the General being elected for life.

The Congregation had thus to legislate under surveillance, and was faced with an embarrassing dilemma: on the one hand, the Jesuits, who had vowed obedience to the Holy See, had just solemnly confirmed their link with the Pope as a distinctive mark of their order; but, on the other hand, they were already in open conflict with Paul IV. To get out of deadlock, they wrote a letter to the Pope informing him, in the most respectful terms, that the decision for life generalship had been adopted unanimously. On receiving this message, Paul IV flew into a towering rage. One can imagine how Laynez and Salmeron felt when, on 6 September, they were received in audience.

Fr Ravier's description of the event is entertaining:

Paul IV did not beat about the bush: he muttered quietly but just loudly enough for the two Jesuits to catch the gist of his rebukes. Ignatius's reign, he said, had been a tyranny, and it was only now that one could talk of electing a General. Since it was the first time, he, Paul, considered it more appropriate for the General to be elected for a three-year period, with the possibility of extending the mandate for a further three years as was done elsewhere.

The old man was getting himself worked up and, when immediately afterwards he started on the subject of the divine office, he became really frenzied. He called the Jesuits 'rebels'

for not having agreed to the choral recitation of the office; by
so doing they were strengthening the heretics' case. He feared
that some day a new Satan would arise from their ranks:
choral recitation of the office was an essential and integral part
of religious life and even of divine law. He, therefore, had
decided to put a stop to such patent abuse. 'I demand that
you sing the divine office in the choir; if you do not you will
become heretics. You must do so, even if it pains you greatly;
and woe betide you if you disobey!'[1]

Laynez let the storm pass over his head and then counter-
attacked. The Jesuits, rebels? But there had never been a
definite order from the Pope. They were heretics, were they?
The companions were persecuted for their attachment to the
Holy See and were already being called papists. The speech
for the defence had its effect. Both sides came to an agreement.
Paul IV would not demand any changes to the *Constitutions*.
His orders were simply added to the end of the text, as codicils
that were not binding beyond his pontificate. The Society was
saved. The storm died down.

Laynez's generalship was extremely fruitful. By his death
the Society of Jesus had 3,500 members in eighteen provinces
and 130 establishments. Unlike Ignatius who, once appointed
General, hardly moved outside the city of Rome, Diego Laynez
was a great traveller. Thus it was that in 1561 he took part
in the Colloquy of Poissy, where he did his best to prevent
Catherine de Médicis from turning to Protestantism. For all
that, he did not forget the interests of the Society. Its implan-
tation in France had been difficult. As early as spring 1540,
Ignatius had sent a small group of students to Paris. In
1550, a party of companions entered Bishop Guillaume de
Prat's house, known as the 'maison de Clermont'. The Cardinal of Lorraine had promised Ignatius naturalization papers,
which he received from Henri II; but the letters patent from
the *Parlement* did not follow. Distrust grew even more after
the foundation of a college at Billom, Auvergne, in 1556. In
spite of violent hostility from the University and the *Parlement*
in Paris, who feared the competition, Laynez managed to get
the Society recognized in France and to open colleges there.
Colleges were in fact set up in Verdun, Bourges, Chartres,
Toulouse, Nevers and Pont-à-Mousson.

Laynez died in 1565, worn out before his time, and was succeeded by Francis Borgia, who led the Society for seven years. He had been Duke of Gandia and viceroy of Catalonia – and also a friend of Charles V – but had given up his titles to enter the Society. His extraordinary background was a tapestry of light and shade. On his father's side, he was great-grandson of Rodrigo Borgia, Pope Alexander VI. On his mother's, he was descended from a Spanish bishop. Perhaps he had wished to atone for the shame hanging over his family by his austere way of life. In any case, he proved to be a most virtuous member of the order.

On his death, the most likely person to take command appeared to be Polanco, who had been Ignatius's right-hand man for so many years, and who had helped to draw up the *Constitutions*. However, in an unprecedented case in the Society's history, the General Congregation gave in to pressure from Pope Gregory XIII and elected Everard Mercurian, a Belgian. There followed a period of relatively calm growth, but the Society once again had to face difficult years during the long reign of his successor, Claude Aquaviva (1581–1615).

This man, who was 37 when he was elected, thought he detected signs of laxity in the order. He reacted with a salvo of instructions: a compulsory daily hour of prayer, an annual week's retreat, regulations for the novitiate, literary studies and the 'third year' (final probationary period coming between the study of philosophy and theology and the taking of solemn vows). Among his best known instructions was the famous *Ratio studiorum*, or study programme, which remains to this day the Society's basic charter for teaching.

Aquaviva also had to withstand further pressure from the Pope. An authoritarian man, Sixtus V wanted to change the *Constitutions* and to do away with the name 'Society of Jesus', which he found offensive to other religious orders. In Spain, moreover, a few Jesuits were seeking to give the Society a more democratic form. A document of reform was even ready when the Pope died in 1590. Under Clement VIII, the Spanish cabal continued unabated; particularly in 1595 when they tried to get Aquaviva appointed to the see of Capua to free themselves of an authority which they considered too overbearing.

Schemes were also afoot to get the Jesuit Curia moved from Rome to Madrid, where they hoped to keep a closer check on his activities. The death of Popes is sometimes providential. This time, it was Clement VIII's death which put an end to the intrigues.

In France, where the situation was far from settled, the first assassination attempt was made against Henri IV. The author of the crime had been for a year a day pupil in the Jesuit college at Clermont, and subsequent searches led to incriminating evidence being found in the room of a certain Fr Guignard: satirical verses against Henri IV dating from the time of the Ligue.[2] The priest was hanged, and all members of the Society were expelled from the realm (1595). They remained however in the south of France, and Henri IV quickly changed his attitude when he learnt that the Jesuits, in particular Cardinal Tolet, the first Jesuit to become cardinal, had helped to get his excommunication annulled. In 1604 the king lifted his ban on Jesuits and entrusted them with the La Flèche college. He even chose the famous Fr Coton as his confessor. Within less than four years there were 30,000 pupils in Jesuit colleges in France.

In spite of this encouraging development, the Society's long line of martyrs was beginning to form. More than 100 Jesuits died for their faith during Aquaviva's time as General, and England did much to help write this bloody page of their history.[3] After a brief return to Catholicism under Mary Tudor, a form of Protestantism had become the state religion. The Jesuits nevertheless sent two priests to Great Britain: Robert Persons and Edmund Campion. The former was suspected and hunted but managed to escape. The latter was arrested, tortured and finally executed in 1581. Notwithstanding the persecutions, the Jesuits continued their activity by living underground: they landed in secret and were then taken in by Catholics who risked their own lives in hiding them. They spent long hours hidden in priest-holes, travelled only at night and were discreetly provided with food. By 1625 there were 150 of them, and they formed a province, but for two centuries the English Jesuits sent their novices to the Continent, particularly to France.[4]

The Jesuits had chosen mobility, but what they got was

a life of wandering, and this despite the relative stability brought about by the colleges. Under the sixth General of the Society, Mutius Vitelleschi, and throughout the seventeenth century, the missionary movement started by Francis Xavier's pioneering work gathered momentum. On 15 January 1544, Francis Xavier had written a moving letter which had caused quite a stir in Rome:

> I am often seized by a desire to cry out against the
> universities – mainly against the University of Paris – as if I
> were at the Sorbonne, and I would rant and rave with all my
> might. I would cry out against those who are obsessed with
> gaining knowledge, rather than using their science to help
> those who have need of it.

The call did not go unheeded. Starting in 1578, Fr Alexander Valignano, who had been appointed visitor and superior of all Jesuits in the Far East, made long and frequent visits to Japan, from where the priests were in fact soon to be banished. People in Europe knew nothing of Japan, and Valignano became convinced of one thing: a thorough study of the language and civilization, the adoption of a Japanese lifestyle and the strict observance of their rules of courtesy were absolutely necessary before daring to introduce the Christian message. The same was true for China. He had Fr Ruggieri called to Macao and set him the task of achieving a perfect knowledge of the language spoken by the Chinese mandarins. In 1582, he also sent for Matteo Ricci, who had studied mathematics and cosmography with Fr Christoph Clau (who latinized his name to Clavius), a Bavarian friend of Galileo's.

To deal with the Chinese fear and hatred of foreigners it was first necessary to find a way to be accepted. Ricci adopted the dress of the lettered class. On ceremonial occasions he would be seen wearing a dark red silk gown, with pale blue embroidered lapels, a red sash and embroidered silk shoes. Ricci let his hair grow so that he was able to plait it. He and Ruggieri obtained permission to reside officially in Chao-Ch'ing province, near Canton. Without hiding their religion, the two men proceeded cautiously and collected a few European inventions that they knew would rouse their Chinese hosts' interest. Little by little, with their knowledge of the Chinese language and history, they became accepted.

At the end of a year, they took the risk of printing a sort of catechism, in the form of a dialogue between a pagan philosopher and a Christian priest. Ruggieri went back to Europe to ask the Pope to appoint an embassy to be sent to the Emperor of China. While he was away, Ricci was expelled from Chao-Ch'ing, a prey to the jealousy from the bonzes – Buddhist priests and monks – and scholars. He tried without success to settle in Ch'ao-Chou or Nanking and finally arrived in Peking (Beijing) on 24 January 1601.

He was detained by the Head of Customs, but was treated with respect and allowed to send a request for an audience at court.

> Your humble servant has perfect knowledge of the celestial
> sphere, of geography, geometry and arithmetic. He observes
> the stars with the help of instruments and knows how to read
> a sundial. His methods are entirely in keeping with ancient
> Chinese methods.

He sent a fine visiting card and some precious gifts, including a clock with a very attractive movement. Li-Pu, of the protocol department at the Ministry of Rites, did not give him a favourable hearing, but the emperor, intrigued, ignored this and received Ricci, listened to him and took a liking to him. Permission was given for a church to be built and the Jesuits were given a dwelling within the 'pink walls', a zone reserved for high-ranking State officials. By 1605 there were 200 Catholics in Peking and, three years later, a new residence was set up in Shanghai.

More a humanist than a scientist, in spite of the claims he had made when seeking an audience at the imperial court, Matteo Ricci implored General Aquaviva to send a real astronomer. His request was granted and in 1607 Sebastiano de Ursis arrived in China, and immediately got down to reforming the calendar. Ricci, for his part, wrote a book introducing the Catholic faith: *A True Doctrine of the Lord of Heaven*. This work was translated into Manchurian, Korean and Japanese.

He became known as the 'new Confucius'. Scholars and government officials adopted his faith. The new converts professed Christianity with a zeal that made a great impression on the people. Among them was Sin, a top dignitary, who himself became a missionary. Ricci did not let himself be carried away. Before arriving in Peking he had admitted to advancing 'on feet of lead' and he never changed. When he died on 11 May 1610, at the age of 58, the emperor gave him a national funeral, an act of friendship which corresponded to an official recognition of Christianity.

The new superior of the Chinese Jesuits, Longobardi, adopted the same principles of adaptation as Ricci, but concentrated on the masses rather than the scholars. Although Jesuit strategy has long been considered as an exclusive approach to the elite, very often it favoured the upper classes only because, through the power they wielded, they prevented contact with the population at large. China is a typical example. Ricci aimed at the top of the social ladder, but his companions opened their field of action much wider. In 1615, Longobardi sent Fr Triganet to Rome to seek permission to use Chinese in the liturgy. He also sought backing for building up an indigenous clergy. Triganet returned with a new team of missionaries. One of them, Adam Schall, a great German astronomer, became the emperor's confidant. This protection gave cause for immense hope. By 1617, the number of Chinese Christians had reached 13,000.

This growth did not occur without meeting obstacles and jealousy. Schall, the victim of an intrigue, was condemned to death – by being cut into 10,000 pieces. An earthquake, a fire in the imperial palace and the appearance of a comet saved his life, with the help of his Flemish colleague Verbiest who, by predicting an eclipse with greater accuracy than his Chinese rival, re-established the Jesuits' authority.

The death of the emperor in 1661 put a child of eight years old on the throne: K'ang Hsi, who was to become both a great head of state and a friend of the Jesuits. At their request, he quelled the persecutions which they often suffered in the provinces, and in 1692 he promulgated an edict for tolerance in favour of Christianity.

Up until the end of the seventeenth century, the mission in China came under the legal jurisdiction of the Indian province, under the protection of Portugal since Francis Xavier's time. A French mission was attached to it in 1688; the reasons for this were largely political and typical of the customs prevailing at that time. Geography was a major field of development in France, and scientific expeditions were essential to it. Jesuit collaboration was required for India and China. Louvois, Colbert's successor as chief minister to Louis XIV, therefore asked the Society for 'six Jesuits who are expert in mathematics'. His intentions were not devoid of ulterior political motives: he hoped to end Portuguese influence in the Far East, and geography served as a pretext. The Jesuits accepted, and the king financed their voyage. In 1700, the French mission in Peking was granted independent status.

This privileged position did not bring about the development hoped for. The French arrived at the height of a crisis that was destroying the work of Ricci and his companions. The Jesuits were not the first to have entered China and were not the only ones there. They had clashed violently with Dominican and Franciscan missionaries who would not tolerate their methods of adaptation. They were reproached in particular with making too many concessions to Chinese morals and, it was said, permitting ceremonies which allowed converts to practise the cult of Confucius and that of their ancestors, something incompatible with Catholic doctrine. Ricci had argued that these rites had no other object than to thank Confucius for 'the excellence of his doctrine'. His accusers claimed, on the contrary, that they were quite simply a form of idolatry. Furthermore, to translate the word 'God' the Jesuits, following Ricci's lead, used a Chinese term, T'ien-chu, which meant 'lord of heaven'. The Jesuits' opponents alleged that T'ien meant the physical heavens, or sky, and that the Jesuits were therefore teaching an idolatrous religion.

Denunciations were sent to Rome, and the 'rites controversy' quickly became a universal issue. In 1645, Innocent X condemned Christians for taking part in Confucian ceremonies. Alexander VII, on the other hand, in 1656 allowed them to do so again. However, that same year, controversy started up again in France. Blaise Pascal, who wholeheartedly backed Jansenist theses that the Jesuits were fighting, launched a violent attack against them. His famous *Lettres à un provincial* (known as *Les Provinciales*) were one of the harshest indictments ever made against the Society. In China, claimed Pascal, the Jesuits 'have allowed Catholics to practise idolatry itself'. In 1669 Clement IX promulgated a new decree of condemnation.

The Jesuits continued to defend themselves. They tried to show what was at stake through the Roman condemnation. They were caught between two lines of fire: on one hand, their enemies who accused them of disobeying the Pope's orders; on the other, the Emperor of China, who, notwithstanding his sympathy for the priests, was becoming irritated by Rome's stand. Whereas he had forbidden foreigners from teaching anything contrary to Chinese traditions in 1706, nine years later Rome decreed, in the bull *Ex illa die* (1715), that missionaries were to give up all 'superstitious' practices, in other words all traditional Chinese rites.

Suffering persecution more and more frequently, in particular from the mandarins, the newly converted Christians finally abandoned the liturgy, and many renounced their faith publicly. Benedict XIV still would not relent: in 1742 he proscribed 'Chinese rites' once again, even demanding a pledge of submission from the missionaries. This disavowal of the Society was simply the prelude to its suppression which, as we shall see, was being plotted at this time on the other side of the world, in Paraguay.

The rites controversy was far from over. It was to reappear in the twentieth century, at the time of new missionary endeavours in Japan and China. This dramatic clash of opinion over the adaptation of Christianity to local cultures was only finally brought to an end in 1939, when the newly-elected Pius XII gave permission for Catholics to take part in civil rites, proving the Jesuits had been right. But the impetus created by Ricci and his successors had long before been halted for good. China has never fully accepted the Catholic Church. In 1982, the Beijing Government refused to take part in the celebrations organized in Rome to celebrate the 400th anniversary of Ricci's arrival in Macao.

The Chinese rites affair was not an isolated episode in the Jesuits' eventful history. From 1605 Roberto de Nobili also tried to use Ricci's methods in India. Noticing the mission's lack of success, he identified one of the causes as the Brahmins' reaction to the type of life led by the Portuguese. With his superiors' approval, de Nobili adopted the Hindu habits and customs and accepted the complex rules of local etiquette. His menu consisted of rice, milk and a few herbs, eaten once a day. He wore a long robe of yellowish cloth, with a white or red veil round his shoulders, and shoes with wooden soles. Finally, he wore a cord around his neck, the distinctive sign of the castes of Brahmins and rajahs, on which he hung a little cross. Since he belonged to a superior caste, not everyone was free to approach him. When possible converts finally gathered around him he let them know that, if they wished to become Catholics, they would be able to keep up the customs of their caste.

De Nobili was not putting on an act. Following Ricci's example, he believed Christianity compatible with cultural rites. Since there were many superstitions mixed up with Brahminic customs: 'We cut out these superstitious ceremonies and replace them with Christian prayers. Thus civil customs are sanctified (...). Gradually, we shall introduce other Church practices.' His two main lines of approach – respect for the culture and genuine evangelization – were clearly defined.

The Jesuit spent 17 years in Madura, where his impact was evident. But his influence remained limited to the members of the upper castes. De Nobili then looked for new forms of adaptation that would allow him to reach all social classes. He found in Hindu culture the solution to his problem. There existed some penitents who could help him enter other castes: the *pandarams*. Although those penitents normally had no contact with the superior castes, they enjoyed a certain religious prestige while being able to mix with the lower castes. Why not create a category of missionaries who would be Catholic *pandarams*? De Nobili contacted the archbishop and the Provincial and obtained their agreement. The first *pandarasami* missionary was Balthazar da Costa. He travelled up and down his mission on foot, and in three years baptized 2,500 adults.

Roberto de Nobili died on 16 January 1656, leaving behind a thriving apostolate, but one that drew criticism. His great plan of 'opening the door' of the Hindu world to the Gospel was thwarted and opposed, despite the constant backing of General Aquaviva and of his successor, Vitelleschi. Nobili's 'method' was repudiated by Rome at the end of the century. Yet in 1979 the Jesuit General, Fr Pedro Arrupe, opened a conference on present-day missions with the words:

Evangelization must give life to that personal and unique being that is a man, a man steeped in the culture that has helped to form him. Evangelization must thus take account of the special, distinct context proper to each people.

It was the glory, and perhaps even the genius, of Ricci and de Nobili to have been the forerunners of this approach.

A more daring – and even more dangerous – attempt at reaching this goal took place in the seventeenth century in Latin America. The story of the Paraguay 'reductions', which, in a completely different context from that of China and India, sought to solve the problems of civilization, shows the degree of risk the Society of Jesus was prepared to take in order to apply to the mission its principles of comprehensive education, already practised in the colleges, and its search for a Christian humanism. One also understands how ambiguous even the most accomplished realizations of the Ignatian spirit were, such as the inculturation of the Gospel message in China and India and the project of the Paraguay reductions. A taste for power – even if it was disinterested – proved to be so powerful that it propelled Jesuits towards absolutism.

Jesuits landed in the New World in 1549. By 1553 there were already some 30 working in Brazil. In 1587, they entered Paraguay, where their first task was to found a college in Asunción. Very quickly, however, they sent out reconnaissance missions into the Indian territories. It was thus that Ortega and Filds made contact with the Guaranis who, far from being the stupid, fierce, cannibalistic, lazy and cruel people that some travellers of the time claimed, showed themselves to be rather patient, quiet and phlegmatic, very sociable and often credulous. And they received the missionaries extremely well.

Relations between the Society and the Spanish settlers in Paraguay were deteriorating. The priests spoke out against the settlers' abuse of their Indian workers and, in so doing, became clearly undesirable. However, a danger threatened the Spaniards: even if the Guaranis were quiet, they were not docile. Why not use the Jesuits to neutralize them? Politics and evangelization, once again, were to find themselves closely entwined – in spite of divergent interests – in the solution adopted. The Indians, it was decided, would be kept apart from the Spanish colony. Cut off from the European world, they would be 'reduced' into separate townships. In exchange, they would be exempt from 'personal service' and shielded from the authority of the royal officials, the Jesuits being responsible for applying the law.

In 1609, Fr Diego de Torres, Provincial of Paraguay, sent Marcel de Lorenziana, hitherto rector of the Asunción college, among the Guaranis. The start was modest: just a few families at first agreed to gather together in what would become San Ignacio.[5] Similar villages appeared along the banks of the river Paraguay and its tributary, the Paraná. The greatest founder of reductions was Antonio Ruiz de Montoya, who became the superior general of the Guarani republic.

Difficulties were not long in coming. The Jesuits moved the reductions away from Asunción to keep them away from the Spaniards, but that brought them closer to the Portuguese in Brazil. War soon broke out with the 'Paulists', the inhabitants of the future São Paulo, a group of ex-convicts, renowned for their ferocity and nicknamed 'Mamelukes' for that reason. The Jesuits parleyed with the Portuguese authorities, but in vain. They then obtained permission from the Spanish crown to arm the Guaranis, who proved to be good warriors, so good that they managed to inflict severe defeats on the Mamelukes, who finally abandoned their harrying. The reductions were then able to expand.

At their height, in the middle of the eighteenth century, there were between 150,000 and 300,000 people living in the reductions – numbers can only be guessed at. They formed a 'republic' that covered an area measuring 400 miles from north to south and 375 miles from east to west, a region almost as big as Great Britain, and which held about 30 townships.

Each reduction was modelled on the draughtboard pattern adopted by the Spanish in the New World. In the centre was the *plaza mayor* and the church; around the square were built the 'people's house', the priests' college, the widows' home and the hospital. Each family had its own house, rudimentary at first, but later built of bricks.

The reduction was independent regarding its internal organization. A municipal council was elected, the voting being effected by acclamation. Private property coexisted with collective production, which paid for communal expenses and the tribute owed to the King of Spain. Collective cattle breeding provided large quantities of meat for distribution. There were police to maintain law and order, and punishment by whipping was carried out; on the other hand the death penalty was abolished. Education was vocationally orientated: the young Guarani learnt a trade rather than academic subjects which served no purpose. Workshops produced essential items. The Guaranis, clever with their hands, forged metal and made weapons. But they also engaged in weaving, pottery and clock-making.

Life in a reduction resembled that of a convent. Woken up at five o'clock to the sound of drums, everyone then went to Mass, and afterwards to work. On feast days there were liturgical and theatrical ceremonies. Scrupulous to excess, the Guaranis sometimes left their occupations to go to confession. They got married very young: boys at seventeen, girls at fifteen. Couples were expected to be completely faithful to each other. Under the priests' watchful eyes no dalliance was allowed.

The Jesuits' role, in this over-organized society, was in principle to advise, supervise and train. In reality, their power was immense. One, at the head of the confederation, had the title of superior general. The confederation was legally qualified to deal with all questions of national defence, justice, overseas trade and legislation.

The reductions filled Europe, and even Voltaire, with admiration. But they also aroused jealousy and, later, hostility: Spain and Portugal joined forces to ruin them. In 1750, the 'Boundary Treaty' handed over to Portugal upper Uruguay, a territory containing the seven richest reductions, essential to the confederation's economy. The Jesuits received instructions from their General in Rome, ordering 'prompt execution of the royal command', but they played for time, asking for a respite.

The affair dragged on, and the Portuguese began to lose

patience. A delegate sent by the Jesuit General landed in Buenos Aires and from there made his way towards the reductions. He received a cold reception. A cordon of Guarani soldiers blocked his way and threatened to shoot if he took another step. A cacique – an Indian chief – informed the indignant visitor that he only took orders 'from the Father Superior and the parish priest'. Rome's representative put the blame on the Paraguay Provincial, who swore obedience. It was better to leave the reductions than to be suspected of rebellion against His Majesty and, especially, against the Father General's envoy.

Several years after the 1750 treaty to their great annoyance the Portuguese had still not succeeded in entering the reductions. A vast smear campaign began in Lisbon; stirred up by the Marquis of Pombal, it quickly spread to the major European capitals. The most outrageous accusations were made against the 'men in black': of possessing occult powers, of permanent collusion with the banks, of dealings with foreign governments. The Spanish and Portuguese courts unrestrainedly fanned the flames of rumoured Jesuit crimes.

In April 1767, not content with expelling the Jesuits from his own realm, Charles III of Spain asked his son, the King of Naples, to do likewise. The Portuguese had preceded them by starting the wholesale deportation of Jesuits in 1759. Charles III signed a further decree in January 1768, banishing the Jesuits from Paraguay. The king's hatred of them was apparent in the wording: 'If, after embarkation, a single Jesuit is to be found, even sick or dying, you will be punished by death. By order of me, the King.'

The reductions were then taken over. The Jesuits put up no resistance to their arrest and the Guaranis watched their departure with a kind of fatalism. Their fighting spirit seemed to have evaporated. Pombal and Charles III had won, the Society was defeated. A flood of traffickers and traders fell on the supposed 'treasures' of the Guarani republic. Jesuit power had been overthrown, the power of greed came into its own. Those Guaranis who survived returned to a nomadic life. The attempt at 'Christian socialism' had ended miserably.[6]

It would be surprising if the Society, attracted by the discovery of new worlds, whether geographical or cultural, had not also shown an interest in North America. Just as the first Jesuits reached the north-east coast of Florida, on 14 September 1566, and prepared to land near the town of St Augustine, a sudden storm tossed the craft back towards the open sea. Two weeks later, having landed on the island of San Juan, Fr Pedro Martínez was begging for food when he was attacked by Indians. He was held under water, then beaten to death. Other tragedies followed, but more Jesuits, not afraid of adventure, continued to arrive. In 1687, a certain Eusebius Kino from the Tyrol founded a mission right in the heart of Indian territory, south of the present town of Tucson. He became a specialist in the Pima language. He could also draw maps and became an explorer, then a farmer and cattle breeder. In his territory, some 30,000 Indians were converted to Christianity.

The story of the Jesuits in 'New France' (as Quebec was called) started with the arrival of Frs Pierre Biard and Edmond Massé in the colony founded by Samuel Champlain in Acadie, present-day Nova Scotia. Three years later, however, they had to go back to France. A fresh attempt was made in 1625, but was reduced to nothing when Quebec was captured in 1629. The third venture proved to be one of the most difficult missions of all time.

In 1632, some 30 Jesuits left the port of Quebec and plunged into the land of the Huron Indians. It was a vast, impossible region with a hostile climate, always under threat from hidden enemies. Three times Jean de Brébeuf travelled the route west that went along the St Lawrence and Ottawa rivers, through Lake Nipissing, down the French River to Georgian Bay, on Lake Huron. It was an exhausting journey that took about a month and was made in canoes of bark that had to be carried through woods when waterfalls and rapids blocked the way. Food was extremely scarce and monotonous, and mosquitoes plagued the travellers.

The Hurons had allied themselves to the French, which was an advantage for founding a mission. Brébeuf got down to work or, more exactly, to study. For five years he observed the social, political and religious life of the Hurons. 'One has to accept the fact', he wrote to colleagues in Europe, 'that, although one may have been a great teacher and theologian in

France, here one is a mere schoolboy, and – O Lord – what teachers one has!' But what disciples! As well as Huron, the missionaries became acquainted with the rudiments of the languages and dialects spoken by some fifteen tribes, including that of the Iroquois.

Brébeuf's patient, unremitting efforts achieved a few results, but his strength of character can be judged from the fact that, after seven years' work and a most uncomfortable lifestyle, the mission in Huron country had only about 60 Catholics. It would have been enough to discourage the most zealous of apostles, but Brébeuf was made of sterner stuff. He proved to be as realistic and good at organizing as he was fervent and intrepid.

During the two years 1647 and 1648, when rivalry between the Hurons and the Iroquois had reached its height of intensity and cruelty, the *Relations des jésuites* – those letters sent regularly by the missionaries to their superiors, formerly full of accounts of conversions and epidemics – spoke only of massacres and pillaging. On 16 March 1649 over a thousand Iroquois Indians attacked the St Ignatius mission and then St Louis, where Brébeuf lived with another Jesuit, Gabriel Lalement. The two men were captured and taken to St Ignatius, where they underwent terrible torture. One of Brébeuf's assistants, who was able to see his body, left us this eyewitness account:

> The flesh had been hacked from Fr Brébeuf's legs, thighs and
> arms; I saw and touched a great many blisters in several places
> on his body: from the boiling water that those barbarians
> had poured over him in mockery of Holy Baptism. I saw and
> touched the wound made from a belt of bark filled with pitch
> and resin which burnt all his body. I saw and touched the
> burns from a 'necklace' of hatchets that they had put on his
> shoulders and stomach. I saw and touched both his lips that
> they had cut off because he was still talking of God while they
> were making him suffer. I saw and touched the hole those
> barbarians had made in him to tear out his heart.[7]

The Hurons were unable to resist the Iroquois onslaught, and their confederation broke up for good. On 10 June 1650, the Jesuits and 300 Hurons set off for Quebec. In the spring of 1651, the remains of the Huron nation settled on the Île d'Orléans in the St Lawrence river, not far from Quebec.

Thus the mission, so dearly paid for by Jean de Brébeuf and his companions, had existed for only fifteen years (1634–49). The Hurons' dispersal meant that the 'rumour' of the faith was spread among the tribes of the Great Lakes of Canada and along the banks of the Hudson River. The converts formed the nucleus of the Catholic communities that the Jesuits were later to found among the fearsome Iroquois.

Beside the noble figure of Jean de Brébeuf, among the cohort of Canadian martyrs, it would be unfair to omit the engaging personality of Isaac Jogues, if only because of the splendid letters he wrote, with details of the life of the Iroquois Indians, whose prisoner he was in 1642–43. He was particularly badly treated: 'They burnt one of my fingers and crushed another with their teeth; they dislocated those that had already been crushed by breaking the nerves, so that, even now that they are healed, they are horribly deformed.' That was how he described the treatment he had endured to his Provincial at the beginning of August 1643. Isaac managed to escape, to reach Albany and from there to go down to New Amsterdam (New York). In 1644, he returned to Canada and took part in the peace talks between the Hurons and the Iroquois in Trois-Rivières, only to fall into the hands of the Iroquois again in 1646. Held responsible for the year's bad harvests, he was chopped to death with a tomahawk on 18 October.

Jesuit activity in North America was not interrupted by these persecutions and deaths. Far from it. Some priests even played a main role in the discovery of the Mississippi in 1673. Others settled in Illinois and in the region of the Great Lakes, some made their way towards Louisiana. The establishment of new missions did not follow any particular plan but depended mainly on circumstances. The Jesuits were often to be found in the front line of the spread of Catholicism, but it was a result of the interplay of protection and persecution rather than any true or supposed strategies devised in Rome. Their prominence was out of all proportion to their numbers. When the Society was suppressed in 1773, there were only 23 Jesuit missionaries in the United States.

The balance of power was somewhat different in Europe. In two centuries the Jesuits had managed to occupy strategic

positions. A constant growth in numbers took the Society
from 17,600 members in 1679 to 22,000 a century later. The
minima societas, as Ignatius used to call it in all honesty when
it had only a few dozen Jesuits, built up a virtual monopoly in
teaching. In France, having been banished in 1594, the Society
was fully re-established in 1603. It took on exceptional and
risky tasks. Jesuits became the appointed confessors of kings:
Fr Coton for Henri IV, Fr Suffren for Louis XIII and Fr de
La Chaize for Louis XIV. On the whole the confessors were
prudent, but the royal temperament, especially that of the
Sun King, did not make the penitent a docile disciple of
St Ignatius's *Exercises*. It was necessary to compromise, bide
one's time, arbitrate and cope with the deep-seated jealousies
of the court.

During the seventeenth and eighteenth centuries, the Society
made an increasing number of enemies. Some reproached it
for its humanism and its ability to adapt, which sometimes led
to excessive casuistry. Others, at a time when the Holy See
wielded political power, saw the Society simply as a papist
force to be felled. If they were to lessen the power of the
Church, the Society had to be destroyed.

In both cases, the accusations were often well-founded. In
the controversy with the Jansenists over grace, the Jesuits
developed an extreme form of casuistry that adapted morals
to each situation and social class. Virtue was made easy for
everyone, in accordance with 'probabilism', by allowing the
penitent to choose, and the confessor to recommend, the less
difficult of two duties, provided that a recognized authority
had declared that choice acceptable. As for the Holy See's
politics, the Society identified itself so closely with the papacy,
in both its good and bad decisions, that the enemies of the
Church of Rome naturally saw it as the first defence to be
removed.

It was a relatively minor incident that sparked things off. The
Society had already been banished from Spain, Portugal and
Paraguay, when a scandal broke concerning a Jesuit in Marti-
nique. Fr Lavalette, having exploited vast plantations and built
up a shipping company, had been forced into bankruptcy, and
his creditors turned on the Society to recover the large sums
involved. The French Jesuits, quite misguidedly, took refuge

behind one of the order's rules which stipulated that each establishment must be financially independent. The Provincial in Paris then made the mistake of appealing to the *Parlement* of Paris, which resulted in a passionate debate on the Society's activities. On 6 August 1762, the *Parlement* not only instructed the French Jesuits to pay Lavalette's debts but also pronounced an act of dissolution of the order, which they described as 'a political body, essentially devoted to a permanent activity whose goal – by all means, direct and indirect, covert and overt – is first to achieve complete independence, and then to seize power'. It only remained to carry out the sentence: on 1 December 1764, Louis XV declared that the Society of Jesus had ceased to exist in France.

Clement XIII, who had protected the Jesuits through thick and thin, died in 1769. The Bourbons immediately brought pressure to bear on the conclave to elect a candidate who would dissolve the Jesuit order. The Spanish cardinals admitted during a pre-electoral meeting with the French that they had come 'not to elect a Pope but to do away with the Society'.

Giovanni Vincenzo Ganganelli was elected on 19 May and took the name of Clement XIV. For nearly four years he was able to withstand the ambassadors from Spain, Portugal and France, but they did not let up: the dissolution of the Society was a necessity, a non-negotiable objective. The new Pope played for time; he tried to treat the Jesuits harshly so as to mollify their enemies. However, that delaying tactic failed after the arrival in Rome of the new Spanish ambassador, Joseph Monino, during the summer of 1772. Monino, with unrelenting vigour, finally managed to compel Clement XIV to give in. On 21 July 1773, the Pope signed the brief *Dominus ac Redemptor* which dissolved the Society of Jesus; though not, it is said, without having sighed: 'I acted under constraint.'

We now know for certain that the papal brief was Monino's personal work. It was he who drew up the 'preliminary draft of the main points' and then the rough draft of the document itself, which he submitted to the Pope's secretary. And it was to all intents and purposes a Latin translation of that which became the final text, except for a few changes made by Clement XIV to incorporate, it appears, last-minute demands made by the Empress Maria Theresa concerning the 'former

Society's' possessions. Moreover it is also known that the brief *Dominus ac Redemptor* was first printed on a secret press at the Spanish Embassy.

Taking everything into consideration, however, Clement XIV cannot be said to have been unduly upset by the dissolution of the Society. His distress, in any case, did not prevent him from throwing the last General, Lorenzo Ricci, into prison. Ricci ended his days in the castle of Sant' Angelo, in spite of having sworn on oath: 'I declare and affirm that the disbanded Society of Jesus has furnished no grounds and no occasion for its suppression (. . .). Secondly, I declare and affirm that I have never given the slightest pretext or the slightest occasion for my imprisonment.' The Society died but did not surrender.

LIFE IN THE CORPSE YET

The Society of Jesus seems to have received a special mission, not only to maintain divine law, but also to defend and protect human freedom.
AMBROISE MATIGNON in *Etudes religieuses*

The Society of Jesus had made a special vow to serve the Pope, and yet it was the Pope's hand that signed its death warrant. It was a strange fate, but what happened next was no less astonishing.

The brief of dissolution took effect only after promulgation by the bishops in each diocese. Rome made the announcement on 18 August 1773, followed by Austria. The Jesuits in China were only informed of the suppression of the order in 1775. A certain number of communities in western Europe and even in Italy were never told of the promulgation. France, considering dissolution as a *fait accompli*, did not authorize publication of the papal brief. As for Prussia and Russia, they maintained the *status quo* both in law and in fact. Thus the Society was never totally wiped out.

In 1773, there were about 2,400 Jesuits in Poland, some under the rule of Catherine of Russia and the others under Frederick II, following the partition of the country in 1772. Because he wished to conserve the Jesuits' service in Silesia,

Frederick opposed promulgation of the brief of dissolution. The Empress allowed no change either, in the status of the 200 Jesuits established on her territory in Russia. Clement XIV tacitly accepted the situation. In any case his authority was greatly limited when dealing with those monarchs, one of them being a Protestant and the other Orthodox. In 1782, the Society surviving in Russia even held a General Congregation. Ten years later Ferdinand, Duke of Parma, sent an appeal to the Jesuits in Russia, who supplied him with three priests. With former colleagues they took over the running of the seminary for the nobility. Pius VI discreetly gave his approval, as he did again in 1799 when a semi-clandestine novitiate was opened at Colorno near Parma.

The Society was re-established in the kingdom of the Two Sicilies in 1804. It had been the new Pope's intention since 1800 to reinstate the Society completely. In fact, Pius VII, a Benedictine himself, was aware that the Jesuits had formed associations whose organization was directly inspired by the Society's *Constitutions*. These associations trained men in Italy and France who would later join the reconstituted Society.

The situation was to remain unchanged, however, for ten years. Napoleon had Pius VII imprisoned in Savona, then in Fontainebleau. As soon as the hostage returned to Rome after the abdication of the emperor in 1814 his first major act was to re-establish the Society throughout the world. On 7 August 1814, Pius VII went to the church of Gesù with all the cardinals who were in Rome, and there celebrated Mass. He then made his way into the chapel of the Marian Congregations where he was awaited by more than a hundred former Jesuits, bowed with age. His secretary then read out the bull *Sollicitudo omnium Ecclesiarum* (The concern of all Churches) which restored the order founded by Ignatius of Loyola in all its rights. After that fraught 40-year wait, the Society was once again ready for service.

Its revival was extremely rapid. In France, Fr de Clorivière, who had entered the Jesuits in 1756 and had made his profession a few days before the dissolution, received nearly 70 novices in the space of two months. But the truce was as short-lived as the hope had been great. As soon as it reappeared on the scene the Society found a new coalition – heterogeneous but efficient – rising up against it: beside the followers of Voltaire and the heirs to the Revolution there were Gallican and Jansenist members of Parliament.

In 1826, François Dominique, the very pious Comte de Montlosier, published a work with a suggestive title: 'A study of a religious system whose aim is to overthrow religion, society and the throne'. It was full of the old accusations: France was not governed by the king (Charles X) but, after the fashion of England under the Stuarts, by the Jesuits. And if only these Jesuits would come out into the open! Instead of which, this mysterious power 'materializes or melts into the shadows according to its aims and intents'. Obviously, at the height of the Restoration, the Society could only be revolutionary: 'Wherever there is movement, unrest, drama, one can be sure of seeing the Jesuits appear. It is their food, their element.' In 1827, Montlosier sent a petition to the upper Chamber in which he stressed that the Society of Jesus was still banned in France – which, strictly speaking, was perfectly true since the 1762 edict had never been repealed. Be that as it may, the king gave in. In June 1828, the Jesuits were once again expelled from the colleges and banned from all teaching.

Two years later, the July revolution broke out and the king was removed. The supposedly 'revolutionary' Jesuits found themselves once more on the wrong side, accused of collusion with the monarchy. It was rumoured that the Jesuits' Paris house in Montrouge was linked by an underground passage to the Louvre. The house was ransacked and set on fire, and this time the Jesuits were expelled from France.

A certain number of them took refuge in Switzerland. This proved a grave miscalculation. In 1847, the Sonderbund (separate alliance) war, with Catholics and conservatives against the Protestant cantons, ended in victory for the Reformed forces. The battle was short, but a scapegoat was needed, and the Jesuits were ideal. The Society of Jesus was banned and its houses closed or confiscated. The federal constitution of 1848 ratified the ban – and it was not until 1973 that the article was revoked from the fundamental law of the country. Even at that late date the anti-Jesuit votes in the popular referendum nearly carried the day, showing just how great was the fear of seeing the Jesuits seize political power, thus fulfilling the prophecy of a radical Catholic of the last century, Augustin Keller, who was a relentless opponent of the Jesuits. 'If we do not banish the Society of Jesus', he exclaimed on 19 August 1844 before the Swiss Diet, 'our country is doomed. Morally, religiously and politically, it is racing to ruin.'

After the exodus of 1830, having met with an equally hostile reception outside their country, the French Jesuits gradually trickled back home and re-opened their houses. They also resumed their apostolate overseas and were to be found in the Americas, India, Syria and Madagascar.

But meanwhile, French Catholicism had changed greatly. Men like Lamennais, Lacordaire and Montalembert had sown the seeds of liberal Catholicism, even if the Pope had condemned their paper, *L'Avenir*, in 1832, and even if the dream of a reconciliation between the Church and modern civilization was a little premature. Lamennais's great idea – 'a free Church in a free State' – was developed brilliantly by Charles de Montalembert (1810–70): 'There is nothing closer to heaven than a monastery inhabited by religious who have freely left the world, but to transform the world into a cloister peopled with unwilling monks would be to create a foretaste of hell on earth.'

Montalembert fought successfully for freedom of education in France. In 1850, a law which owed much to him was passed granting the Church – and therefore the Jesuits – the right to open primary and secondary schools. Even though theoretically the Jesuits had been expelled from France, they enjoyed a relatively peaceful period between the revolution of 1848 and Napoleon III's downfall in 1870. There was hardly a town of any size that did not want to have its own Jesuit school. The 'good fathers' may have been fearsome, but they were certainly in great demand, particularly because the bourgeoisie, worried by the aftermath of 1848, believed they should join forces with the Church against nascent Socialism, which – in their eyes – represented a threat. They hoped to find valuable support from the Society.

The Jesuits were indeed hesitating between hard-line Catholicism and the temptation of liberalism, between

old humanist traditions and modern ideas. The conflict
between ultramontane leanings and the Gallican trend, still
very noticeable, complicated their dilemma even more.

In 1863, Fr Ambroise Matignon, a writer for *Etudes religieuses*,
a Jesuit magazine founded in 1856 (now *Etudes*), became de
Montalembert's confessor. Without adopting all the latter's
audacity, he did publish eleven articles, between 1864 and
1867, under the general title 'The Society of Jesus's doctrines
on freedom'. His aim was to reply to the accusations that the
Society was the ally of all forms of political, spiritual and
religious tyranny. Fr Matignon showed that Jesuit teaching
had defended doctrines favourable to freedom and reason:

> The Society of Jesus seems to have received a special mission,
> not only to maintain divine law, but also to defend and protect
> human freedom. Whenever anyone has tried to deny, or
> threatened to destroy, this freedom the Jesuits have risen to
> defend its rights . . .

Not everyone thought so, for the article came right in the middle
of the controversy that divided Catholics over the legitimacy
of 'modern freedom'. Its plea was fervent, brilliant, cogently
argued, but ill-timed. In 1868, Pius IX himself did not fail to
mention this in an audience with a delegation of Jesuits, when
he stressed the duty not to compromise on Catholic principles.
Had he not written in the encyclical *Quanta cura* (1864) that
freedom of conscience and religion was simply 'utter delirium',
only good for spreading 'the plague of indifferentism' and for
'throwing people into moral corruption'? The Pope added to
his general warnings a personal remark for Fr Matignon, saying
that 'had he been present I would have said the same thing
and would have asked him if he wished to alter the doctrines
of the Church to suit modern doctrines'. Truth and error were
irreconcilable.

The affair did not stop there. In 1869, the First Vatican
Council opened in confusion. The liberal members of the
assembly were in the minority, making up only a fifth of
the numbers. They wished to reconcile the Church with
what was best in modernity, but the majority were deaf to
their plea. For the latter, the Church had to be defended
against the excesses of free thought by the reaffirmation of

the authority of its leader: to counter liberal relativism, vote for papal infallibility!

On 19 July 1870, soon after the dramatic vote giving the Pope primacy by right and infallible authority 'not only in matters concerning faith and morals, but also in those affecting discipline and government', France declared war on Prussia. *Etudes* stopped publication, and then resumed it at the end of 1871. The editorial board moved to Lyons, and its former writers were evicted to make room for people considered to be less favourable to Catholic liberals. The tone changed noticeably and Fr Matignon's pleas gave way to Fr Ramère's indictments. This judgement, published in 1875, shows the extent of his severity: 'The failure of Catholic liberalism is summed up in these four words: deception, cowardice, rebellion and betrayal.'

Pius IX asked Jesuit writers in 1873 to put themselves at the service of the Church, 'their eyes fixed on the chair of Peter'. He was heard, and not only by the writers of *Etudes*. In 1876, Fr Jules Morel, a canon of Angers cathedral and a consultant for the Congregation of the Index, could write: 'Throughout the world, a liberal Jesuit is a contradiction in terms that one no longer meets, except perhaps for two or three stubborn Belgians.'[8] The Jesuits had chosen their camp: that of ultramontanism.

The decree of 29 March 1880 brought about a fresh dispersal of the Jesuits from France. To be precise, the measures affected all 'non-authorized' religious congregations. The Marists, the Dominicans, the Assumptionists and many others were also to be expelled. However, they were able to procure the necessary authorization to stay, whereas 'it would be neither dignified nor proper for the Society of Jesus to request authorization, since one knows in advance that such authorization would be refused'.

Anti-Jesuit hostility was extremely persistent, but at least had the merit of being sometimes, as in this case, rather half-hearted. The decrees of 1880 were so disputed and badly applied that the Jesuits were able to maintain, or return to, their communal life, however precarious. They formed four provinces (Paris, Lyons, Toulouse and Champagne), with over 3,000 members, and had 29 colleges and schools;

over a quarter of their strength were deployed in overseas countries.

The history of these incessant foundations – which varied enormously in size, from a modest little seminary to a university like the one in Beirut – display common characteristics. Contrary to the popular view, these establishments were not wealthy but heavily in debt. The priests spent part of their time collecting money, just to survive. And they undertook many pastoral duties. Curiously enough, these hated Jesuits could not supply all the needs of those requiring their services everywhere they settled, most of the time at the request of bishops and local authorities. They also gave a great many spiritual retreats inspired by St Ignatius's *Exercises*. They preached and heard a great many confessions, mainly through the *missions populaires* (missions among the working class). They also founded numerous fraternities, devout associations and even religious congregations. On the other hand, they always refused to create institutions directly affiliated to the Society. The Jesuits, unlike the Dominicans, Carmelites and Franciscans, never had a feminine branch nor a third order.[9]

The French Jesuits were not the only ones to fall victim to the troubles of the nineteenth century. The persecutions of their European confrères were many and violent. In Spain, they were killed, banished or hounded at least seven times between 1820 and 1936. In Portugal, their situation has been legal only since 1933. In Italy, they suffered the repercussions of the troubles of 1830 and had to close their Roman establishments in 1848. The order was suppressed in Piedmont, Naples, Venice and Sicily ten years later.

The Jesuits were first driven out of Germany in 1848. The exile imposed by the *Kulturkampf* Church–State clash from 1872 to 1917 was even harsher. Under the Nazis the number of closures and requisitions of their establishments increased, especially from 1938 onwards. During the Second World War their fate was bound up with that of the Jews.

Alfred Delp, one of the distinguished figures of internal resistance to the Führer, was executed on 2 February 1945. He was born on 15 September 1907 in Mannheim and entered the Society of Jesus in 1926. He began writing for the magazine

Stimmen der Zeit, in Munich, just before war broke out, and became responsible for articles on sociology. After the Nazis banned the magazine in 1941, Alfred Delp found work in one of the parishes in the town. In 1942, Count von Moltke was beginning to form a group of men capable of rebuilding the nation after the collapse of Nazism. The Provincial of Munich suggested Fr Delp, who thus joined the 'Kreisau circle'. Some members of this circle had personal relationships with the conspirators of the failed assassination attempt against Hitler on 20 July 1944. On 28 July Delp was arrested by two members of the Gestapo as he left church after celebrating Mass. He was tortured and then sent to Berlin where, on 12 September, he was shut up in the sinister Tegel prison. Imprisoned with him were some of Germany's great men: Ernst von Harnack, Erwin Planck and Dietrich Bonhoeffer.

Alfred Delp had not yet pronounced his final vows. In a pile of linen that he was given on 7 December 1944, he found a note telling him that he was to be visited the next day by a colleague, Fr Franz von Tattenbach. This priest, a former captain in the Wehrmacht, with which he had fought in Norway, had just been turned out of the army for disgraceful behaviour (that of being a Jesuit). Tattenbach had been assigned by the Society to receive Alfred Delp's vows and so, at the risk of his life, he had made his way to Berlin, requested and obtained permission to visit Delp.

On 8 December the two men found themselves face to face in the prison parlour. They were separated by the guard, who followed every word of their conversation. Fr Tattenbach mentioned a few innocuous items of news and then explained to the incredulous guard, who was luckily ill-versed in the classics, that he was going to say some prayers in Latin with his friend. Every Jesuit's vows, to be valid, have to be written down and signed. The text was therefore placed on the table and a rough translation given to satisfy the gaoler. The conversation continued, broken by phrases in Latin: Alfred Delp was making his vows of poverty, chastity and obedience, for all time, in the Society of Jesus. When he had finished, he signed the paper.[10]

The day before his execution, Delp wrote:

My crime is to have believed in a Germany beyond this hour
of distress and darkness, to have refused the religion of pride
and violence, and to have done it as a Catholic and as a Jesuit.
If I am here awaiting the hand that will take me to the gallows,
it is because I have believed in a new Germany, superior to
the Germany of today, because I have seen in Christianity
and in the Church the secret aspirations of this country and
its people, because I have loved, in the Society, a family of
men of character. Men who are hated because people do not
know them, because their free obedience is not understood or
because they are feared, like a living reproach thrown in the
face of arrogant tyrannies.[11]

At different times in history tyranny has taken on a variety
of guises, and has wielded brutal but far from blind violence.
The blows dealt to the Society's men and institutions did
not spare the 60 Jesuits based in the Lebanon, where they
were mainly involved in running the Notre-Dame de Jamhour
secondary school (3,000 pupils) and Saint-Joseph University
(6,000 students), both in Beirut.

On 13 August 1989, the school was hit by more than
200 large shells, after several days of almost continuous
bombardment. On 11 August one of the elderly teachers,
Fr Dupré-Latour, sent a report on the situation to France:

The blockade for us means the shelling that we suffer every
day: shells which rain down in series of forty at a time,
sometimes on residential areas, sometimes on the sea and the
coast to stop trading vessels from reaching the 'Christian' zone,
destroying homes and factories, hitting even the hospitals and,
some days, leaving over a hundred dead, without counting the
injured.

The Jesuit's unemotional reporting nevertheless ended with:
'What is certain is that we feel that we are in God's hands!'

It was an act of faith shared by Nicholas Kluiters, a Dutch
Jesuit, abducted on 14 March 1958 in the Bekaa valley, where
he was parish priest for several villages. His mutilated body
was found in a 70-foot-deep chasm a fortnight later. According
to the forensic surgeon's report: 'Fr Nicholas suffered torment
and forms of torture of a kind that I have never seen in the
course of years of war.' A few years before, Fr Kluiters had

written in a letter to the Netherlands: 'The justice that we need here must be at the service of wounded mankind: it is above all a moral element. It is a matter of curing people's souls, of restoring confidence in relationships that appear impossible.' The factions bent on ruining the Lebanon could not afford to spare such a man. So they killed hope.

On the morning of Thursday, 24 September 1987, Fr André Masse, former editor of *Etudes* (1975–81), was killed in Sidon 'by persons unknown' (who in fact knew their victim). André Masse, 47, ran a south Lebanon unit of Saint-Joseph University which taught adminstration, engineering and nursing. That study centre was attended almost entirely by Muslims, and Fr Masse is one of a long list of people who have been killed by the very people they were trying to help. André Masse was the eighth Jesuit to die in the horrors of Lebanon.

But, as regards repression and persecution of the Society, let us return to the example of France, crucial for the whole Society. In 1878, Fr Pierre Beckx, from central Belgium, celebrated the 25th anniversary of his election as Jesuit General. It was a rare event; of his 21 predecessors only two had enjoyed such a long time in power: Claude Aquaviva (1581–1615) and Mutius Vitelleschi (1615–45). Fr Beckx could look back on his years in office with satisfaction. Under his rule the order had increased from 5,194 members to 9,795, with French Jesuits alone making up a good third. However, the shadow of anticlerical repression was hanging over France, and the General, a good tactician, sensed that the threat would come from there. Beckx wrote to the Provincials: 'It could be that our training establishments will be closed; in that case, we must provide ourselves with places of refuge, as from now, outside the country for the novices and scholastics.' And no-one was to do anything foolish, the General warned: 'Do not allow yourselves to do anything that might be taken as a provocation.'

The warning was necessary; events soon confirmed the General's fears. On 16 May 1877, Marshal Macmahon, the President of the Republic, dissolved the Chamber of Deputies in France. The Jesuits prepared themselves for battle, although their tactics appeared quite derisory. One such was the vow

to build a church on Montmartre and another the promise
of prayers, on condition that 'the storm spare us'. Nor were
material interests neglected. The Society's buildings were
mortgaged and the French Jesuits began secretly to prepare
for their retreat to England.

On 30 January 1879, Macmahon resigned, Jules Grévy
became President and Gambetta succeeded him as head of the
Chamber. On 4 February, Jules Ferry was given the portfolio
for State education in William Waddington's government. A
few weeks later he submitted a bill concerning 'the freedom
of higher education'. The minister had laid his cards on the
table. Article 7 of his bill read:

> No-one is allowed to take part in State or denominational
> education, or to run a teaching establishment of any kind
> whatsoever, if he belongs to a non-authorized religious
> congregation.

Ferry admitted himself that that article, hardly compatible with
freedom, was aimed mainly at the Society of Jesus, which at
that time ran 29 schools, teaching 11,000 pupils.

Jules Ferry's show of strength did not go unnoticed on the
other side of the Channel. The Anglican paper *The Guardian*
stated bluntly that: 'the character of French radicalism has
always been idiotic and violent, stupid and tyrannical.' In
France, both in Paris and in the provinces, petitions against
the government grew in number. The episcopate mobilized
their troops and the bishops found themselves being treated
as 'seditious' by the minister. Ferry stood firm, coming back
at the slightest pretext to the main motive for his bill:

> We are only aiming at the unauthorized congregations;
> and, among them, I say loud and clear, a congregation that
> not only is not authorized, but that has been prohibited
> throughout our history, namely the Society of Jesus. Yes,
> it is from that that we want to wrest the souls of French
> youth.

The parliamentary commission was fully behind him. It accused
the Jesuits, already 'masters of spiritual power', of now wanting
to 'pursue their dream of temporal domination'. The reporter
did not pull any punches:

The Jesuits (...) wish to abolish the French Revolution, to
wipe out its moral and material triumphs. The writings of their
theologians, their preaching and sermons, their periodicals
and various works all show that they consider themselves as
missionaries and soldiers of the counter-revolution.

The debate on the commission's report opened on 16 June
1879. Bombarded with questions, Ferry explained himself
unwillingly and did not succeed in arousing the Assembly
until, in a burst of inspiration, he suddenly cried out: 'Where is
the danger? It is in the Jesuits, it is in their growth, it is in their
progress, it is in their indisputable and undisputed power.'
Meagre at first, a ripple of applause broke out. The voluble
minister was able to add – without being contradicted –
'Horror of Jesuits is an integral part of French national
sentiment.'

Ferry's bill was passed by the Chamber of Deputies on 9 July
1879. In the Senate, the Right opposed it and finally won the
day: article 7 was rejected on 15 March 1880. Although beaten,
the government did not consider itself defeated. It decided to
govern by decree and, on 29 March, ordered the application
of existing laws providing for the expulsion of non-authorized
congregations. The Jesuits were given 'preferential treatment'.
Article 1 in the decree of 29 March 1880 states: 'A delay of three
months is granted to the non-authorized association, so-called
"of Jesus", to disband ...'

There remained a delicate problem. How was the Holy See
going to react to this decision? *A priori*, it should defend the
Jesuits, its shock troops. The situation was complicated by a
diplomatic imbroglio. Two days after the promulgation of the
March decrees, Ambassador Desprez presented his credentials
to the Pope. Desprez wished to treat Leo XIII tactfully, and the
Pope had no desire to antagonize the Republic. The Society
of Jesus was in trouble: traditionally committed to the Pope's
cause, it had now become his chief embarrassment. 'We
are standing in his way', complained the future General Fr
Anderlédy. Fr Morier, former Provincial of Paris, sent to Rome
with a delegation representing the religious orders that were
threatened by the decrees of 29 March, had to wait two months
before being granted an audience with the Pope. This was an
unmistakable signal for the Jesuit: France had suggested a deal

to the Holy See. The Society was to be sacrificed so that the other congregations might be spared.

On 30 June 1880, once the three months' delay had run out, the expulsion of the Jesuits was put into effect. Their residences and schools were broken into by the police, sometimes with the help of the army. The Jesuit peril, from which Ferry wanted to 'wrest the souls of French youth', faded away. The 1901 law concerning associations, and that on the separation of Church and State in 1905, would confirm the government's hostility to the 'power' of the Jesuits.

Here, then, are a few episodes of the four eventful centuries of history during which Ignatius's 'little company' grew, against every hope, was opposed, even put to death, came back to life and continued in the face of all obstacles to work for 'the greater glory of God'.

In the course of this rapid survey, I have touched upon certain themes dealt with much more completely and competently in Fr John O'Malley's book, *The First Jesuits*.[12] And I was pleased to discover (I read his book after writing mine) that he confirmed certain of my intuitions. Namely, and here I quote Peter Hebblethwaite's review of O'Malley's book:

> Three tenacious myths bite the dust. The first is that Ignatius
> had a detailed blueprint for his companions. O'Malley shows
> convincingly that Ignatius did not found a teaching order.
> He improvised and responded to needs. A second myth is
> that the Jesuits were founded to combat the Reformation and
> to spearhead its Catholic riposte, the Counter-Reformation.
> O'Malley shows this is a partial view. If they thought about the
> Reformation, the early Jesuits saw it as a spiritual rather than a
> theological problem. The third myth is that they were founded
> as the Pope's shock troops. True, Ignatius devised the 'fourth
> vow', but it is a vow to God not to the Pope; and its essential
> content concerned mobility and availability for mission rather
> than anything else.

Alternately held in contempt and flattered, maligned and admired, the Society of Jesus has had its hours of glory, when its sons did not recoil from martyrdom, and its dark hours, when cowardice and the thirst for power of some of its members led it to betray its original ideals. Bruised but not beaten, determined to go forward, it was soon to discover, in a twentieth century marked by war, industrialization and de-Christianization, that it was going to have to adopt a new strategy.

NOTES

1 André Ravier, *Ignace de Loyola fonde la Compagnie de Jésus* (Desclée de Brouwer, 1975), pp. 330–1.

2 A Catholic association founded by the Duke of Guise in 1576. Its aim was to defend the Catholic faith against the Calvinists and, as an indirect consequence, to overthrow Henri III and put the Guises on the throne of France. By renouncing Calvinism, Henri IV put an end to the Ligue, which had been brought into discredit by its alliance with Philip III of Spain.

3 See Part II, Chapter 1, pp. 106–10.

4 By a strange quirk of fate it was in Britain, particularly in Jersey, that the French Jesuits found refuge when they were chased out of their country at the beginning of the twentieth century.

5 Ignatius of Loyola and Francis Xavier were canonized in 1622.

6 The saga of the Reductions has inspired many writers. Two recent examples of works dealing with the subject are: *On Earth as in Heaven*, a play by Fritz Hochwalder (1952) and *The Mission*, a film by Roland Joffé (1986).

7 R. Latourelle, 'Jean de Brébeuf' in *Dictionnaire biographique du Canada*, 1, p. 217.

8 *Somme contre le catholicisme libéral*, quoted in *Etudes* (November 1956), p. 208.

9 Many women's religious orders nonetheless modelled their rule on the Jesuit Constitutions, and there is even one, admittedly isolated, case of a woman becoming a Jesuit. In 1554, Juana of Austria, a Spanish princess of the House of Habsburg, became a Jesuit, as Fr John Padberg noted in the *National Catholic Reporter*: In Ignatius's lifetime, Paul III had commanded him to accept Isabel Roser and three of her companions as members of something like a women's branch of the Society, but the experiment did not last. Juana entered the Society almost ten years later. Born in 1535, at the age of seventeen she married the heir to the Portuguese throne. He died two years later and she returned to Spain.

She informed the Spanish grandee Francis Borgia, himself a Jesuit, that she wanted to join the Society of Jesus. The idea was full of danger: her father Emperor Charles V and her brother Philip would be furious with her and the Jesuits. Such a decision could wreck future dynastic marriage plans for Juana. But the Society, still small and weak, could not afford to alienate Juana, depending in part on her good favour for its existence in Spain. So perilous was the project that all existing Jesuit correspondence about the matter never uses her name, but a pseudonym: Mateo Sanchez or Montoya. Ignatius appointed a committee to advise him. It recommended that Juana enter the Society as a permanent scholastic: truly a Jesuit but still in formation.

When Juana pronounced her three religious vows as a Jesuit, absolute secrecy was enjoined on everyone. She could make no obvious change in her manner of life. So, for her, poverty meant leading a rather austere life at her already simple court. Chastity meant never marrying again. Obedience – well, her letters show her sometimes trying to give orders to Ignatius and Borgia. The secret was so well-kept that no-one ever suspected it. And as far as it is known today, she lived the rest of her rather short life (she died in 1573) as the only woman Jesuit.

10 Account based on an interview with Fr von Tattenbach, now working for a Catholic radio station in Costa Rica.

11 *Alfred Delp, honneur et liberté du Chrétien*, p. 208.

12 John O'Malley, *The First Jesuits* (Harvard University Press, 1993).

PART II

THE NEW STRATEGY

1

Jesuits, politics and the State

ENGLAND: CAMPION'S BRAG

*And touching our Society, be it known to you
that we have made a league – all the Jesuits
in the world, whose succession and multitude
must overreach all the practices of England –
cheerfully to carry the cross you shall lay
upon us, and never to despair your recovery,
while we have a man left to enjoy your Tyburn,
or to be racked with your torments, or consumed in your prisons. The expense is reckoned,
the enterprise is begun; it is of God, it cannot
be withstood. So the faith was planted: so it
must be restored.*

EDMUND CAMPION

So much has been said about the Jesuits, especially about their
meddling in politics, that one is at a loss to choose among such
a rich crop of quotations. Here is a short selection. The authors
of the following judgements will probably come as a surprise.
Try and guess who said what:

'The quickest way to a good education is to consult the
Jesuits: their schools have never been bettered.'

'Wherever Jesuits are admitted, they must have power at
any cost. Their Society is domineering by nature and, for that
reason, is the implacable foe of all other powers.'

'Under the specious pretext of saving souls, the Jesuits
meddle in secular affairs. They worm their way into the courts
of princes and statesmen; but their true motive is love of self
and of worldly possessions.'

'The Jesuits want to reconcile God and the world, but they only succeeded in winning the contempt of God and of the world.'

'The Society is always to be found where the need is greatest, even if it has to run the greatest risks and face the gravest dangers.'

'Speak little, listen much, reply to each point in turn, then take your leave. Win the affection of the great and the noble by humouring whoever you are speaking to, whether he be choleric, melancholy or ponderous. The aim of these conversations is to win the person over and bring him into our net for the greater service of God. And, to that end, act towards him as the devil does with a virtuous soul. He wants to pervert that soul entirely, whereas we wish to sanctify it totally, by using the same wiles as the devil, who knows how to enter one door, leave by another and come in again by a third when need be.'

'I confess the atrocious lies – I can call them nothing else – which are circulated against myself, have led me to feel how very false the popular impression may be about Jesuits.'

'We are the Young Turks of the Revolution, with something Jesuitical for good measure.'

These quotations are by: Francis Bacon, Napoleon, Fr Aquaviva (a General of the Society in the sixteenth century), Pascal, Fr Arrupe, Ignatius of Loyola, John Henry Newman (when he was still an Anglican) and Lenin. One could add to the list an anonymous inscription I noticed on a wall in Ulster, on entering the town of Cossgar, in the spring of 1989: 'Speed limit: 30 mph. Jesuits keep out!'

What lies behind the cliché of the scheming, Machiavellian Jesuit, ready to play any trick to worm his way into a closed *milieu* in order to exercise his influence? We have seen how from the start, and especially in France, the Jesuits tried, as Ignatius put it, to 'win the affection of the great and the noble'. Louis XIII had four Jesuit confessors and Louis XIV five, including the wily Fr de La Chaize, and Henri IV the no less cunning Fr Pierre Coton.[1]

Furthermore, the network of colleges run by the 'good fathers', which soon covered the whole of Europe, and its colonies, proved to be extraordinarily effective in moulding the ruling classes. Hence the saying (wrongly) attributed to the Jesuits: 'Give me a child until the age of seven, then you can do what you want with him.' One shouldn't exaggerate the lasting effects of a Jesuit education, however. For every Descartes and de Gaulle there was also a Voltaire and a Marquis de Sade. Excellent intellectual training doesn't automatically guarantee piety or religious faith.

As regards politics as such, it obviously is not easy to draw the line between temporal and spiritual matters, especially as the characteristic of Ignatian spirituality is to live one's faith in action. Even so, it cannot be denied that Jesuits have often overstepped the bounds of political commitment. This was especially true during the Renaissance and the Reformation periods, when religious quarrels were inseparable from political conflict and wars between nations. The Jesuits were rumoured to have been involved in numerous assassination plots throughout the world: Henri IV in France, Elizabeth I and James I in England, Joseph I of Portugal, William of Orange, and even Abraham Lincoln. They were credited with such deep designs because of the justification of regicide made by some of their members. Their detestable reputation throughout Europe led to their expulsion 74 times from the various countries where they had been established, and finally to the dissolution of their order.

To take the example of England, the image of the equivocating, cunning Jesuit sent by Rome as a spy to bring about the downfall of the realm was a standard Protestant myth, from the arrival of the first Jesuit in 1580 to the 'Popish Plot', for which six Jesuits were hanged, drawn and quartered at Tyburn. English recusant history is a complex one. The English Jesuits, trained abroad, returned to their native country to face persecution and death during one century, then ostracism and distrust for another hundred years. They were criticized and distrusted, not least by their fellow Roman Catholics. Yet, as the Jesuit Fr Bernard Basset wrote,

in 1829, when Catholic Emancipation gave room for a modest
expansion, the Jesuits were ready with an enthusiasm
unquenched by two centuries and more of unrelenting
hostility. They entered England as ogres, fit only for the
gallows, and lived to see Fr Bernard Vaughan, in the early

twentieth century, calling at Buckingham Palace to sip a cup of Imperial tea.[2]

Even so, prejudice died hard. As late as 1900, Sir Arthur Conan Doyle, who was standing for Parliament in Edinburgh as a Liberal-Unionist, was defeated by bigotry even though he had long since abandoned his Catholic faith. The 'Dunfermline Protestant Defence Organization' campaigned against him, proclaiming that he was a 'Papist conspirator, a Jesuit emissary and a subverter of the Protestant faith'. He was beaten by 569 votes. Had it not been for that smear campaign he would have won outright.

As for the real Jesuit emissaries, from Edmund Campion to John Carroll, first Archbishop of Baltimore, they were indeed crusaders against the Protestant faith, but their tactics were preaching and piety, not subversion. Edmund Campion was one of the ten Jesuits among the Forty Martyrs of England and Wales canonized by Paul VI in 1970. The son of a London bookseller, he became a Junior Fellow of St John's College, Oxford, in 1557. Nine years later he was chosen by the university to welcome Queen Elizabeth I to Oxford. In spite of his Catholic sympathies he was ordained deacon in the Church of England, but pangs of conscience led him to seek exile in Dublin, and then Douai, where he was received into the Roman Catholic Church. He made a pilgrimage to Rome, became a Jesuit in 1573 and was ordained in 1578.

After his novitiate in Bohemia, he taught in Prague until 1580 when he joined Robert Persons[3] in the first Jesuit mission to England. He was barely forty years old and knew that he was going to die. When William Allen, the founder of Douai College, told him that his talents would be more useful to his countrymen than to his students in Prague, he replied: 'As for me, all is one and I hope I shall be ever indifferent for all nations and functions, whatinsoever my superiors under God shall employ me.' Just before he sailed he wrote to a friend:

> Yet our minds cannot but misgive us when we hear all men, I will not say whispering but crying the news of our coming. It is a venture which only the wisdom of God can bring to good

and to His wisdom we lovingly resign ourselves ... but in any case, I will go over and take part in the fight though I die for it. It often happens that the first rank of a conquering army is knocked over. Indeed, if our Society is to go on with this adventure, the ignorance and wickedness against which this war is declared will have to be overthrown.

A war which was to last a hundred years.

Campion preached extensively in London and Lancashire for a year, always in hiding, always on the run. As he wrote at this time,

> I ride about some piece of the country every day. The harvest is wonderful great. On horseback, I meditate my sermon; when I come to the house I polish it. Then I talk with such as come to speak with me or hear their confessions. In the morning after Mass, I preach; they hear with exceeding greediness and very often receive the sacrament.

If the laity welcomed the Jesuits enthusiastically, the Catholic clergy were more reticent and, at a secret meeting with some priests in Southwark, Persons and Campion could only insist that they had come to England under obedience and that their written instructions barred them from politics.

The object of their mission was clearly defined and limited, namely 'the preservation and augmentation of the faith of Catholics in England'. In his biography of Edmund Campion, Evelyn Waugh writes

> So far from active proselytizing among heretics, the missionaries were charged not only to avoid disputes with them, but to shun their company. They might treat with Catholics who had lapsed through compulsion or ignorance, but this work was subordinate to their primary duty of ministering to those who remained constant. They were forbidden, absolutely, to involve themselves in questions of State or to send back political reports. They must permit no conversation against the Queen in their presence, except perhaps in the company of those whom they held to be exceptionally faithful, and who had been tried a long time; and even then not without serious cause.[4]

The position of Catholics with regard to Queen Elizabeth was a delicate issue for loyal Englishmen. As early as 1573, during his first visit to Rome, Campion had spoken to Cardinal Gesualdi of the difficulty in which English Catholics had been placed by the bull of deposition, *Regnans in Excelsis*, by which in 1570 Pius V had excommunicated Elizabeth I. After Pius's death word was sent to Rome to ask whether the bull was still in force. The reply was embarrassingly casuistical:

> The Bull had been issued in the hope of the kingdom being
> immediately restored to Catholicism, and therefore, as
> long as the Queen remained *de facto* ruler, it was lawful for
> Catholics to obey her in civil matters and co-operate in all
> just things; that she might honourably be addressed with
> her titles as Queen; that it was unlawful for any private
> person, not wearing uniform and authorized to do so in
> an act of war, to slay any tyrant whomsoever, unless the
> tyrant, for example, had invaded his country by force; that
> in the event of anyone being authorized to put the Bull
> into execution, it would not be lawful for Catholics to
> oppose him.

In 1581, Campion secretly published a pamphlet entitled *Decem Rationes*, defending the Roman Catholic position. His *Ten Reasons* had been planned for some months. To write it, Campion travelled north at Easter 1581, and went to ground in Catholic Lancashire. When the manuscript was completed it was sent to Persons in London to be printed. Campion was arrested later in the year, charged with conspiracy against the Crown, and was forced to ride into London, his arms pinioned and the inscription pinned to his hat: 'Edmund Campion, Seditious Jesuit'. He refused to return to the Church of England, was put on the rack and executed at Tyburn on 1 December 1581.

Shortly after his arrival in England, Campion was asked by two Jesuit colleagues to commit his story to paper, to check any attempt at false propaganda by the government. At first he refused, and then suddenly rose from the table, went into an unoccupied corner and there, in half an hour, dashed off the kind of explanation that he would like to see published after his arrest. That is the origin of what became known as 'Campion's Brag'. No Jesuit other than he could have written such a stirring text, with its clarion call:

And touching our Society, be it known unto you that we
have made a league – all the Jesuits of the world, whose
succession and multitude must overreach all the practices of
England – cheerfully to carry the cross you shall lay upon us,
and never to despair your recovery, while we have a man
left to enjoy your Tyburn, or to be racked with your torments, or
consumed in your prisons. The expense is reckoned, the
enterprise is begun; it is of God, it cannot be withstood. So the
faith was planted; so it must be restored.

A hundred years after the publication of 'Campion's Brag',
1680 marked the height of the 'Popish Plot', the supposed
conspiracy to murder Charles II. Seventy-five years earlier, the
'Gunpowder Plot', an attempt to blow up the Houses of Parliament, had been laid at the door of Catholic conspirators, led
by Robert Catesby and Guy Fawkes, and produced an upsurge
of anti-Catholic feeling. It was a mysterious affair, possibly
government-sponsored, but the Popish Plot was a fabrication,
from start to finish. Titus Oates, who revealed the so-called
plot to the Privy Council in 1678, was the son of an Anabaptist
preacher. He had tried to join the Jesuits but had been rejected.
In revenge, he inflamed public opinion by spreading stories of
alleged Roman Catholic intrigues to assassinate Charles II and
put his brother James on the throne. The public panic lasted
from 1678 to 1681 and many innocent people were executed
on his false testimony. As Bernard Basset writes,

Hundreds of innocent people died through the Oates Plot. One
Jesuit reckoned that four hundred perished in prison, some
of them victims of the plague. King Charles, knowing full
well that the plot was a fraud, made no effort to stop it. The
Jesuits were stunned by this royal indifference but they never
condemned the King. They saw his dilemma, for Charles could
have stood for justice only at the risk of a second civil war. In
the Jesuit papers are preserved two unusual letters concerning
the portraits of the martyred Jesuits which the Queen kept in
her retiring-room. A nobleman of rank urged her to remove
them lest she offend the King. The Queen, instead, asked her
husband, who gave her two reasons for retaining them. In the
first, Charles is said to have answered that 'he himself was
fully convinced of the falsity of the charge'. In the second, the
King is reported to have kissed the portraits, remarking that
the Jesuits were now in a place where they would know that

he was forced so to act. After years of temporizing, Charles died a Catholic.[5]

In the United States, matters were very different. Since the founding fathers had fled persecution in the Old World to find tolerance in the New, the Jesuits were free to evangelize these vast territories, with material hardships, great distances and hostile Indians as the main obstacles to their mission in Canada and the United States. A good example of a great pioneer American Jesuit is John Carroll, the first bishop of the American Roman Catholic hierarchy. A native of Upper Marlborough, Maryland, he was educated in Europe, at St Omer's College in Flanders. He left Maryland at the age of thirteen and only saw his mother again after 26 years of absence, catching the last boat to sail for the Potomac, at the start of the War of Independence.

He entered the Society of Jesus in 1753, was ordained in 1769, and taught philosophy and theology during the next four years at St Omer's and Liège. When he was 36, just before the suppression of the order, he went to Rome, where he was disgusted at the decadence of the papal court. He sailed in 1774 for Maryland, where he led the life of a missionary and actively supported the movement for political independence. In 1776, he took part in the embassy of Benjamin Franklin to Canada and, partly through Franklin's influence, was appointed superior of the missions by the Pope in 1784, a step which made the Church in the United States independent of the apostolic vicars in England. Carroll and the other ex-Jesuits were also planning to found a college at Georgetown.

The priests of Maryland having petitioned Pius VI in 1788 for a bishop for the United States, Carroll was appointed in 1789. A year later he was consecrated – in the chapel of Lulworth Castle, Dorset – to the see of Baltimore. It is of note that those ex-Jesuits who at the time of the suppression had experienced clerical corruption distrusted the Congregation of Propaganda and all its minions. Too much had been stolen at the time, too many unworthy men had feathered their private nests through the suppression of the Jesuits, for men of the calibre of Carroll to feel any lasting confidence. The first Archbishop of Baltimore and father of the American hierarchy had seen enough of the Old World.

'Napoleon was still on the Isle of Elba and the Bourbons were wholly preoccupied with their own restoration when Pius VII published his Brief *Sollicitudo Omnium Ecclesiarum*, in 1814', writes Bernard Basset.[6] 'The Gesù in Rome once more wore all its trappings and some 80 ex-Jesuits stood behind the line of cardinals when the Pope celebrated Mass at the tomb of St Ignatius, after which the brief of restoration was read aloud. *The Times* (13 October) informed its readers that an ancient Jesuit was rejoining the order at the advanced age of 126. 'Notwithstanding his great age, he hopes still to render some service, submitting himself to go wheresoever his superiors think proper to employ him', added 'The Thunderer'.

FRANCE: SOLIDARITY WITH HUMANITY OR FELLOW-TRAVELLERS OF THE COMMUNISTS?

> *The old dream of the Jesuits, cherished for a hundred and fifty years: to organize Christianity along the lines of a totalitarian dictatorship and the raison d'Etat.*
>
> GEORGES BERNANOS

The nineteenth century was particularly disastrous for the French Jesuits. Scattered by the government and banished several times, they were accused of many things: 'Jesuitism! What a hideous sight', exclaimed Michelet. 'A police mentality and delation, the sneaky habits of the telltale schoolboy transferred from college and convent to the whole of society.' Their crime was political: allegedly that of siding unconditionally with the monarchy, and then with the Empire. When Napoleon III abdicated after his defeat at Sedan, the Commune, which seized power briefly in Paris, immediately attacked the Church, singling out the Jesuits in particular.

In the face of this ingrained habit of equating the Catholic cause with that of the monarchy, Leo XIII himself tried to rally French Catholics to the Republic. But the harm was done. The monarchists of the Action Française movement, together with the Catholic members of the army who had hounded Captain Dreyfus because he was a Jew, had triggered off an anticlericalism among the politicians of the Third Republic that was not only implacable but directed mainly against the Jesuits, who were held responsible for the intellectual formation of the Catholic bourgeoisie.

The last years of the century, and of the reign of Leo XIII, afforded the Jesuits a brief respite. They returned to France in 1890, but ten years later the controversies over education, and then the separation of Church and State, led to a new expulsion of the Society, on 9 September 1901. It reappeared officially 22 years later, as a reward, so to speak, for the patriotism of the 855 French Jesuits who returned to France from the four corners of the earth to fight under the French flag in the First World War.

The period between the two World Wars marks the beginning of the difference of opinion that would soon separate the *avant-garde* of the French Jesuit province from the Roman authorities. Faced with the new threat of Russian Communism, Pius XI and Pius XII had adopted an uncompromising stand: for them Communism was 'intrinsically perverse' representing absolute evil. But at the same time, no doubt partly blinded by their obsessive anti-Communism, these two Popes were half-hearted in their condemnation of Fascism, both Italian and German, which they considered as a lesser evil, or even as a bulwark against atheistic Communism. To make matters worse between the Society in France and the Holy See, certain Jesuits played a crucial role in Vatican politics, whether it was in negotiating a concordat with Mussolini, under Pius XI, or in the relations between Pius XII and the Nazi regime, conducted by the German Jesuits in whom the Pope, formerly Eugenio Pacelli, the nuncio in Berlin, placed his trust.

In France, on the contrary, leading Jesuits were exploring quite different avenues. On the one hand, they were interested in intellectual pursuits: philosophy and theology. The young Teilhard de Chardin was at the start of his quest of the 'Omega point', and his questioning of the traditional doctrine of original sin had brought him the first of many warnings from the Roman theological watchdogs. On the other hand, they were showing an interest in Marxism, not in a polemical way, but with a political and analytical approach. Leading figures in this field were Fr Jean-Yves Calvez – afterwards editor of the Jesuit monthly *Etudes* – who was writing his impressive work *La Pensée de Karl Marx* (The thought of Karl Marx), Fr Villain, engaged in theorizing on the collaboration between Christians and Marxists, and Fr Bigo, author of a study entitled *Marxisme et humanisme, introduction à l'oeuvre économique de Karl Marx* (Marxism and humanism, an introduction to the economic writings of Karl Marx).

Furthermore, on their return to France in 1923, some Jesuits engaged in the apostolate to youth, in the Catholic Action movements which were just beginning. Already, at the end of the previous century, Jesuits had acted as chaplains to the Catholic Association of French Youth, which had contributed to the reconciliation of Catholics with the Republic, the development of social action among Catholics, and the founding of the Christian Democrat Party. Among the leaders of the Catholic Youth movement were men such as the future politicians Georges Bidault and René Pléven.

In 1929, the Young Catholic Farmworkers' movement was created together with the Young Christian Students' movement, on the model of the Young Christian Workers, founded by a Belgian priest, Joseph Cardijn. In these circumstances too, the Jesuits made enemies. The influence exercised by the Society on these movements was considered by certain members of the hierarchy, and by certain among the clergy, as unfair competition, and after the crisis that shook these youth movements in the 1950s the Jesuits were obliged to distance themselves from Catholic Action. This is but one example of Jesuit activity which shows the evolution of the Society's mentality, especially among the younger generation. There was a move away from teaching towards a more social commitment, with the temptation to flirt with politics. This tendency was obviously accelerated by the Second World War and the upheavals it brought, especially as a number of Jesuits distinguished themselves in the Resistance. The clandestine magazine *Témoignage chrétien* (Christian witness) – whose first issue carried the famous warning: 'France beware! You are in danger of losing your soul' – was founded by a Jesuit, Fr Pierre Chaillet.

With time the Jesuits diversified their activities. In addition to the traditional activities, such as teaching, scientific research, publications on spirituality and general news, preaching, parish work, retreat centres and chaplaincies, the Jesuits turned their attention to the industrial and social sectors, either to analyse them, in the specialist magazines of the Centre de recherche et d'action sociales (Social research and action centre) in Paris, or to take an active part in them, through the Mission ouvrière (Workers' mission). Thus the French Jesuits gradually deserted the institutional Church, seeking a place for themselves in professional, secular life, with the aim of living in solidarity with their fellow men.

This social commitment inevitably led to a greater political awareness. It has already been pointed out that those who joined a Catholic Action movement tended to vote Socialist. By the same token, the fact of counselling youth movements and, even more, of becoming a paid worker among others, automatically brought with it a greater 'conscientization' and a quite different political commitment from that to be found among the Jesuits who led a sheltered college life, teaching the sons of the monied classes.

And even in the field of education as such, the priorities laid down by the Jesuits have changed radically over twenty years. Not only has the Society fewer men to devote to this work – in France they have dropped from 200 to about 60 – but 'elitism' is out of fashion. Of the fifteen colleges run today by the Jesuits, two are devoted to higher education (an agricultural college near Toulouse and an engineering college in Lille) and a third is a technical college in Saint-Etienne.

It could be argued that Opus Dei has replaced the Society of Jesus by its occult influence among the right-wing elite. Fr Henri Madelin was prudent:

'I know little about Opus Dei, except by hearsay. But, as people often compare it with the Society of Jesus, I can only say that we have learnt a lot in over four centuries of history; during that time, we have often had to face adversity, which has given us food for thought. It is true that the Society was tempted, on several occasions, to devote itself entirely to the training

of elites. At a time when the political and civil society was
built on a pyramid model, it was understandable – and more
effective – that the Jesuits should concentrate their efforts on
the leaders, as long as they did not forfeit their own evangelical
freedom in the process. It was the Jesuits, for example, who
introduced the practice of granting bursaries in their colleges,
which was a way of making the rich pay for the education of
the poor. But in today's democratic society our mission, in the
name of Christ, is directed both to the country's leaders and to
the least privileged of our society.'

Like most lucid Churchmen, the Jesuits have realized that
a large portion of modern society has completely escaped
evangelization, namely the working classes. This is why, adds
Fr Madelin,

'in the French Province of the Society, we have a Workers'
Mission which employs over 50 Jesuits, a technical college
20 per cent of whose students are sons of immigrants, and
numerous missionaries in Chad, to take but one example. This
explains why we have abandoned a rather facile elitism which
would otherwise prevent us from serving all men, who are
called to an equal dignity in God's sight.'

The shift of emphasis cannot be denied. This is obvious when
one considers the astonishing diversity of the sons of St Ignatius
in the mission field. In fact they are simply returning to their
origins, when Jesuits could be found equally at home as a
Brahmin among the priestly caste of Hinduism in India, a man-
darin in the imperial court of China, an astronomer in Italy or
a tutor in Germany. Even today, if the majority of Jesuits are
to be found within the Church's structures, an active minority
have left the beaten track, in search of untrodden paths that
will lead them closer to mankind.

Fr Edmond Vandermeersch, a Jesuit journalist and soci-
ologist, sums up the situation in France thus:

'Whether he is 35 years old or 60, the Jesuit in this country
is a hospital orderly in Paris or Marseilles, a taxi driver, an
engineer, a driver of a steamroller for public roadworks, a
country priest, a hospital or prison chaplain in Antananarivo,
Marrakesh, Amiens or Nancy, a professor of literature or
handicraft in a provincial college or technical school, a social
counsellor helping immigrant workers, a student of languages

in Beijing, a catechist for the mentally retarded on a cargo ship ...

'Not to mention those, whose number is increasing, who live alone, or in twos and threes in an apartment building, working part-time, often in the social services, and eager to help their neighbours in small ways: material help, advice in dealing with civil service red tape. This desire for a communal life and for an active solidarity with mankind leads these Jesuits to join trade unions, more often than not the Communist-run CGT. If a few are even Communist Party card-holders, the majority are active in the defence of migrant workers, foreign tenants and other underprivileged citizens.'

French Jesuits are to be found across the whole spectrum of politics, from the classical Right to the extreme Left. One might imagine that these opposite tendencies cancel each other out, but this is not so for two reasons. Firstly pluralism is a new phenomenon and indicates a leftward shift in the Society for, traditionally, Catholics in general and Jesuits in particular tended to favour the monarchy, then the liberal bourgeoisie. Secondly, the leftward-leaning Jesuits are usually the youngest and the most dynamic, that is to say those who represent the Society of tomorrow.

One Jesuit, a specialist in political science and French Provincial Superior of the Society in France for a term, has studied the political evolution of French Catholics. In his book *Les chrétiens entrent en politique* (Christians enter politics) published in 1975, Henri Madelin starts from the discovery that of all the variants that affect voting habits, religious membership is the most significant. The more regularly French Catholics practise their religion, the more they vote for the Right. Statistically, a non-believing businessman will be more likely to vote Communist than a churchgoing worker.

And the role played by the Catholic electorate is an important one: since 1945, and especially since the Fifth Republic (1958), practising Catholics have voted massively for the Right (an average of 80 per cent), whereas the greatest support obtained by the Left in this same category of the population was 23 per cent in the presidential election of 1974. Generally speaking, in France the less people practise their religion the more they vote for the Left. Is this a result of cause and effect? To a certain extent, replies Fr Madelin, adding that 'the fact of joining the Socialist family often implies that one has left the Catholic one'. But, since the French bishops gave their blessing to political pluralism in a pastoral letter published in 1972, numerous Catholics vote Socialist with a clear conscience. The arrival of a Socialist government in 1981 could be linked to a decline in churchgoing, but also to a new political awareness among Catholics. Some practising Catholics have contributed to the renewal of the Socialist Party even if they remained a minority in their Church.

The reasons for this conservatism in politics – so different from English Catholics, largely composed of Irish immigrants and of the working class – are twofold. First there is the negative image of religion projected by the Communist Party, so long dominated by the Soviet Union. And then, one should not underestimate the lasting effects of the division of France into two warring camps, dating from the French Revolution of 1789, the Commune (1871) and the separation of Church and State (1906).

The rivalry between State schools and Catholic schools is still very much alive today, as was shown by the massive demonstrations in favour of private education when the Socialists planned to nationalize religious schools in 1984, and then again by the equally impressive crowds who turned out in 1993 to protest against the favouritism shown by Edouard Balladur's government towards Catholic schools. Two deep-seated principles running through the French tradition, which any government should think twice before tampering with, are: freedom of choice in education, and the right to a free, public education system. The balance between these two correlative principles should never be upset.

Nevertheless, this Catholic support of conservatism may be short-lived, in view of the rapidly declining rate of religious practice in France. In 1986, 88 per cent of the adult population declared a belief in the existence of God and 81 per cent described themselves as Catholics; in 1994, these figures dropped respectively to 72 and 64 per cent. The proportion of 'convinced Catholics' has fallen from 30 to 24 per cent while those who practise their faith regularly represent a mere 9 per cent of the overall population. This disaffection for the Church

may well be a result of the new Roman dogmatism enforced
by John Paul II, since 83 per cent of French people hold that
conscience is the sole criterion of moral actions and only 1 per
cent look to the teaching of the Church for moral guidance.

In his latest book, *Dieu et César, essai sur les démocraties
occidentales* (God and Caesar, an essay on the Western
democracies), published in 1994, Fr Madelin examines the
politico-religious situations in the United States and reunified
Germany. In the USA the Roman Catholic Church is rooted in
a democratic and pluralist society. Its first bishop, the former
Jesuit John Carroll, was *elected* by his fellow priests, whose
choice was ratified by Rome, and today many of the documents published by the hierarchy are drawn up collectively,
the result of public debate, and they represent a consensus.
The 'simple faithful', to use the derogatory Roman expression,
participate in formulating the 'mind of the Church', or what
theologians call *sensus Ecclesiae*.

Fr Madelin warns, however, that the unprecedented growth
of the Hispanic-American Catholic population threatens the
status quo:

> Spanish-speaking Americans are Catholic and poor; more than
> anyone, they are prey to the new cults which offer instant
> solutions to their problems. They represent more than 40 per
> cent of practising Catholics and in the year 2000 they will be
> the largest ethnic group in the USA. The biggest challenge for
> the American Church will be their integration into a democratic
> and individualistic society, bearing in mind that their mentality
> is Latin, with a different appreciation of freedom of conscience
> from their Anglo-Saxon colleagues. (...) The bringing about of
> the country's two-centuries-old motto, *E pluribus unum*, will be
> the acid test of the Church's credibility.

As regards the new Germany, the reunification of the two
States has produced a country with a Protestant majority,
whereas West Germany was slightly more Catholic than Protestant: in 1990 there were 42.5 per cent of Catholics and 40.6 per
cent of Protestants. But the real danger for the churches, Fr
Madelin points out, is secularization, especially in former East
Germany, where 71.9 per cent of the population declare themselves to be 'without religion'. In the new Germany, people are
officially leaving the churches in droves; Fr Madelin writes that

In 1992 a record 300,000 people left the Protestant Church and 200,000 the Catholic Church, for various reasons, not least financial, since they refuse to pay the *Kirchensteuer* (ecclesiastical tax).

Religious statistics are equally eloquent: in 1967, 94 per cent of West Germans described themselves as Christian, and 25 per cent of Catholics practised regularly. In 1992, the first figure had dropped to 84 per cent and the second to 10 per cent. One wonders whether the prediction of the Jesuit theologian Karl Rahner is not coming to pass. He foresaw Germany as 'a pagan country with a Christian past and a few Christian vestiges'. And yet, paradoxically, the unorthodox writings of the Catholic theologian Eugen Drewermann are read by thousands.

Such lucid analyses as those of Fr Madelin are typical of the younger generation of French Jesuits, but they are not to everyone's liking in the Church, even within the Society of Jesus. There as elsewhere conservative and progressive factions coexist. During his term of office, which coincided with the postconciliar era, Fr Arrupe encouraged debate and freedom of speech. This new openness not only displeased the papacy, it also attracted criticism from fundamentalist movements.

A good example is that of the right-wing polemicist and lone sniper Fr Bruckberger – a Dominican to boot – who summed up eloquently the criticism most often levelled at such Jesuits:

> The Jesuits have only managed to adapt themselves so admirably to the modern world because it is their creation! Their trace is to be found everywhere and their influence is omnipresent. The Jesuits were born with the modern world. They were its midwives, and they share its triumph.

And after describing Lenin and Trotsky as 'imitators of the Jesuits', he concludes:

> Insofar as they follow Christ, the Jesuits cannot go the whole way with their disciples. But they remain fellow travellers. Thus their thirst for power, so often disguised as humility, threatens to bury them in the ruins of the very civilization they helped to build.

The Jesuits have often been accused of being 'Communist fellow-travellers' or 'crypto-Communists', and certain traditionalist movements have gone so far as to accuse the Society of Jesus of hatching a worldwide plot aimed at fostering Christian–

Marxist collaboration, when it isn't simply marrying Christianity with Communism. This was of course before the defeat of Marxism in Eastern Europe, but at the height of the courtship between liberation theology and Marxism during Fr Arrupe's generalship he was often accused of leniency towards atheistic Marxism. Without foundation, as we shall see in the following section.

THE THIRD WORLD: FROM REACTION TO REVOLUTION

> *Inculturation is a concept that has evolved. Christ himself acknowledged that at its beginnings the Gospel was clothed in Jewish spirituality and culture. The message may have been intended for all cultures and languages, and its content may be transcultural, but it remains that the message can only be mediated through a given culture.*
>
> PETER-HANS KOLVENBACH

In seeking to rediscover its roots at the end of the twentieth century, the Society of Jesus stresses more than ever the missionary character of the Ignatian intuition. But whereas the first companions dreamt of reconquering the Holy Land from the infidel and of baptizing the heathen populations of the Far East, today's Jesuits are eager to help Third World countries in their religious, cultural, social and economic development. They attempt to do so while avoiding, as far as possible, both proselytizing and political interference.

This new approach is also visible in the industrialized countries. Young Jesuits take an interest in sectors that were neglected before, like the factory or the urban ghetto. They have founded industrial missions in France, as we have seen, but also in Italy, Spain, Belgium, the Netherlands and Germany. In the United States, neglecting the colleges and universities, some of the younger generation of Jesuits have chosen to work in the Black ghettoes and to educate the poor. And even those who remain in the traditional structures of higher education have adopted a radical change of style.

In the 1980s the ten American provinces collaborated to run three large theological faculties in Massachusetts, Illinois and California. These theological centres for the formation of Jesuit priests are open to students from other churches: notably Lutherans, Presbyterians and Episcopalians, whose colleges are situated nearby. The Jesuits also collaborate more closely with the state universities of Harvard, Chicago and Berkeley. This has resulted in some serious reflection on human rights, on women's rights in society and in the Church, on liberation theology and non-violence. Members of the Jesuit university of Georgetown, in Washington, contributed to the American bishops' document on nuclear arms, and the Kennedy Center of Ethics, another Jesuit institution in Washington, has become one of the leading centres of research on questions of bioethics.

In 1990, Fr Kolvenbach's then assistant for the United States, the late Fr Joseph Whelan, told me that American Jesuits should be reconsidering their priorities:

> 'Should we be investing so much energy in our high schools,
> when our numbers are falling and our average age is
> increasing? At the present time, the proportion of Jesuits in
> education is constant, and yet our field of activity is growing, to
> include the Hispanics and the Blacks. In the year 2000, 50 per
> cent of American Catholics will be Spanish speaking. There lies
> our real challenge: the problem of immigration. In California,
> in the diocese of Orange, a third of the 90 seminarians are
> Vietnamese. This is why Fr Kolvenbach is right to stress the
> necessary internationalization of the Society. On the whole,
> our relations with the American Church are excellent, even if
> Rome's present policy of episcopal appointments is leading to
> a right-wing shift in the Conference of bishops ... The new
> generation of Jesuit novices is much more conservative than
> mine. I consider myself as a "moderate" whereas my students
> see me as dangerously progressive.'

Four years later, I met Fr Whelan's successor in Rome, Fr John O'Callaghan, who seemed to confirm his predecessor's remarks. More conservative, he refused an on-the-record interview. The problems he sees facing the Society in America, as in Canada and especially Australia, are secularization, materialism and consumerism. He considers the Society's mission to be not primarily social nor directed exclusively to the poor, but to the middle class and the intellectuals. Above all, education is the priority of priorities, and Fr Kolvenbach has laid a greater emphasis upon this than Fr Arrupe. Finally the Jesuits in America have a duty to work on the government, by a system of lobbying, through non-governmental organizations and through Congress.

But it is in the Third World that one can measure the extent to which the Society of Jesus has radically changed its strategy. Its major priorities can be summed up as inculturation and the promotion of faith through justice. The respect for different cultures, so rare during the whole saga of colonization, appeared essential to the first Jesuit missionaries in India, China and Paraguay. It was another return to the origins, therefore, when Fr Arrupe launched an appeal in 1971 for a profound reform of Jesuit colleges. In a message sent to Mexico, where a congress of former Jesuit students from the whole of Latin America was taking place, he pointed out that 'education is essential for finding a true solution to poverty', and invited his audience to turn their colleges into 'instruments for forming men who are aware of the need for radical change'.

The General's words were a confirmation of a decision taken the year before by the Mexican Provincial to close the Patria Institute, a college of 2,500 students which was reputed to be one of the best in the country. 'The culture which is transmitted in our colleges is decidedly unfitted for a country that can only find a solution to its problems through participation and co-operation', the college's governing board stated at the time. 'It is an education which smacks of privilege and encourages an elite mentality, bolstering up the powerful right-wing forces in the country. We believe this to be contrary to the harmonious growth of our nation.'

No slight confession! Traditional policy was admitted to be harmful and those in charge were ready to relinquish their power in exchange for 'participation'. This about-turn was one of the fruits of Fr Arrupe's generalship. Having spent 27 years in Japan, he was well equipped to understand the necessity of an inculturation of the faith. Having learnt to respect, and then to love, Japanese culture, he had quickly realized that the Christian message, in its traditional scholastic form, could not be grasped by non-Latin minds. In a book of memoirs, he asked

What path should I take to reach the Japanese soul? The paths (*do*) of zen. Namely, the manner of preparing and presenting tea (*chado*), the tea ritual, a ceremony which has nothing to do with our Western rules of politeness; the manner of handling a bow and arrow (*kyodo*), which is not a sport but a veritable philosophy; the art of arranging flowers (*kado*), which requires five years of study before receiving one's diploma; the art of self-defence (*judo*), which allies elegance with efficacity; the art of fencing (*kendo*), which is done equally with sticks as well as swords and which is not so much a fight as an art. And finally *shodo*, the art of composing and writing a poem, which entails not only the sentiments expressed but the calligraphy used to convey these sentiments.[7]

Thus, Fr Arrupe reversed the traditional method. To reach another person, it is first necessary to enter into his mentality and to love him for what he is. According to Fr Arrupe, 'inculturation requires a "trans-culturation", that is an opening to and an exchange with other cultures, which itself requires a partial "de-culturation", that is to say a questioning of certain aspects of one's own culture'.

Pushing the argument even further, he claimed that, to render Christianity credible today, inculturation is necessary in all countries, including traditionally Christian Europe. 'A new and ongoing inculturation of the faith is unavoidable', he added, 'if we want the message of the Gospel to get through to modern man, and the new members of his subculture (down and outs, immigrants, intellectuals, scientists, students, artists, and others).'

It is not surprising, then, that the 32nd Congregation entrusted the General with 'the task of encouraging and promoting the work of inculturation throughout the whole Society'. But one can also understand why such an undertaking, undoubtedly necessary but difficult to carry out and leading to excesses by the inexperienced or over-zealous, aroused the suspicion of the last three Popes, even though this new policy was not imposed on the Society by a handful of hotheads, but represented the collective answer to a universal situation. Fr Kolvenbach has not only pursued the same policy

concerning inculturation, he has gone even further than his predecessor, advocating what he calls 'interculturation'. When I
asked him whether relations between the Society and the Holy
See had improved, he answered:

'Relations are at present cordial and based on mutual trust.
The Holy Father recently expressed his confidence in our
forthcoming General Congregation. Even if the Holy See seems
resigned to the shortcomings of certain individual Jesuits, it
is convinced of the collective responsibility of the Society as
a whole. We too have come to understand the Pope better.
For example, when he first launched his plan for a "second
evangelization" of Europe many people were afraid of a new
crusading spirit of conquest, or even of a neo-imperialism. Once
one has understood the phrase correctly, one cannot but adhere
to the idea of a new mission to spread the Gospel. We even
have an advantage over the Pope. It is no longer possible to
address the whole Church in identical terms, as he tries to do.
And this is where our theory of "inculturation" comes into its
own. It is necessary to translate the Gospel message into the
different cultures throughout the world, as we have been doing
for centuries ...'

To the question: What are the limits to inculturation? Fr
Kolvenbach replied:

'Inculturation is a concept that has evolved. Christ himself
acknowledged that at its beginnings the Gospel was clothed
in Jewish spirituality and culture. The message may have been
intended for all cultures and languages, and its content may
be transcultural, but it remains that the message can only be
mediated through a given culture.
   'Today, we are aware that language and culture are not
simple matters of packaging and that people cannot change
their culture or language the way they change their clothes. As
a linguist I am reminded of Wittgenstein's remark: "Whatever
we don't have a word for doesn't exist." Thus, the idea of
inculturation implying that an entity with its own culture
comes into another culture to transform it, is increasingly being
challenged. There is a new emphasis on a meeting between
cultures, in which witnesses of the Gospel, having a given
culture, take part in an exchange of their experience of Christ's
message with people of another culture. They know that the

Gospel will be a process of purification and challenge not only for the receiving culture but also for the culture that is communicating the message.

'Maybe a new word will be coined. It is better to speak of "interculturation" – we already say "cross-cultural". On a practical level, it is much more an encounter of cultures than the imposition of one culture on another, even with the aim of helping. It is really a sharing of cultures, and done in the spirit of the Lord. I myself have had problems with inculturation, because I lived most of my life in the Arab world and I have no Arab blood. What did I do about it in the Middle East? In fact I did nothing. But I had the good fortune of being parachuted into real Arab surroundings, and I just had to live with it. Not everyone can do this. We had Jesuits coming to the Middle East who panicked and left after two weeks ...

'You are not really inculturated until you have acquired not only the qualities but also the defects of the people you are with. My eyes are blue and in the Koran devils have blue eyes, probably because of the Arabs' bad experiences with people with blue eyes. Once you go back to Europe – a mere three hours away by plane – you really feel the difference. For example, in Arab culture one is never direct, and so when you come back to Europe and listen to the language it seems really harsh and rude.'

Fr Giuseppe Pittau himself – who was Provincial in Japan when he was chosen by John Paul II to assist Fr Paolo Dezza as his personal delegate at the head of the Society – is convinced of the necessity of opening up Christianity to other religions:

'Thanks to the Council, for the first time Catholicism entered into a proper dialogue with the great religions of the world. Until then, it was confrontation rather than dialogue. We denied any value to these religions the better to destroy them. By its open approach to Buddhism, Hinduism, Shintoism and Islam, the Society has contributed to this new spirit of dialogue. I could quote, among our contemporaries, Frs Lasalle and Kadowaki in Japan, Fr Raguin in Vietnam and Taiwan, among many others. These efforts not only enrich our Christian experience, they also serve to modify the understanding these religions have of Christianity. This is vital, especially in Asia where Christians have a real impact on the history of this continent, even if they only make up 3 per cent of the population.'

What is more, the future of the Society of Jesus lies in the Third World. According to Fr Madelin,

> 'Vocations are down everywhere in Europe: even in Poland
> they have dropped by a third. Spain, Italy, France – even
> Ireland – are faring badly. England seems an exception.[8] On the
> other hand, things are going well in Asia: in Indonesia, India,
> the Pacific region. The problem there is one of formation and
> the true motivation behind vocations.'

After a grave crisis, numbers are increasing slightly in the West, but they are climbing more rapidly in regions such as India, Central and South America and Africa. In the view of Fr O'Keefe,

> 'There has been a steady decrease in the total number of
> Jesuits, especially in Europe and North America, since Vatican
> II. India and Africa have done well. A key statistic is the
> number of scholastics (seminarians) for each priest. This ratio
> is very good for India and Africa, which have large numbers
> of young Jesuits. The largest concentration of Jesuits is in the
> United States, followed by India, but this position will most
> likely be reversed in seven years or so.'

The President of Georgetown University, Fr Leo O'Donovan, is more worried about those leaving the Society than about those not entering it:

> 'Vocations have dropped sharply in Western Europe and French
> Canada, not quite so sharply in the United States and English-
> speaking Canada and have increased in other parts of the world
> like India, Indonesia and sections of Latin America and Africa.
> In the part of the Society I know best, the United States, most
> provinces have received a respectable number of novices in the
> years since the decline began – roughly the late sixties.
>   'A disappointing number of young Jesuits, however, still
> leave the Society after pronouncing their first vows, and one
> of the questions that might be addressed to the upcoming
> Congregation is whether the Society wishes to continue
> regarding these first vows as "permanent" in nature. In any
> case, the history of the Society has always shown a substantial
> number of departures after first vows, so this is nothing new.'

In the United States, vocations are down, to about 60 or 65 Jesuit novices a year. There are approximately 4,000 Jesuits spread over ten provinces. This is down from the peak figure of 10,000, but the situation is better than in Europe. Fr Salvini, the editor of *Civiltà cattolica*, thinks the rhythm of diminution is slackening:

'In Italy we have between ten and fifteen novices per year, but between 30 and 35 deaths. The crisis affects the traditional Christian countries (Belgium, France, Italy). What does the future hold? Fr Kolvenbach resorts to his legendary humour: "Prediction is a difficult art, especially concerning the future."'

Some Jesuits don't see the drop in vocations as catastrophic. Fr John O'Malley, author of the recent and widely appreciated study *The First Jesuits*,[9] who teaches at the Weston School of Theology in Cambridge, Massachusetts, admits that

'thirty years ago I thought that the Society was accepting too many people who were marginally qualified, so I would not idealize that aspect of the past. Very little in modern culture supports the kind of life Jesuits are called to ...'

And Fr Padberg, director of the Institute of Jesuit Sources in St Louis, puts the matter into an historical perspective:

'The very large classes of entrants, not only to the Jesuits but to the religious life in general, both male and female, to which we were long accustomed, is a special phenomenon of the 150 years from the French Revolution to Vatican II. A longer historical perspective on the Church and on religious life over the centuries could lead to a lot less pessimism than is common today.'

Especially since the Third World appears ready to take over from the spiritually drained West. Fr Julian Fernandes, an Indian Jesuit and assistant to Fr Kolvenbach for India, is optimistic about the shifting of the Society's centre of gravity to the Third World:

'There are at present 3,500 Jesuits in India (including the novices). This has produced a renewal of theology, of inculturation and missiology. Inculturation is constantly developing and growing. During the colonial period, India received much: we studied theology industriously, and now we live it. We have a new awareness of what we learnt. The Church has asked us to do this. We are re-experiencing the

Gospel, within the limits of orthodoxy and in an ambience of loyalty to the Church.

'There is necessarily some tension ... We are a small minority surrounded by a number of living religions. Some Hindu political parties want to impose a Hindu nation, but we consider ourselves to be as Indian as they. The problem is caused by certain fundamentalists. Fortunately, there is a swing back from the extreme right wing to the centre, both in political and religious matters.

'In practical terms, we celebrate the liturgy in an Indian manner and we now have access to more serious scholarship, both in terms of the written word and in dialogue with Hinduism and Islam. Among our leading intellectuals, I could quote the name of Michael Amaladoss SJ, an expert in inculturation, who is here in Rome. As regards Indian Jesuits, I could mention T. K. John, president of the Jesuit theological faculty in Delhi, who has developed close contact with the people; Ignatius Puthiadam, a brilliant intellectual at the "House of Friendship" at Varanasi; Sebastian Painadath, director of the Dialogue Centre at Sameeksha, an expert on social and spiritual questions; and Ignatius Hirudayam, who lives like a *sadhu* (holy man or guru) in Madras.'

I asked him how Rome had reacted to this experimentation.

'We have received the encouragement of the Pope and the General regarding our work amongst the poor, with a reminder, however, that we should show caution in our contacts with the population, avoiding confrontation or engaging in party politics. We are expected to show loyalty to the Church and the hierarchy. Obviously, some political overtones are inevitable, especially among our non-Jesuit collaborators.'

Vocations are plentiful, but changing in nature, as Fr Fernandes explained:

'We have an intake of about 150 a year, of whom 70 to 75 per cent persevere. In addition to the 3,500 Jesuits in India, Nepal has 80 and Sri Lanka 90. People are attracted to the Society from the lower middle classes, in the hope of doing something about the social situation. Others come from good Catholic families. Their vocation is initially wholly religious – they wish to spread the Good News of the Gospel – but soon they prefer simply to bear witness to the values of the Gospel. They no

longer wish to convert people, but simply to bring them the
Christian message. If conversions follow, all well and good. If
preaching the Gospel is the ultimate goal, it is first necessary to
create a favourable human context. Will this lead to baptisms?
I don't know, maybe ... Paul VI said that "the new name
for evangelization is development". And even John Paul II
realizes that there is no going back, although he is worried
that orthodoxy will fall prey to secularism. The present Pope
is conservative doctrinally, but progressive socially. He has
condemned consumerism as being opposed to the Gospel.'

Fr de Vera, who runs the Jesuit Press Office in Rome, is
equally enthusiastic. According to him,

'Decentralization is a fine thing. We have been much too
European-centred in the past. It is time we changed. Personally,
I have learnt a lot from my stay in Japan. Even if the number of
conversions there is very low (there are only 450,000 Catholics
in a population of 127 million), the Japanese are as open to
Christianity as any other culture.

'As for the declining number of vocations, this is no
problem. When we had a maximum of 36,000 members this
was an abnormally high number. Fr Arrupe thought that our
numbers would level off at 14,000. Our vocation is to act as a
ferment in society. Of course we are asked to carry out many
commitments, but the laity should take an increasing part in
our activities, such as running our schools. I believe that the
Holy Spirit is leading the world: not thanks to us Jesuits, I
hasten to add, but through history. The monastic monopoly
must disappear ... Which Pope will have the foresight – and
the guts – to see this? There are so many good ways to serve
the Lord – not just in religious life.

'Ignatius saw his Society of Jesus as a small number of
dedicated brothers. At the recent symposium in Loyola I
noticed twelve portraits of Jesuits who looked as though they
were living dangerously. They were dressed as Egyptian priests,
as Chinese mandarins, as scientists and explorers ...'

Fr Fitzpatrick, professor at Fordham University in New York,
sees the centre of gravity shifting

'not only in the Society but in the whole Church. In the
United States, we have the phenomenon of the Third World
(Hispanics) coming in large numbers and contributing to the life
of the Church. The Society has always functioned well as an

international organization and I think it will continue to do so
despite the shift in numbers to the Third World.'

Fr John Padberg is less sanguine. Although he welcomes the
challenge to the Society of the religious insights of Jesuits who
have grown up in the non-Western world, adding that 'probably
within the next generation a non-Western Jesuit will either be
elected General or will be one of the leading possibilities for such
an election', he also foresees 'vigorous differences of opinion on
how far to go in inculturating the insights, policies and practices of non-Westerners into the life and work of the Society'
as well as a drop in revenue:

> 'The economic resources at the disposal of the Society will
> decrease as the number of Jesuits from the West decreases.
> Those from the Third World will not have supporters with as
> much disposable resources as were previously available from
> the West.'

And finally,

> 'Because the Roman Catholic Church in its central government
> does not usually change as rapidly as the Society of Jesus as
> a whole, there will be the occasion for misunderstandings and
> friction between them.'

Fr O'Keefe points out that

> 'the influence of India, other parts of Asia, and Africa is
> already being felt on account of their presence at General
> Congregations. Previously, these countries had been
> represented by Europeans and North Americans. The influence
> of the Third World was seen at the 32nd General Congregation
> which defined the faith/justice mission of the Society. The voice
> of the poorer world will be heard more as we understand the
> importance of inculturation. Theological reflection will be quite
> different from the more usual European and North American
> approach, where the context was Judaeo-Christian. The world
> of Islam and Hinduism will be much more in view.'

Fr Leo O'Donovan also points to the new geographical
composition of the Congregation:

> 'The upcoming Congregation will prove instructive for two
> reasons: (1) its delegates will be distributed according to a new
> representational scheme decided upon at the 33rd Congregation,

so as to honour better the population patterns of the Society; (2)
therefore, the tipping of the scales towards Third World power
in the Congregation of the Society – already visible, but not
yet decisive, in the 32nd and 33rd Congregations – will become
even more pronounced, and a study of the documents and
decrees coming out of the 34th Congregation can be expected
to reflect more obviously the shift in the Society's "centre of
gravity".'

Fr Michael Campbell-Johnston sees the move from Europe
to the Third World – which he made personally by leaving
England for Central America – as an opportunity for renewal.

'The shift applies, of course, to the Church as a whole and
not just to the Society. I personally have great hopes that it
will bring about new forms of ecclesiastical and religious life
and give new vitality to existing ones. The condition is that
Europe – and Rome – do not cling to power of privilege and
acknowledge that the periphery can be as important as the
centre. But I also believe that some elements in the charism of
St Ignatius are timeless and valid for all cultures. The challenge
is to disentangle these from historical/geographical accretions in
such a way that they are free to be inculturated into others.'

As for the General, Fr Kolvenbach is equally enthusiastic
about the emergence of the Third World in the Society:

'This will undoubtedly enrich us. At its origins the Society was
very Spanish, but soon the Pope wisely approved the election
of the first non-Hispanic General, and then a Frenchman, a
Slav ... This opens windows onto worldwide horizons. Pedro
Arrupe looked towards Asia, having spent many years in Japan.
The Society intensified its dialogue with Buddhism and Islam.
With regard to India, where Jesuit vocations are numerous, the
country is far from homogeneous: between the "Tribal belt"
and Westernized Bombay, the differences are immense. Will we
have an Indian General one day? Why not? He would surely do
better than the present one! ...

'There are five principles characteristic of the Jesuit apostolate,
established by my predecessor, Fr Arrupe, and confirmed by
the 32nd General Congregation. They are: theological reflection,
social action, education, the mass media and, pervading them
all, the *Spiritual Exercises*. These together make our preaching
of the Gospel most effective. They sign our labours with the
seal of the Society of Jesus. Whatever a Jesuit's daily work is,

and wherever he is in the world, I think that one of these five
should be the dominant note, the other four completing it and
filling it out.'

The last two Generals have been keenly aware that the future
of the human race lies in Asia. Fr Arrupe once said that

'Europe used to be at the centre of the world. Today, America
occupies that place, but tomorrow it will be Asia. Since the
Gospel reached Asia through the missionaries, at present
Christianity is considered by the inhabitants of the Far East to
be the religion of the West, an alien religion that they cannot
accept. Tomorrow, however, the new generations will not
have experienced colonialism, for them the West will simply
represent the origin of colonialism and, hopefully, the Gospel
will no longer be considered as a foreign body that must be
eliminated from their culture.

'No other civilization is better equipped to receive the Gospel
than the Oriental civilization. Asians hold the Gospel values
in the highest esteem; I would go as far as to say that they
have them in their blood. It is in their tradition to respect
poverty, simplicity, authenticity, wisdom, contemplation. They
have a natural sense of the divine. Christ's Gospel will reveal
them as they really are and, by penetrating their spirit, will
transform them.'

Equally obsessed by Asia, Fr Kolvenbach is less optimistic
about its conversion to Christianity.

'Asia and Africa are a source of riches for us but when
one realizes that Christians represent only 3 per cent of the
Asian population, one wonders if the Lord wants them to be
converted ... It is hard for Asians to accept the Incarnation and
Latin theology. The fear that Hindus might take communion
gives nightmares to the cardinals of the Curia. I suggest that
Christians content themselves with bearing witness.'

An example of this witness to the Gospel values was the
creation, by Fr Arrupe in 1980, of the Jesuit Refugee Service,
already mentioned in the opening pages of this book. The
General's intuition was prophetic: the number of refugees in
the world has been multiplied by ten in as many years.[10]
In reviewing the first ten years of its operations in 1990, Fr
Kolvenbach spoke of the JRS as 'a characteristically Ignatian
apostolate'. He saw the JRS not as one special project within

the Jesuit order but as a task shared by the whole Society of Jesus.

I asked Fr Mark Raper, the International Director of the JRS, to describe his work.

'The most striking development is our increasing collaboration with the laity. The current generation of youngsters, a product of the eighties, are less "institutionally minded" but just as devoted as their predecessors. Our overall staff comprises 200 committed Jesuits, of whom 80 to 100 work full time and the rest part time. There are approximately 60 non-Jesuit religious working with us, and this figure will soon reach 100.

'The number of lay people is more difficult to evaluate. Over 100 have been recruited internally by means of a volunteer programme (they are not well paid). In local refugee situations, a large staff is recruited and we run 22 primary schools and 22 nursery schools. The Jesuit lay volunteer is given a specific mission to accomplish, but we also need Jesuits to accept long-term commitments. These are from 45 different provinces or regions. They tend to be middle-aged (in their forties and fifties). We are not affected by the drop in vocations, I am thankful to say.'

Regarding the General Congregation, Fr Raper considers it

'vital that the 23,000 Jesuits realize the importance of the Refugee Service for the Society. Our work is a profoundly disturbing experience, and a salutary one ... We are not alone in this, of course. We work closely with other refugee services and with the UNHCR (High Commission for Refugees of the United Nations). We are sometimes critical of the control exercised by governments on their own organizations. We, on the other hand, receive strong support from the Vatican, especially Cardinal Etchegaray, president of Justice and Peace, and the Council of Pastoral Care for Migrants. But we have to be careful to steer clear of political or ideological – or even doctrinal – controversies.'

In spite of this last remark, Fr Raper does not mince his words. In a recent talk he gave in Rome he summed up the situation thus:

Reflecting on the new world order that is emerging, we can observe that the field is now open for the United States to exercise unprecedented hegemony. Even when, in response

to a 'humanitarian' crisis, the UN system, kept at near
bankruptcy by its host country, is empowered to act, it is now
at ever-greater risk of manipulation by the US. (...) During
the last few years, we have witnessed large-scale intervention,
during the Gulf War as well as in Liberia and in Somalia. The
Somalian operation, at least its military aspect, turned out to
be an unfortunate experiment in 'humanitarian' intervention.
The military cost of the operation in Somalia was at least
ten times the amount spent on humanitarian assistance and
reconstruction.'

Fr Kolvenbach's wholehearted support of the JRS was spelt
out plainly in the letter he addressed to the whole Society in
1990 on the tenth anniversary of the creation of the JRS.

I consider our work on behalf of the refugees to be an
essential part of our commitment to serve the faith through
the promotion of justice. We have too often neglected the
basic question: why are there fifteen million refugees,[11] for the
most part from the poorer regions of the world? Granting aid
to these refugees is usually considered to be an act of charity
rather than justice, thus avoiding the fundamental question I
have just asked. (...) For this reason, I consider more urgent
than ever the work of the JRS, with its political analyses, its
research work and organization of public debate, in order to
answer the above question.

Such a statement leaves little doubt as to Fr Kolvenbach's
backing of the 'Arrupe line' in dictating the Society's social
policy. But it cannot be denied that this 'promotion of justice'
is a minefield. It is almost impossible to carry out such a
delicate task without engaging directly in politics. And there
are instances where the Society's activities have laid it open to
the accusation, sometimes with good reason, more often not, by
reactionary forces within the Church, of 'engaging in politics'.
Or worse, of joining forces with the diabolical Marxists.

One example of a Jesuit's name being unjustly blackened by a
right-wing smear campaign was the infamous 'Pellecer affair'
in Guatemala. Luis Eduardo Pellecer, a young middle-class
Guatemalan, entered the Society of Jesus after his medical
studies. Ordained in 1976, he worked with the poor and
oppressed in El Salvador and Nicaragua before returning to

Guatemala. There he engaged in three activities considered 'subversive' by the ruling junta: he edited a magazine called *Diálogo*, devoted to human rights; he worked for an organization which cleaned up shanty towns; and he provided humanitarian aid for Salvadorean refugees. Above all, he had links with the clandestine Guerrilla Army for the Poor (EGP), not as an active member but as a sympathizer.

Despite death threats, he persevered in his work until 9 June 1981 when he disappeared, kidnapped by six armed men who dragged him from his car in the centre of the capital, beat him until he lost consciousness, and drove away with him. There was no news for 113 days, and his friends believed him to be dead. Then on 30 September, he appeared on television where he delivered a lengthy, self-critical confession, in the presence of the Minister of the Interior and the country's military and religious authorities. The 'public' included representatives of the Diplomatic Corps, Guatemalan and foreign journalists and, in an adjoining room equipped with closed-circuit television, were the President, General Lucas Garcia and members of the Episcopal Conference.

For two hours he confessed his errors in public. In a monotonous voice, scarcely recognizable by his friends, he described himself as a 'repentant revolutionary'. He explained how he had belonged to the EGP, with the blessing of his religious superiors, how he had organized his own kidnapping in order to make a clean break with the guerrilla movement and give himself up safely to the police. He criticized, pell mell, liberation theology, the 'Marxist practices' of certain committed Christians, the 'Marxist formation' given systematically to Jesuit novices, the 'preferential option for the poor' – an option he judged 'unilateral and dangerous', although it was the actual expression adopted by the Latin American bishops at the conferences of Medellín in 1968 and Puebla in 1979. He levelled accusations against several Christian movements of social action, asked forgiveness for having 'betrayed' his country, and finally announced his decision to leave the Society of Jesus and Guatemala. After which he replied to the questions of the press.

Luis Pellecer's friends who were present at the press conference, or who later saw the videocassette, were convinced that the Jesuit had been brainwashed. Not only did he speak in a toneless, staccato voice – 'as though he had lost his soul', as a close friend put it – but his statement was full of errors and contradictions.

Firstly, he claimed to have given himself up voluntarily to the police on 8 June 1981 (it was actually the 9th), whereas eye witnesses had seen him beaten unconscious, then taken away covered in blood. It was discovered later that his 'accomplices' even broke his jaw, and one of his young Jesuit friends, Carlos Perez Alonso, a hospital and prison chaplain, had seen him in the military hospital of Guatemala City, before disappearing in his turn on 2 August of the same year. Secondly, he spoke several times of his '122 days of absence', instead of 113. Why this error of ten days? Could it be that his televised confession had been planned originally to coincide with that of another repentant guerrillero made ten days later?

In any case, those Jesuits who knew him, as well as two Central American bishops, Mgr Marcus McGrath, Archbishop of Panama, and Mgr Arturo Rivera Damas, Bishop of San Salvador, all said that they were sure that Fr Pellecer had been reciting a lesson which he did not believe. A statement published by the Society of Jesus in Central America on 2 October 1981 speaks of 'declarations obtained under very strong pressure', adding that 'Fr Pellecer was imprisoned for 113 days, without any guarantee of his physical and mental well-being for such a long period'.

Four months later Fr John O'Callaghan, then president of the Jesuit Conference of the United States, wrote, on behalf of the ten North American Provincials: 'I am convinced that Fr Pellecer was the victim of an ideological conversion obtained by psychological means. The "robot" who appeared several times on television in Guatemala, El Salvador and Honduras is not – psychologically – the same Fr Pellecer who was kidnapped on 9 June 1981.' On the basis of a report on the 'Pellecer Affair' made by two psychiatrists, Dr Frederick Allodi from Toronto and Dr Martin Symonds from New York, and submitted to the 38th Session on human rights in Geneva in March 1982, Fr Henri Madelin, then French Provincial, denounced what he called 'an ideological conversion, obtained under duress by psycho-physiological means', and warned that Fr Pellecer's 'profoundly disturbed state might lead him to commit suicide'.

Even the Guatemalan bishops – except Cardinal Mario Casariego, Archbishop of Guatemala City, who had publicly called Pellecer 'Judas' – made a statement on 3 October 1981, in spite of the pressure brought to bear by the government, in which they appealed to 'the critical judgement of the people', whom they trusted to 'discern what is true and false in the accusations made by the priest in question'. Mgr Eduardo Fuentes Duarte, Auxiliary Bishop of Guatemala City, confided in private to a journalist that 'although it is possible that Fr Pellecer's confession was beneficial to the Church, I do not believe in its sincerity'.

Such forced confessions are not rare, especially under totalitarian regimes. What is more surprising is that the right-wing press in Europe, notably *Le Figaro Magazine*, launched a violent anti-Jesuit campaign, in favour of Fr Pellecer's 'conversion from Marxism'. Writing in this magazine, the Dominican Fr Bruckberger published the following diatribe:

> The following questions require the answer yes or no: has
> the progressive wing of the Catholic Church in Latin America
> simply joined the Marxist-Leninist Revolution? Do certain
> priests bear arms and take part in guerrilla warfare? Do
> Jesuits recruit and train this progressive and revolutionary
> wing of South American Catholicism? Do these Jesuits enjoy
> the complicity, the sympathy and even the authority of the
> superiors of the Society? After the 'Pellecer Affair' it is
> impossible to answer 'no' to these questions. The conclusion
> to be drawn is obvious. In Central America, a young man who
> felt called by God to enter the Society of Jesus was unaware –
> since no-one had told him – that the obedience he would
> offer and the education that his Jesuit teachers would give
> him would turn him into a Marxist-Leninist revolutionary, and
> possibly a guerrilla fighter.

The mind boggles at such sophistry – such Jesuitical casuistry, and by a Dominican! Are the Jesuits in Latin America really dangerous revolutionaries? First, it is impossible to generalize. Not all Jesuits have abandoned their traditional teaching apostolate: the Jesuit University of Guatemala, for example, still provides a classical education for the sons of the ruling class. It is true, however, that, given their dwindling numbers, the

Jesuits collaborate more and more with the laity, especially with the poor and the underprivileged, in associations which seek to promote social justice and naturally come into conflict with the conservative political forces.

But to deduce from this that they are 'Marxist-Leninist revolutionaries' or 'subversive guerrilla fighters' is patently absurd. As for the complicity of Jesuit superiors, it is best simply to listen to them. The late Fr Cesar Jerez, for example, former Provincial of Central America and Panama, does not beat about the bush:

> 'Those who oppose any change have launched a campaign to discredit us. They call us Marxist-Leninist, pro-Marxists or philo-Marxists. Such accusations even emanate from within the Church, which makes them all the more wounding.
>   'Certain Latin American countries suffer from social inequality, political strife and intolerable injustice. Violent repression has provoked corresponding violence – revolutionary or subversive according to opinion – in a context of corruption and structural violence. All of which has resulted in much suffering and many deaths. Some Jesuits have tried to play their part in finding solutions to these problems. It is obvious that some of us have made mistakes at certain times, mistakes which have provoked violent reactions against us. We wish merely to carry out our apostolic apostolate *ad majorem Dei gloriam*, by bringing our Christian contribution to the needs of our country.'

And Fr Jerez spoke from experience. He was not debating in the salons of the 'New Right' in France or pontificating in the plush offices of the Roman Curia; he spoke out from the midst of his suffering people. His life was threatened in his own country and he had to go into hiding during a visit to El Salvador, after the assassination of a Jesuit priest, Fr Rutilio Grande. His verdict was pessimistic:

> 'Persecution is rife and disunity between supposed brothers is hard to bear. The mistrust shown by members of the Church is especially painful. We have had many trials. Here are several examples: first of all, the assassination of Mgr Romero, Archbishop of San Salvador, in 1980. He was a good friend and a great bishop. The time of his glorification will come, in spite of the slander spread through jealousy.

'Before that, I was very affected by the death of another
holy man, Rutilio Grande. There were also arrests, tortures,
expulsions, bomb attempts against our houses and institutions,
searches, slander campaigns in the press, death threats against
many Jesuits, including those of a whole country.'

Fr Jerez is alluding here to El Salvador, where the Jesuits of the
José Simeón Canas University in San Salvador were accused of
teaching Marxism. The 47 Jesuits of the university had been
threatened with expulsion but were defended by Mgr Chavez,
former Archbishop of the capital, and were finally reprieved
by Colonel Molina. In 1976, the university threw its weight
behind Molina's proposed agricultural reforms, and when,
under threat, he abandoned them, the Jesuits continued to
defend the project. A year later, Fr Rutilio Grande, a Jesuit
in charge of a rural parish, was murdered. The same year,
sixteen Jesuits were expelled and the others 'invited' to leave
the country under pain of death. In July 1977, the army
occupied the university. From 1976 to 1981, the university
and the Jesuits' residence were the object of eleven bomb
attacks. At the beginning of 1981, the university was once
again occupied by the army and the residence ransacked.
Finally, on 16 November 1989, six Jesuits in charge of the
university were brutally murdered (see the Introduction).

Fr Jerez's outspokenness was not to everyone's taste, especially as he did not spare the Church. He said bluntly:

'I think that the greatest obstacle to the Church's mission
is the divisions within the Church itself. We live in deeply
divided societies and these dissensions are reproduced in the
hierarchy and the religious orders – often at war with each
other. We should, on the contrary, seek a common vision of
our fragmented world.'

Fr Michael Campbell-Johnston, former Provincial Superior of
the British Jesuits, took over, in April 1994, as director of the
Servicio Jesuita para el Desarrollo Pedro Arrupe in El Salvador.
He sums up the situation of the Jesuits in Central America
succinctly:

'In the 1960s, Jesuit schools and colleges were very traditional
and typical of Jesuit education throughout the world: a very
high academic standard, strict discipline and students from

the middle and upper classes. All this changed with the
Conference of Medellín in 1968, when the Latin American
bishops undertook to work with the poor. "This solidarity with
the poor", they wrote at the time, "should manifest itself by
a criticism of oppression and lack of justice and an attempt to
change the intolerable situation which the poor are often forced
to tolerate." When these courageous words were put into
practice, they provoked a negative reaction from the rich and
the powerful.

'At the end of the 1960s, on his return from a whirlwind
tour of twenty Latin American countries, Nelson Rockefeller
wrote a report denouncing the Catholic Church as a threat to
the interests of the United States on this continent. Another
document, the Santa Fe Declaration which defined President
Reagan's Latin American policy, unequivocally identified
liberation theology with "a growing threat to the geopolitical
interests of the United States in the region", and suggested
launching a campaign to discredit the proponents of this
school of theology "by all necessary means". Two examples
of the methods used: the promotion of fundamentalist right-
wing cults in order to undermine the work of the mainstream
Churches and the support of each country's national security
system, to control the peasants' organizations and the unions.

'Eleven years later, at the Puebla Conference, the Latin
American bishops renewed their commitment by adopting a
"preferential option for the poor". On this occasion, Fr Pedro
Arrupe explained at a press conference how "the defence of
justice implies a sign of contradiction". In the same way,
when the 32nd General Congregation in 1974 was discussing
the Society's new commitment for "the promotion of justice
as an integral part of the service of faith", Fr Arrupe warned
of the consequences of such a choice in these prophetic words:
"Our Congregation should be conscious that evangelical justice
can only be preached on and through the Cross. If we work
seriously in favour of justice, the Cross will immediately
appear, bringing intense pain."'

But some Jesuits have undoubtedly overstepped the mark.
Nicaragua is probably the Latin American country where
the Church is most bitterly divided. The Catholic hierarchy had finally condoned, if not helped, the Sandinista
revolution which overthrew the Somoza dictatorship. But it
quickly changed its mind and, under the leadership of the

conservative Archbishop of Managua, Mgr Miguel Obando
y Bravo, it constituted the main opposition force to the
Marxist-inspired regime of Daniel Ortega, before he lost the
elections of 25 February 1990 to Mrs Violeta Chamorro and
her National Opposition Union (UNO), a coalition grouping
fourteen political formations, ranging from Conservative to
Communist. Nonetheless the grass-roots Christians who
had taken part in the revolution continued to support the
Sandinistas, insisting that their faith and their membership
of the Church was not incompatible with their political commitment.

Here too, the Jesuit university of Managua worked openly in
favour of the co-operatives in poor areas, helped to train technicians for government projects and even took part in certain
of those concerning agriculture. Apart from the university and
parish work, Nicaragua's 59 Jesuits ran two colleges and a rural
technical college in Estelí.

But the most evident sign of polarization between the grass-
roots Christians and the hierarchy – or, to quote John Paul
II, between the institutional and the popular Church – was
the presence in the Sandinista government, or in sub-
sidiary posts, of five priests or religious, of whom two
were Jesuits: Fr Alvaro Arguello, representative of the
clergy in the Council of State, and Fernando Cardenal, in
charge of the Sandinista Youth Movement (Fernando is the
brother of the priest-poet Ernesto Cardenal, who was also a
minister).

In May 1980, John Paul II signed a decree forbidding priests
to seek elected office in politics. It was but a reminder of an
article of canon law, which had been repeated at different
synods. But this new warning by the Pope signalled his
determination to prevent priests from engaging in politics
(on the Left, it goes without saying). This general ruling
of 'no priests in politics' has always had numerous exceptions and in certain circumstances special permissions. The
Archbishop of Kigali, the capital of Rwanda, Mgr Vincent
Nsengiyumva, who was murdered in 1994, was a member
of the Central Committee of the ruling dictatorship for ten
years, until the Vatican finally persuaded him to step down
in 1985.

In this instance, the Pope's decree had an effect ... in the United States, where two priests who were Democrat members of Congress – the Jesuit Robert Drinan was one – resigned their seats. In Nicaragua, on the other hand, the priests and their religious superiors judged the situation to be too complex to obey the papal command. After lengthy negotiations, speeded up by the impending visit of John Paul II to Central America, an agreement was reached through the good offices of Cardinal Agostino Casaroli, then Secretary of State of the Holy See, whereby the priests concerned renounced their right to celebrate the sacraments, including saying Mass, during the term of their public office.

It would appear that this compromise solution did not satisfy the Pope. On his arrival at Managua airport, he was disconcerted to discover Fr Ernesto Cardenal kneeling before him on the tarmac. The Pope admonished him, shaking his finger at him and saying: 'Put yourself right with the Church!' Matters finally came to a head with the general elections in Nicaragua on 4 November 1984. This put an end to the truce, and Fr Fernando Cardenal, appointed Education Minister of the Sandinista government, preferred to keep his post rather than remain in the Society of Jesus. When he refused to obey the Pope, he was expelled from the Society. He stated that the reasons for his departure were 'political, not religious'.

Fr Cardenal cannot say he was not warned. On 18 July of that year, Fr Kolvenbach had told him that his political office was 'incompatible' with his status as a Jesuit. On 10 August, the Holy See asked him, along with the other three religious who were members of the Sandinista government, to renounce their posts: namely his brother, the Trappist Ernesto Cardenal, Minister of Culture; Fr Miguel d'Escoto, a Maryknoll Father, Minister of Foreign Affairs; and Fr Edgar Parrales, Nicaragua's ambassador in Washington to the Organization of American States. Notwithstanding Fernando Cardenal's claim that 'there isn't the slightest contradiction between my Christian faith and my commitment in the Sandinista Revolution', the disciplinary measure had been communicated to him by the Provincial for Central America, Fr Valentín Menendez.

In October 1984, Fr Kolvenbach had insisted on meeting Fr Cardenal in New York. He had done everything he could to avoid severing relations with the refractory Jesuit by flying, the same month, to Rio de Janeiro and Caracas to meet the Provincials of Central America. But the Jesuits of the region were divided over the presence of their colleague in the Sandinista government, and Fr Kolvenbach finally put Fr Cardenal face to face with his responsibility, according to the Ignatian principle of 'discernment'. 'My decision caused suffering to him, and to a great number of Jesuits', stated Fr Kolvenbach's communiqué of 10 December. The General had hoped to find another solution, and still hopes that Fr Cardenal will one day return to the Society.

Be that as it may, the hope of finding an acceptable compromise with Cardinal Casaroli came to nothing. It is no secret that Paul VI's former confidant was never really won over to John Paul II's policies, especially in Latin America. The meteoric rise of the ultra-conservative Cardinal Alfonso Lopez Trujillo, former Archbishop of Medellín and president of the Latin American Council of Bishops (CELAM), now president of the Pontifical Council for the Family in Rome, coincided with Casaroli's fall from grace. It was on account of pressure brought by the reactionary elements of CELAM that Fr Jerez was not appointed as rector of the Jesuit University of Nicaragua at the end of his term as Provincial, as had been planned.

But the most authoritative voice on the question of Jesuits in politics was naturally that of Fr Pedro Arrupe. When he was General, he spoke on several occasions of the Society's attitude to revolutionary violence and Marxism. At a press conference given at Puebla in 1979, he addressed both of these problems. In reply to a question on violence, he said:

> It is true that revolutionary violence can be legitimate, as
> Paul VI states in his encyclical *Populorum progressio*: 'In the
> case of evident and prolonged tyranny which would violate
> the fundamental rights of the human person and attack the
> common good of the country'. These are the words of the
> Holy Father, not of the revolutionary Fr Arrupe! But it is
> equally true – not only according to the Gospel and to the
> Church, but also to experience – that violence gives birth to
> new forms of violence which are even worse. This is a fact

which is evident throughout history.

It is obvious that I am against violence. I do not believe that violent means are appropriate. Recent events confirm how inhuman and counterproductive are operations based on armed violence. Therefore, if one of the exceptional situations described by Paul VI exists in a Latin American country, those who envisage the use of violence against an even greater violence are assuming, in conscience, a grave responsibility, which they will have to justify before God, their fellow men and the history of their own people. It is up to each to decide according to his own conscience.

As regards Marxism, the General declared:

The Society of Jesus can never accept an ideology based on, or defending, atheism. We cannot identify ourselves with this. Perhaps, and this is very different, some hold that certain elements of the Marxist analysis are useful for examining our society. This does not mean defending the Marxist ideology, but studying its positive elements, which may exist in other ideologies and religions. Vatican II referred to this when it spoke of *semina Verbi* (seeds of the Word), that is, the valid elements of Hinduism, Buddhism, Islam or other religions. We should study these elements as a starting point for constructive dialogue with other religions and ideologies.

The preceding year, in his report on the state of the Society, Fr Arrupe had been even more forthright:

Without excluding *a priori* the possibility of a certain dialogue, and even of critical collaboration with Marxist-inspired groups and movements, we certainly cannot accept Jesuit involvement with Marxism nor public support of its ideology by Jesuits. Such acts undermine our credibility and our apostolic efficacity; it is a motive of scandal and misunderstanding not only for those suffering oppression and persecution under Marxist regimes, but for many others. The occasional attempts to introduce Marxist methods of group pressure and political manipulation into our meetings or assemblies must be resisted with the utmost vigour, for such methods are diametrically opposed to an authentic communal discernment and to the spirit which animates the government of the Society.

But it was in his letter to all the Provincials of Latin America of 8 December 1980 that Fr Arrupe developed most fully his

thinking on Marxist analysis. It is obviously impossible to sum-
marize such a balanced document, but here are the main ideas.
To the initial question: can a Christian, or a Jesuit, accept Marxist
analysis, as opposed to Marxist philosophy or ideology, he
replied: 'In analysing society, we can accept a certain number
of methodological points more or less taken from Marxism,
as long as we do not consider them as exclusive.' And Fr
Arrupe gives examples such as economic factors, structures
of ownership, the interests of the ruling classes, the exploitation of the lower classes, the place occupied in history by
class warfare, the criticism of religion, 'which can be useful in
opening our eyes to cases where religion is wrongfully used
to cover indefensible social situations'.

But he also warns against the dangers inherent in the use of
Marxist analysis.

> If one claims that everything finally boils down to forces
> of production, considered as the sole reality, the content of
> religion and of Christianity is soon relativized and weakened.
> Faith in God our Creator and Jesus Christ our Saviour will be
> considered of little use. Christian hope will tend to become
> unreal. A distinction is sometimes made, it is true, between
> faith in Jesus Christ, which is intangible, and its diverse
> doctrinal or social manifestions, which can be criticized. But this
> often leads to a dangerously radical attack on the Church, far
> beyond the 'fraternal correction' implied by the saying *Ecclesia
> semper reformanda* (the Church is always in need of reform). At
> times we are tempted to judge the Church from without, as
> though we no longer considered it to be the place where we
> live our faith.

There are other mirages in the Marxist vision, said Arrupe:

> If we are to be realistic and admit the existence of disputes and
> class warfare, we must avoid generalizing: it is by no means
> proved that the whole of human history, past and present, can
> be reduced to this struggle. (...) Even if Christianity recognizes
> the legitimacy of certain conflicts, and doesn't exclude recourse
> to revolution in extreme cases of hopeless tyranny, it cannot
> accept that the best means to get rid of conflict is conflict itself.
> (...) We are not permitted to adopt Marxist analysis as such,
> but only certain methodological elements.

Relations with Marxists were another matter, for Fr Arrupe.

We should be fraternally disposed to dialogue with Marxists.
And we should not refuse to collaborate with them when the
common good requires it. (...) We should also firmly oppose
all attempts of those who use our reticence towards Marxist
analysis to brand as 'Marxist' or 'Communist' a legitimate
commitment for the poor and for the just demands of the
exploited. How often 'anti-Communism' is simply an excuse for
injustice!

One can scarcely in all honesty accuse Fr Arrupe of crypto-
Communism. If some Jesuits have been tempted to enter
politics in the Third World, sometimes rashly siding with
Marxists, it is the price paid for their new-found interest in
the fight against injustice, misery and the exploitation of the
poor. The famous 'preferential option for the poor' advocated
by the conferences of Medellín and Puebla, and embraced by
the 33rd General Congregation of the Jesuits in 1983, is not
undertaken lightly. The Jesuits have paid the price of their
courage. Fr Arrupe spoke of the Cross, and one only has to
read the recent martyrology of the Society (see note on pp.
26–7) to see what he meant.

If I have dwelt at such length on the situation in Central
America, it is because it is not only a region where the Jesuits
are most exposed to political temptation, it is also a seedbed
for the future of the Society, and the Church as a whole: in
the next century, the majority of the world's Catholics will be
Latin American. I have also stressed Pedro Arrupe's role, and
his courageous but balanced approach to Marxism, since they
were vital to the thinking of the Society on the continent in the
crucial postconciliar years. What of his successor in the post-
Communist period?

In an interview given to the Canadian magazine *Compass*,
published in Toronto in 1993, Fr Kolvenbach is utterly open
on his commitment to social justice:

I am always enlightened by people who may have led a
splendid life, but who remained blind to certain things. Thérèse
of Lisieux, for example, lived at the time of Karl Marx – think
of all the injustices that were going on at the time! – and once
she saw a poor man and brought him a piece of cake! The man
just threw the cake away. In Thérèse's writings I think there

is nothing about the need for social justice. In spite of her holiness, this aspect is completely missing ...

Take this famous sentence of Fr Arrupe's: 'It is becoming clearer and clearer that despite the opportunities offered by an ever more sophisticated technology, we are simply not willing to pay the price of a more just and humane society.' Today, thanks to technical progress and modern know-how, we can really change many situations in the world that should not exist. We can ... but we don't! Something in our hearts has to be converted. And we ourselves know that it is not something that depends on machinery. It is *we* who have to grow.

With the 1991 encyclical *Centesimus Annus*, the Church celebrated a hundred years of sustained reflection on such difficult questions. In the light of the Gospel and of tradition, the Church both announces and denounces. The Church denounced the blindness of our ancestors – and our own – whether wilful or ignorant. This blindness takes permanent shape in sinful social structures with their terrible consequences for those who are 'poor' in every sense of the term: those whom society throws out, thinks of as 'non persons' and treats as mere things to be used for the pleasure, power or profit of a few. The Church should criticize all such examples of injustice and, at the same time, it should call and guide Christians effectively to incarnate (or inculturate!) the teaching of Christ in the social realm.

The neoliberal form of capitalism currently spreading everywhere, with its refrain of 'let the market decide', does enhance some human and even spiritual qualities: creativity, initiative, courage. It promises to avoid the corruption and mistakes often associated with centralized government planning. But it also seems to entail very self-centred consumerist attitudes, the idolatry of money, the spoliation of nature and the reduction of human and social goods to market values.

The Pope himself is quite outspoken in his social teaching. He has even taken the wind out of the sails of liberation theology. Nowadays, John Paul II speaks so strongly about all these issues that some of its polemical sting has been removed, because the whole Church has to teach it. There are many schools of liberation theology, but I think the most important thing is not so much what the theologians have worked out as what the people have got out of it. It has certainly brought about a tremendous change. No longer can one speak about 'the poor' as was the case twenty years ago: 'Life is short and, as the Lord said, the poor you will always have with you, so be nice and good and count on eternal life!' This kind of resignation has completely gone. Everyone knows that the Lord came to fight against poverty, that he really felt ashamed of what people had made of his creation. And that is why he himself made a preferential option for the poor.

It is true that the Church has condemned certain aspects of liberation theology. The first is the tendency to reduce everything to the socio-economic situation. If we really respect them, the poor are more than just economic beings. They also have a need for culture and for a spiritual life and for the sacraments. The second thing is that there was sometimes too much hate. Now 'love' and 'charity' are loaded words no doubt. But the Church refuses to create a better world through hate.

These are hardly the words of a traditionalist. But Fr Kolvenbach is above all a subtle strategist who knows how to smooth ruffled feathers and disarm suspicion by his candour and good humour.

Fr Alvaro Restrepo has worked with both Generals – he was appointed Provincial by Fr Arrupe and Assistant General for Latin America by Fr Kolvenbach. He is full of admiration for the 'Kolvenbach method'. On his election, the new General began by getting to know the whole Society. He spends a quarter of each year travelling, and by 1990 had visited the Society's 80 provinces. Fr Restrepo:

'In spite of his shyness, Father General likes meeting people. He puts them at ease by his humour and begins every meeting by saying: "I am prepared to hear every request, possible or impossible!" He also has a gift for languages but, unlike Fr Arrupe, he dislikes improvising. He prepares each meeting, each short sermon which he writes out on a small sheet of paper in his meticulous hand, without crossing out a line.'

How does Fr Restrepo think the situation has changed in Latin America since Fr Arrupe's era?

'There is greater stability. After the years of turmoil, the Medellín and Puebla conferences and the various experiments we have made, to the extreme limit of what is permissible – and sometimes beyond – we are better integrated in our

surroundings. The young generations of Jesuits are very close
to the poor, and even our universities – like the UCA in El
Salvador – are engaged in the fight for justice. Thanks to
movements like Fe y Alegría, social justice is in the hands of
responsible lay people. Fr Kolvenbach speaks of liberation
theology in his homilies, making a clear distinction between the
different schools of thought, but without closing any doors.

'Inculturation too is making progress. Provinces which were
linked closely to Spain are less so today, and we are making
an effort to preserve ethnic groups in Bolivia, Paraguay,
Guatemala and Panama. Our collaboration with the local
bishops is more successful, except for a few glaring examples.
A new problem is appearing, however: secularization is making
its appearance in Latin America.'

John Paul II made a pastoral visit to Central America from 2
to 9 March 1983, a voyage he described as the 'most difficult'
of all those he had made up until then. His strongest words
were spoken in Nicaragua, where he denounced the 'absurdity'
of a 'people's Church' existing alongside the hierarchical one.
As chance would have it, he was speaking in the only country
of the region where a large part of the Church had taken
sides with the poor.

The protests provoked by the papal warning during Mass in
Managua were ill-timed. It was no doubt unseemly of those
who were denied access to the Pope to voice their discontent
during the ceremony. But, to speak of incidents 'close to profanation', as John Paul II did on his return to Rome, was patently
exaggerated. Especially as the Pope had remained discreet
when confronted with the real 'profanation' represented by
the thousands of people executed in El Salvador, kidnapped
in Guatemala and humiliated in Haiti.

CENTRAL EUROPE, CHINA, VIETNAM: THE 'UNDERGROUND SOCIETY'

The Uniate Church is no longer a bridge but an obstacle.

PETER-HANS KOLVENBACH
(in an interview with the author in 1990)

The controversy has made little progress since 1983. Certain people in the Church, often those who wield power, continue to confuse social and political commitment. They also assume that the fight for justice leads necessarily to socialism, claiming that the order founded by St Ignatius is still attracted by the siren song of Marxism, even today after the Communist débâcle. It is they who contrast the realism of the Polish Pope, former Archbishop of Cracow, with the dangerous daydreams of revolutionary religious. These inquisitors would do well to reflect on the clandestine role played by the Society of Jesus in central Europe, China and Vietnam. The Jesuits, as we shall see, had a great influence, often at the risk of their security, their freedom and their lives, and are promised an even greater future.

On 2 September 1983, at the opening of the 33rd General Congregation, nearly all the participants, elected or summoned to this assembly, arrived on time in Rome. Absence or delay were not tolerated without an excellent reason. On that day, however, the Romanian representative was awaited in vain. From Hungary, the provincial was the only Jesuit allowed to attend. The Provincial Congregations of Bohemia, of Slovakia and of Lithuania, who should have elected their delegates, were prevented from meeting. They were represented by compatriots living abroad, appointed by the papal delegate, Fr Dezza. These absences reveal an unknown truth: the Society of Jesus had always been present in Eastern Europe, even if its forces were depleted because of the political circumstances, except in Poland (with over 750 members). Yet the official Jesuit catalogue for 1994 contains statistics which are far from negligible: 79 Jesuits in Lithuania, 155 in Hungary, 122 in the Czech Republic, 68 in Slovakia, 187 in Croatia and 22 in Russia.

Officially, the Society is poorly represented in Romania, with only seventeen Jesuits. But the figures here are intentionally misleading. A secret novitiate existed under Ceauşescu, in spite of the ban forbidding religious orders to receive new candidates or to lead a communal life. According to Fr Kolvenbach, who is at last in a position to contact the tiny Romanian Province, the number of Jesuits is 'much greater' than the official figure. He refuses to say more; the long Jesuit tradition of persecution and expulsion creates certain reflexes. And this attitude is understandable on hearing one of the rare witnesses of life under Ceauşescu tell the story of his life as priest and religious: 'I have been a priest for more than 30 years, and yet I have only been able to exercise my ministry during one year.' Another 80-year-old Jesuit confessed, just before his death: 'The richest period of my life as a Jesuit was ... the fourteen years I spent in prison.'

In the 1994 Jesuit Yearbook, published in Rome, an Austrian Jesuit, Fr Georg Sporschill, writes about his experience with the 'street children of Bucharest's North Railway Station'. With three colleagues from Vienna, he has opened several homes for these abandoned urchins, victims of Ceauşescu's dictatorship, including a 'Children's Farm', 50 miles from Bucharest, with 50 adolescents saved from 'violence, stealing, glue-sniffing, sickness and sexual abuse'. 'The ongoing formation of our educators', writes Fr Sporschill, 'is fostered by seminars and exchange programmes with shelters for the homeless in Austria and England.'

But it is without doubt Albania which suffered the most under Communism. The first self-proclaimed atheist state, for 45 years Albania attempted simply to wipe out religion and any reference to God. Of the twenty Jesuits in the country in 1946, only three survivors were discovered in 1991: Fr Anton Luli (81 years old), Fr Gjergi Vata (75) and Br Filip Luli (73). It should be noted that the Society was present in Albania as long ago as 1841, where it founded a Pontifical seminary, a college, some magazines and – in keeping with tried Jesuit practice – a botanical museum, a physics laboratory, a meteorological observatory and a theatre. In 1941 the Jesuits were able to inaugurate the cathedral of the Sacred Heart in Tirana. After that, silence once more descended on their work.

In 1991 a delegation from the Holy See visited the country, including an Italian Jesuit, Fr Pietro Maione, who celebrated the first midnight Mass to be said in 46 years, in the restored Jesuit cathedral of the Sacred Heart in Tirana, which has now become the permanent residence of the Jesuits. In February 1992 the seminary of Scutari was reopened, under the direction of the Society of Jesus; today 50 seminarians study there.

If the Romanian and Albanian Jesuits were among the hardest hit by Communist repression, those in Poland seem to have flourished extraordinarily, in spite of 40 years of a hostile regime. It was no doubt the advantage of having a long religious history. At the beginning of 1989, the two Polish provinces totalled more than 750 Jesuit priests and 40 novices. Five years later, however, this figure has dropped to 714. The vocations crisis is even affecting the Pope's homeland.

In 1974, the Society celebrated the 400th anniversary of the creation of the Polish Jesuit Province. The first Jesuits arrived in Poland only ten years after the death of Ignatius of Loyola. This generation of pioneers preached in Polish and German, organized sumptuous liturgical ceremonies and put on plays and concerts. Two centuries later, when the Society was suppressed, Poland possessed 56 Jesuit colleges, twenty residences and 65 mission stations. This important network permitted a rapid restoration of the order in 1814 and, since then, it never looked back. Apart from their traditional activities (teaching, spiritual retreats), Polish Jesuits publish magazines in Warsaw and Cracow. And, in the autumn of 1989, Cardinal Glemp, Primate of Poland, asked them to run the country's Catholic radio and television broadcasts: it was the first time in the Communist bloc that a government allowed the Church to have access to state broadcasting.

This Jesuit activity in one of the most Catholic countries of Eastern Europe is hardly surprising. But what about the other side of the border, in Russia? The Society of Jesus in the Kremlin? It sounds fantastic, but it happened, 400 years ago. The hero of the story was Antoine Possevin, 'the most eminent diplomat of the order, and even one of the cleverest negotiators of his century', as he is described by René Fülöp-Miller, in his

Histoire de la Compagnie de Jésus, published in 1933. Possevin went to Moscow to negotiate an alliance between Rome and Ivan the Terrible. The Tsar and the Jesuit engaged in a theological battle, to no avail, and Possevin was almost beheaded when he attacked the king for having criticized the Pope. Then they made peace, the Jesuit obsequiously asking permission to kiss the Tsar's hand. When they parted company, with protestations of undying friendship, Ivan heaped Possevin with presents and asked him to lead his envoy to Venice and to Rome, where he would pursue the negotiations. Which is how the Italians came to witness a strange sight: a Russian diplomatic mission on its way to western Europe under the leadership of a Jesuit.

Travelling in the opposite direction – from Rome to Moscow – another Jesuit underwent a bizarre and painful adventure in the middle of the twentieth century. A French Jesuit, Michel d'Herbigny, was appointed in 1922 to head the Oriental Institute in Rome by Pius XI. Pius's dream was to bring about a rapprochement between the Roman and Eastern Churches, better still, to evangelize Lenin's country. Little by little, d'Herbigny became the Pope's counsellor on Russian affairs. In 1926, Pius XI had him consecrated bishop in secret by Cardinal Pacelli, the future Pius XII, with a mission to 'enter Russia by all possible means' in order to consecrate some Catholic bishops.

Mgr d'Herbigny arrived in Moscow on 1 April of the same year, and consecrated three bishops. His mission accomplished, he returned to Rome where, at the beginning of the 1930s, he found himself at the heart of a plot. His enemies accused him of having conspired with Pius XI to condemn the Action Française[12] in 1926, which was obviously false, and of having transmitted to the Soviets some compromising documents on Pius XI's Russian policy. It was obvious that some Polish Jesuits had added fuel to the fire, because of an obscure personal quarrel with this Frenchman, who had prevented them from contacting the Polish General of the Society, Fr Vladimir Ledochowski. Their manoeuvres were successful. Stripped of his episcopal dignity and exiled to a French Jesuit residence, Mgr d'Herbigny died in disgrace in Aix-en-Provence in 1957.

This sorry episode illustrates the ambiguous position of the

Society with respect to the Soviet Union. It never gave up the hope, if not of a Catholic reconquest of Holy Russia, at least of regular contacts with the Jesuits who survived in Lithuania, Latvia and Estonia through all the vagaries of history. In 1985, Fr Kolvenbach created a delegation *pro rebus russicis* (for Russian affairs), under the responsibility of a German professor at the Centre of Marxist Studies of Rome's Gregorian University. This delegate is responsible for the co-ordination and formation of Jesuits who will devote themselves to 'the Russian apostolate'. In France the Centre of Russian Studies in Meudon, run by the Jesuits, is a study centre of Russian culture and of the Slav-Byzantine religious tradition. It has a library of 30,000 books and its aim is still 'to prepare a Christian elite for the Russia of tomorrow'.

But Fr Kolvenbach does not trust the new regime in Russia, neither that of Gorbachev nor that of Yeltsin, in spite of the promise to restore religious liberty in the Ukraine. Eight hundred parishes, converted to Orthodoxy by force in 1946, are said to have reverted to the Uniate Church with its Byzantine rite, in full communion with Rome. But the existence of a Uniate Church poses a personal problem to Fr Kolvenbach, who has adopted the Eastern – Armenian – rite. 'The Uniate Church is no longer a bridge but an obstacle', he told me, 'which poses serious ecclesiological problems.'

The religious situation in the former USSR is, however, improving. Between 1983 and 1988, three Lithuanian Jesuits were imprisoned for their collaboration with the clandestine Catholic press or conducting religious services outside churches. Today, they have been freed and the principal church of the Lithuanian province, that of St Casimir in Vilnius, which had been converted into a museum of atheism, was handed back to the Society at the beginning of 1989. It is open once more to religious celebrations. In Kiev, in July 1988, twelve Italian Jesuits took part in a delegation of artists who were visiting the city on the occasion of the celebration of the millennium of Christian Russia. While in the Ukrainian capital, they were able to meet local artists, who said openly: 'Make no mistake, we are all believers here.'

The tenacity of the Jesuits is at last bearing fruit. A new independent 'region' of the Society was established in Russia on 21 June 1992, with civil recognition following on 30 September.

Fr Stanislaw Opiela, a Polish Jesuit, gives details in the 1994 Yearbook:

> Now we can function openly and legally. Reinforcements are arriving steadily: two Jesuit fathers and a brother from Poland are in Novosibirsk; a Canadian has arrived in Tomsk [where Jesuits from Byelorussia had set up a parish as long ago as 1806]; a Frenchman, a Mexican and a Pole are in Moscow; and a Lithuanian and two Poles have gone to Byelorussia and the Ukraine. We also have young Russians, Ukrainians and Byelorussians wanting to join the Society. (...) While we prepare men for the ministry, we must get inculturated ourselves and find suitable projects, like the socio-cultural centres in Moscow and Novosibirsk. (...) We have to create a climate that is favourable to dialogue with the Orthodox Church, as well as other Christian and non-Christian groups.

There are 27 Jesuits dispersed across the thousands of miles that make up this new Russian Jesuit region, comprising the whole of the former Soviet Union (except for the existing Province made up of Lithuania, Latvia and Estonia), with its great cultural diversity.

This relative breakthrough, or at least a promising start, would have greatly surprised the Jesuits whose mission was in the vastly different context of the sprawling conurbations in the East German Democratic Republic, before the Wall came tumbling down. Of the 38 members of the Society then working in this mainly Protestant country, a dozen were in Dresden, where they ministered to a community which had tripled in size, growing from 30,000 to 90,000 in a few years. Under the Communist regime, they limited their apostolate to a door-to-door campaign. With little result, as one of them recalls:

> 'In five years we knocked on all the doors of the new buildings, saying that we represented the Church and suggesting a chat. In 60 per cent of the cases, the people would have nothing to do with the Church. We began to be ashamed of our lack of persuasion, but decided to stick it out. The "comrades" finally got used to us, and we gradually managed to broach certain religious questions. In fact, 80 per cent of the population had severed all links with the Churches.'

Today things have changed for the better. In 1994, there were 264 Jesuits in former East Germany, compared with 353 in former West Germany.

This dogged tenacity was also the hallmark of the Hungarian Jesuits, who had greatly suffered from the suppression of their Province in 1950 and their subsequent dispersion after the invasion of Budapest by the Soviet army in 1956. The young Jesuits, often still students, found themselves scattered throughout the world and formed a Hungarian 'vice-province' in exile. In Hungary itself, there were only 63 Jesuits left in 1988, most of them elderly. But as soon as they were allowed to re-open a novitiate, in 1989, life began again: in 1994 there were 155 Jesuits.

In former Yugoslavia, when the university they had founded in 1669 in Zagreb was taken from them, the Jesuits devoted themselves to the press. They launched *The Sacred Heart Messenger*, a title chosen not to arouse the government's suspicions, while *Life Renewed*, published by the Philosophical and Theological Institute of Zagreb from 1971, is a highly intellectual magazine which discusses the Church's teaching on atheism, ecumenism and the family. At present, of course, it has more tragic topics to consider.

The Society in Croatia is having to face up to the dramatic events taking place in the Balkans. The Jesuits are particularly vulnerable since, after the establishment of new independent countries in former Yugoslavia, the Jesuit Province of Croatia (187 members in 1994) covers three separate States, with houses and missions not only in Croatia, but also in Bosnia-Herzegovina, in Serbia and in Montenegro. When war broke out in 1991, 'ethnic cleansing' was accompanied by the destruction of religious and cultural monuments. In Croatia the historic cities of Vukovar and Dubrovnik were badly hit. Among the damaged buildings was the 300-year-old Jesuit college and the adjacent church of St Ignatius. Faced with the human catastrophe of the war, all the Jesuit residences have established relief centres. Thanks to the generosity of the aid agency Caritas, especially in Germany, Austria and Italy, Jesuits have been able to provide food, clothing and medicine to all comers, irrespective of nationality or religion.

The Jesuit Refugee Service is also very active in former Yugoslavia, and a Croat Jesuit, Fr Vladimir Horvat, repeats the message of reconciliation preached by John Paul II when he visited Zagreb in September 1994, when he says: 'The Province regards its commitment to the refugees as a witness to Christian solidarity. (...) We are paving the way for future collaboration in an atmosphere of reconciliation. In wartime, one may rightly defend oneself; but no-one should foment hatred among peoples.'

At present, the Province has fourteen novices and 42 scholastics. In 1992, Fr Kolvenbach paid a two-day visit to the exhibition in Zagreb entitled 'The Croatian Legacy of the Jesuits', to express his solidarity with the sufferings of the people. He was interviewed on television at peak viewing time, and great publicity was given to his gesture in visiting the country. The role of the media in spreading the Church's teaching must not be underestimated, especially in Eastern Europe, where Communist censorship had driven the press underground. It is hard for us in the West to realize how backward Eastern European Catholics had become regarding Church matters, after decades spent confined to liturgical and parish life. Their hunger for reading matter and conciliar theology, stifled by forty years of official propaganda, belies the impression given to foreign visitors of a conservative, or even reactionary Church, one living in the past.

We should be indulgent. Take the case, for example, of Jan Korec, appointed bishop in secret, on 24 August 1951, when the Czechoslovak government had just expelled all the religious from their convents and monasteries. Korec, who had been ordained a year before and was working at the time in a chemistry laboratory, was consecrated in a clandestine ceremony, at the dead of night, in a locked, dimly lit room. His true identity was only discovered in 1959, while he was still working at the laboratory but had been downgraded to night watchman. His 'crime' was punished by twelve years of hard labour. Set free during the brief Prague Spring, Jan Korec managed to reach Rome in 1969. Warmly received by Paul VI, who gave him his own pectoral cross, he was only able to take up office, at the head of the diocese of Nitra, in

eastern Slovakia, on 25 March 1990. Forty years had elapsed
since the night of his episcopal ordination. Is it surprising that
today, the ex-night watchman bishop should be somewhat
old-fashioned?

All the countries so far mentioned have now emerged from
a sombre period when the Church's influence was all but
wiped out. But there are other countries under Communist
dictatorships where Jesuits worked silently. The silence is
slightly less deafening if we move from the European continent eastwards towards Asia, and consider the destiny of
Indo-Chinese and Chinese Jesuits. In the spring of 1957,
when Fr Fernand Lacretelle, former superior of the Shanghai
mission, arrived in Vietnam, he was renewing ancient history. The Jesuits had settled in the country in 1615, and Fr
Alexandre de Rhodes became famous, twenty years later, for
his work on the Vietnamese language. The Jesuits had not
returned to the country since the suppression of the Society
at the end of the eighteenth century, and they found it
had been divided into two, by the Geneva Agreement
of 1954.

Lacretelle realized that the success of the Jesuits' return
to Vietnam depended on their acceptance by the young.
He opened a novitiate in 1960 and gradually organized
formation centres. In March 1975, just before the fall of
Saigon, there were 69 Jesuits in Vietnam, of whom 30 were
Vietnamese. When the Communists took over the whole of
the country, reunified in 1975, strict measures were taken
against the religious in general, and the Jesuits in particular.
All pastoral activity was forbidden, and recruiting of new candidates banned totally. Seven Jesuits, imprisoned towards the
end of 1979, were not tried until 1983. Other arrests were
made in 1984 and 1985, just before a slight liberalization
took place.

Fr Joseph Nguyen Cong Douan, Provincial of Ho Chi
Minh City, had been arrested in June 1983 and sentenced,
with twelve other Catholics, to fifteen years of prison. He
was freed in 1990. Some time later, a prayer in the form of
a poem reached the West, in which this Jesuit, free at last,
speaks without rancour of his heartfelt desire:

Lord, set me down where you will,
so that I may bring happiness
to those I meet who are unhappy.
Let me never be afraid to serve the world
with a heart like a volcano,
and hands as gentle as those of a mother.

The jail sentences did not put a complete end to the Jesuits' pastoral activity in Vietnam, where the dynamism and loyalty of the Catholics were stimulated by their trials, to the surprise and grudging admiration of the regime. The government has authorized the opening of several major seminaries, but still refuses to allow the young Jesuits who have finished their philosophical and theological studies to be ordained. 'We have sacrificed our religious vocation to our country', said one young student, moved to tears by the visit of a European Jesuit who had brought him a suitcase full of books of theology and spirituality.

'Here you are at last!' It was in almost identical terms to those used by the Vietnamese scholastic that Mgr Aloysius Jin Luxian welcomed a European delegation in the spring of 1987, led by a Jesuit, Fr Denis Maugenest, then director of the Institute of Social Studies of the Catholic Institute in Paris. Mgr Jin Luxian, himself a Jesuit, is Assistant Bishop of Shanghai, but a bishop elected by the Patriotic Association of Chinese Catholics, an organization controlled by Beijing and not recognized by Rome. Since 1958, 40 bishops have, like himself, been appointed and consecrated in China without the Pope's permission.

According to canon law, they, and their priests and faithful, are considered to be schismatic. When he received this first visit of European Catholics, including several Jesuits, Aloysius Jin Luxian could not hide his emotion, or his bitterness. 'Schismatic, me?' He considers the term too legalistic, too Roman. Were not China's three million Catholics obliged, since 1949, to organize their own means of survival? And the tragedy was all the more painful in that, alongside this official 'visible' Catholic Church, there exists a clandestine one, placed strictly under Roman jurisdiction, which has become a rival to her schismatic sister.

The personal destiny of Mgr Jin illustrates this tragedy, which is still far from being resolved. Born in 1916 into an old Catholic family, he entered the Society of Jesus in 1938, was ordained in 1945 and studied in Europe, where he made friends with, among others, the Archbishop of Lyons, the late Cardinal Albert Decourtray. Having obtained a doctorate of theology at the Gregorian University in Rome, with a thesis on Christian unity, Fr Jin Luxian returned to China in 1951. He knew the situation of Catholics to be perilous. The Society of Jesus had reached its apotheosis in 1949 – the *Yearbook of Catholic Missions in China* recorded the presence of 888 Jesuits, of whom 267 were Chinese, [13] but the Communists had already started dismantling the Church.

On 8 September 1955 Jin Luxian was arrested. He spent eighteen years in prison, or in a re-education camp. It was a time of reflection for him:

'First of all I applied Pius XII's rules to the letter: absolute opposition to the Communist regime. But, in prison, I began wondering if confrontation was the only way. Several years after my liberation, in 1982, the diocese of Shanghai asked me to become rector of their seminary. After six months of inner struggle, I accepted.'

In January 1985, Aloysius Jin Luxian was consecrated bishop. He was perfectly well aware of the canonical situation in which he was placing himself. But he does not regret it. In March 1988, he succeeded Mgr Louis Zhang Jiashu, who had died, in the episcopal see of Shanghai. Meanwhile Rome still recognizes as the legitimate bishop of that diocese Mgr Kung Pinmei who, at 94, is living in exile in the United States.

In the autumn of 1993 Mgr Jin travelled to France, where he stayed in Lyons with his old friend Cardinal Decourtray. On the second floor of the archbishop's house, on the hill of Fourvière which dominates the capital of the Gauls (Lyons is the primatial see of all the Gauls), the chubby Chinaman granted an interview to Claude-François Jullien, which appeared in the *Nouvel Observateur*. Beaming, in his strict black clerical suit, Mgr Jin explains why he finally agreed to join the 'open Church' – he doesn't like the expression 'patriotic Church':

'We are not "schismatic", in fact we are probably more "Roman" than many Western Catholic Churches. It is simply that, trapped between Rome and Beijing, we were obliged to organize our religious life on our own. Don't forget that we are a Tridentine Church – we are still living according to the Council of Trent, since we were unable to attend the Vatican Council. We have tried, however, to study the conciliar documents and the papal encyclicals ... Since becoming a bishop, I have ordained 81 priests from 40 dioceses, I have managed to invite professors from France, Germany, the United States and Taiwan. I also send my students to study abroad. I have spent 300,000 dollars to build, or repair, the churches in my diocese, and in 1994 I shall spend the same sum to publish missals, breviaries and prayer books for the 4,000 churches that have been built throughout the country in the last ten years.'

Where does the money come from? Mgr Jin chuckles:

'That is why I have just been to Germany. I needed the other 300,000 dollars, and I got them there. At home, the 155,000 Catholics of Shanghai contribute 20 per cent of the diocese's running costs. The rest comes from ... Church property. Incredible though it may seem, the authorities gave back 70 per cent of the property belonging to the foreign missionaries, and we rent it out. We are a capitalist Church in a Communist State. But Shanghai isn't the whole of China. The south has always been more open, and less repressive, than the north. What is more, I know everyone: the Party Secretary, the Vice-Mayor ... I almost always get what I want. In China, personal relations are more important than the laws. Everything depends on discussion, on persuasion. Five times I went up to Beijing to get permission for foreign professors to visit. The trick is to persuade the official before you that your request is good for the image of the Party, of China, that he will avoid losing face. In the West, you like simple, clear-cut situations. We prefer a more complex "oriental" approach. I sometimes receive visits from priests belonging to the clandestine Church, accompanied by a State official. As we say: "It is sometimes necessary to close one eye, or even two."'

Mgr Jin is president of the 'Patriotic Alliance' in Shanghai, and vice-president of the national movement. He explains, ingenuously,

'In this way I can control everything. But I know some areas
where the Patriotic Church rules supreme. It depends on the
personality of the bishop and the severity of the authorities.
Recently, the Bishop of Wuhan made a trip to Great Britain,
accompanied by two members of his Church, but the Bureau
of Religious Cults insisted that three Party members went along
too. Nothing is simple in China!'

He is less outspoken about the tragedy of Tiananmen Square,
four years before.

'At the time, I was in a parish many miles away. It was wiser
to keep a low profile. What could I do or say? I knew the
government would adopt a very hard line ...'

His main problem today is his relations with Rome and with
the underground Church.

'In the first half of this century, the foreign missionaries
didn't understand that they had to choose between us and
our colonial oppressors. Rome made the same mistake in the
1950s. It ignores us, and pretends to be unaware that, since
1992, the married bishops have been deposed. In my diocese,
I had seven married priests. Now they carry out administrative
tasks, but no longer say Mass or celebrate the sacraments. And
yet, when I last came to France, in 1987, on the invitation of
my friend Cardinal Decourtray, I was denounced beforehand
by Cardinal Casaroli, which is why I received a cold reception
from the Archbishop of Paris who refused to put me up. This
time I avoided calling on Cardinal Lustiger, although I *was*
welcomed by the Provincial of the Jesuits!'

Mgr Jin explains his annoyance with Rome for having granted
the red hat to the Bishop of Hong Kong.

'The Vatican hopes that Mgr Wu will become the head of the
Chinese Church in 1997, after Hong Kong is returned to China
by the British. But this is a mistake. Hong Kong will long
remain separated from the Republic of China. Rome should
recognize Beijing, not Taiwan. When Cardinal Etchegaray came
to China to attend an important sporting event, he was invited
by Mgr Fu Tieshan of the official Church, which was obviously
a cruel blow for the clandestine Church. And when the Pope
visits China, it is the official Church he will meet ...
   'I can understand the suffering of the underground
Christians. I too have suffered, and am sometimes awoken

by nightmares. But I have forgiven my tormentors and look towards the future. The clandestine Church lives in the past, and it wouldn't even listen to the Pope if he asked it to change. Its clergy is ignorant, having had no seminary training, but they are as numerous, in the north, as the official clergy, and there are at least fifteen bishops still in prison. The problem appears insoluble: I think only time and tolerance can bring about change. As for the future, I think there will be no more persecution. The Chinese leaders are much too intelligent. They are more intelligent than the Russians.'

Has religion a future in China? According to Mgr Jin,

'the Chinese are much more religious than the Japanese, even if they don't like a faith that is too demanding. They believe in a God who allows them great freedom. Some, for example, would like to be both Christian and Buddhist. Confucianism has been criticized and ridiculed by the Communists for 50 years, but now it is Marxism which is called into question. Even if it is still theoretically the official ideology of the State, no-one believes in it any more. Therefore, the young turn increasingly to philosophy and religion. Not all of them, however: most think only of money or leaving the country. But many do come and see us, and some of them take their catechism seriously.

'Rome should understand our difficult situation, accept the new circumstances and put "inculturation" truly into practice. Instead of which the Pope is hardening his position; he keeps repeating the teaching of *Humanae vitae* forbidding birth control, for example, whereas in China it is not permitted to have more than one child, otherwise the mother is deprived of work and she cannot feed her family. The Church cannot help financially all those families with more than one child, and anyway non-Christians would not accept it. So my position is clear, I have chosen the lesser of two evils: I refuse abortions and accept contraception.'

On the hill of She Shan, not far from Shanghai, the French Jesuits built a basilica at the end of last century that can accommodate 2,000 people. The neo-Gothic style of the building, reminiscent of Lourdes rather than the Far East, bears witness to a religion that is totally alien to the local culture. Inculturation was far from the minds of the Jesuits of that generation, who had forgotten their illustrious forerunner Matteo Ricci, and by no means prefigured the present position of the Society. Be that as it may, in 1982 the site was chosen for a new seminary, which in 1987 contained 116 students. It is one of the seven seminaries open at present in continental China.

The seminary of She Shan was built from nothing. Almost all the works on theology had been lost during the Cultural Revolution, but the library was restocked thanks to gifts from abroad. In 1985 Jin Luxian also opened a research centre and printing press there. Its aim is to 'study the problems of inculturation and theology and to furnish information of the Church throughout the world'. One can find publications there like *The Month*, *La Croix*, *Stimmen der Zeit*, *La Civiltà cattolica*, *Etudes* and even *L'Osservatore romano*. Mgr Jin has himself translated the four Gospels into Chinese from the Jerusalem Bible, the commentary of St Mark by Fr Huby, the works of Daniel-Rops and of Cardinal Martini, the Jesuit Archbishop of Milan. Three hundred thousand copies of the translation of the Gospels were printed, and 10,000 copies of the other works, all 'sold out in a month'.

How are these 'schismatic' Jesuits regarded by the Society? Whether it be the Bishop of Shanghai, with his anti-Roman attitudes, or the other Jesuits who have held posts in Communist China since the break between the Vatican and the Patriotic Association, the Society's policy towards them has not varied: as was confirmed officially by the Jesuit Curia, not a single Jesuit has been struck from the register as 'schismatic', even if they no longer appear on the official list.

This approach creates problems and a certain amount of tension. First of all the Society, which had designs on the Chinese Empire in the sixteenth century, was rebuked by Rome for its missionary audacity, and then by the Chinese authorities for its excessive loyalty to the Holy See, but today it finds itself in the paradoxical situation of having some of its members in Chinese prisons or under strict surveillance by the regime, while others occupy official posts, either in the Patriotic Church or even in government organizations. Thus it was that, on 30 April 1988, Mgr Aloysius Jin Luxian was elected, together with Mgr Michael Fu Tieshan, Bishop of Beijing, to be member of the Permanent Committee of the Consultative Conference of the Chinese People, a creation of the 'United Patriotic Front' and composed of Communists and non-Communists.

At the other extreme, another Jesuit, Mgr Dominic Tang, 86 years old, the legitimate Bishop of Canton who is at present exiled in Hong Kong, was appointed as one of the leaders of the clandestine Episcopal Conference of continental China, created in November 1989, in mysterious circumstances. The initiative, it seems, was taken by the last bishops still living to be appointed by Rome before 1958. But Rome expressed its 'dissatisfaction' with an act which closes the door to Vatican diplomacy in its attempts to restore relations with Beijing. When John Paul II visited Manila in January 1995, the presence of a delegation from the Chinese Patriotic Association raised high hopes of a *rapprochement* between the Holy See and Communist China. Unfortunately, the 24 Patriotic Catholics walked out of the papal Mass, in protest against a display of the flag of Taiwan.

Having fallen back on strategic positions in Taiwan, Macao and Hong Kong, the Jesuits are not fighting a rearguard action. The year 1997 looms as a threat to the former British colony of Hong Kong, it is true, but the Jesuits are as active as ever. The Society runs two highly regarded secondary schools in Hong Kong, and the university residence Ricci Hall is a Catholic centre ministering to 7,000 students. Jesuits, including the Canadian Maurice Brosseau and the French Yves Nalet and Dominique Tyl, who have had years of experience in the Chinese Republic, publish *China News Analysis*, a magazine which is highly thought of by the diplomatic corps, who consider it to be one of the best informed and most credible sources of information on the economic, political and cultural life of the Chinese 'continent'.

One thing seems clear: the Jesuit committed to the promotion of faith and justice is neither the naïve Trojan horse of international Communism, in spite of his tenacious reputation, nor the blind opponent to all that is modern. When he finds himself immersed in a Marxist system, he doesn't refuse to enter into dialogue, whenever humanly possible, or avoid head-on confrontation when that is inevitable. His strength is never to retreat *for good* in the face of an obstacle.

A final example of this stubborn policy of the Society, which usually succeeds in wearing down resistance: in May 1988,

Peter-Hans Kolvenbach met Fidel Castro, a former Jesuit student even if he is not a shining example of Jesuit education. Thirty Jesuits are working on the island. They are scattered over the whole territory, engaged in the most diverse tasks: they run houses in Havana, Matanzas, Cienfuegos, Camagüey and Santiago. They publish a magazine, *Vida Cristiana*, with a print run of 40,000 copies, and organize retreats. They are mainly restricted to parish work and youth counselling, since the State has taken control of education. In 1990, there were 22 Jesuits in Havana, four in Cienfuegos, two in Camagüey and seven in Santiago and their average age was over 54 years old. In 1994, the number of Jesuits had dropped to 29.

The meeting of the General of the Jesuits and the *líder máximo* ended in an agreement. The following 26 July, five more Jesuits were permitted to go and work in Cuba.

NOTES

1 Hence the puns that were made: 'Le prince est assis sur une chaise dangereuse' (the prince is sitting on a dangerous chair), and 'Le roi a du coton dans les oreilles' (the king has his ears stuffed with cotton). Jokes about Jesuits abound: 'A Jesuit was lost. When he asked his way, he was told sadly: "You'll never find it, it's straight ahead."'

2 Bernard Basset SJ, *The English Jesuits, from Campion to Martindale* (London, Burns and Oates, 1967).

3 Founder of the English college in St Omer, the ancestor of Stonyhurst College.

4 Evelyn Waugh, *Edmund Campion, the Famous Elizabethan Jesuit Scholar and Missionary* (Penguin Books, 1935).

5 *The English Jesuits.*

6 Ibid.

7 *Pedro Arrupe: Itinéraire d'un jésuite, entretiens avec Jean-Claude Dietsch SJ* (Pedro Arrupe: a Jesuit's itinerary, conversations with Jean-Claude Dietsch SJ) (Paris, 1982).

8 According to Fr Yarnold, of Campion Hall, 'In the British Province, entries seem to have reached an average of five or six a year, compared with 25 or so pre-war.'

9 John O'Malley, *The First Jesuits* (Harvard University Press, 1993).

10 Of a world population of almost 5.5 billion, there are 45 million displaced persons (20 million refugees and 25 million internally displaced). Currently it is estimated that 0.75 per cent of the world's population are forcibly displaced. (Source: *1993 World*

Refugee Survey, US Committee for Refugees.) More recent figures (September 1994) give a much higher estimate, with 125 million people living outside of their frontiers.

11 Twenty million in 1994.

12 A French political right-wing association, associated with the brilliant writer Charles Maurras, who admired the Roman Catholic 'system' although he was a freethinker.

13 In 1994, there were 315 Jesuits in China.

2

Jesuits in society

A TURNING POINT: FROM ECCLESIAL QUESTIONS TO SOCIAL CONFRONTATION

> *As the Society was once at the forefront of the cultural movement of the Renaissance should it not now be at the forefront of the working-class movement? Can it not now find a formula to plunge its priests in among the workers just as it set up colleges to Christianize humanism?*
>
> JEAN LACAN SJ

'Discover God in all things', 'contemplation through action' – these two precepts epitomize the intuition that drove Ignatius of Loyola to found a new order, combining as they do both efficacy and mysticism. But even the highest mysticism can degenerate into politics, and the Society of Jesus was more prone to such lapses than any other religious order. Ignatius had foreseen, and even welcomed, persecution, while wishing to avoid providing a pretext for it. The Society has been spared nothing: neither expulsion nor martyrdom, hate nor slander. And yet, on their own admission, the Jesuits have known, and are still experiencing, even greater long-term perils.

In the course of their eventful history the Jesuits have not always resisted that taste for power which comes close on the heels of the pursuit of influence. They have resorted to an excessive use of human means and have curried favour with the social elite. Their mistakes in evangelization are as unquestionable as the honesty of their intentions. And therein lies their frailty. The combination of humanism and the Gospel lent a splendour to the Society's achievements that brought lustre to mere human glory while tarnishing the 'greater glory of God'. Fr Emile Rideau, a French Jesuit whose attachment to his order cannot be doubted, has no indulgence for the Society when he states:

> The Society of Jesus is guilty of inertia and laziness rather than the pride and ambition of which it is so often accused. The Society, whose intelligence is extolled and whose 'cleverness' is jeered at, has, overall, been lacking in clearheadedness in the light of history. This order, whose initiative and creativity is so admired (. . .), has got into a rut in Europe. (. . .) Instead of advancing it is standing still.[1]

In short, the shock troops, once in the vanguard, have dropped back towards the rear. The power the Society won in the Church and the world at large has come close to overwhelming it. As is evident from its recent history and present-day evolution, the Society's efforts are directed less towards winning back the influence it has lost than to regaining the vitality it squandered in overcoming its many enemies and the force of resistance within its ranks.

The surprising lecture given by Fr Arrupe on 18 January 1979 is sufficient illustration of this. Speaking to a packed auditorium of Jesuits on the subject of 'the way we behave', he sketched portraits of Jesuit deformations as merciless as any views from outside the order. After warning his companions of the age-old temptation of vanity, he presented his 'rogues' gallery':

1 The born contradictor. While protest can be considered a prophetic and evangelical duty, self-satisfaction, systematic militancy, slovenliness and coarse behaviour or language do little to promote sound personal convictions.
2 The professional. The Jesuit know-all. Please do not disturb. Completely immersed in his profession, absorbed by his commitments, he lives unattached to any community and cut off from his superior. Fr Arrupe is

adamant: the Jesuit who recognizes himself in these traits must be aware that he is distorting the Society's image.

3 The irresponsible 'absent-minded professor'. Characteristics: order, punctuality, the value of money and moderation are unknown to him. 'One finds in him an unwarranted allergy to any checking of results, in either his studies or any other activity.' Very suspicious ...

4 The political activist. Who thought to find him here? It is surely considered a virtue for a Jesuit to be involved in politics? Not in the opinion of the 'progressive' Arrupe: 'When the struggle for justice takes such a Jesuit out of his proper sphere of Christian activity, assistance and sharing, and leads him into politics – perhaps even to join a party and sometimes even to give up his priestly mission – then it can no longer be said that he is acting as the order's envoy, nor that his political or trades union activism provides authentic evangelical mediation.' These remarks are surprising, considering the high proportion of Jesuits belonging to unions[2] and the fact that, like any citizen, they have every right to join political parties. In fact Fr Arrupe is objecting to 'political activism' when it implies seizing and confiscating power. A French Canadian Jesuit was forced to leave the Society in 1976 when he was made a minister in René Lévesque's Government. After several years in power he resigned from the government and was then reinstated in the order at his request.

5 The tendentious traditionalist. This last 'identikit' aroused the greatest ferocity in Fr Arrupe. His overriding fault is that 'he flaunts conspicuously the external trappings and symbols of a bygone age'. This Jesuit, 'a blend of bitterness and nostalgia', is the almost perfect hypocrite. 'He boasts that he will never have a bank account but is only too happy to be waited on hand and foot by a few obliging families. He may well be unhappy about empty churches and fewer people coming to him for spiritual guidance, but he is unlikely to wonder if this is partly due to his spiritual narrowness of view or to his refusal to keep up with changing ideas.'

With this attack from their own General, the Jesuits were invited to put their house in order. Nothing new here: 'fraternal correction' has long been a tradition in the order. Even though it is carried out less rigorously than in the past, it is necessary to check both the power of superiors and the independence of individuals and communities. A contemporary expression of this is the 'Annual Report' that has to be sent to Rome by every Jesuit director, the superior of each community and also the 'consultors' of each Provincial. The information collected is analysed and collated to give a significant, if not exhaustive, assessment of the Society's accomplishments. Many of those responsible are more interested in getting on with their jobs than in the tedious business of filling in forms; 3,600 reports were received by the order's Curia in Rome in May 1979: slightly over 55 per cent of those expected. Jesuits sometimes really do display obedience *perinde ac cadaver* – when they play dead.

The survey instigated by Fr Arrupe in 1966 had already produced a wealth of information about attitudes throughout the Society. Contributors did not mince their words. The official recorder of the North American Assistancy, for example, had no scruples about writing:

> Religious life as we have known it is totally at odds with modern life in America. It appears stationary in an era of change; it stresses absolute obedience in a world of freedom and autonomy; it advocates celibacy in a world deeply attached to emotional experience; it speaks of poverty without being poor; it demands commitment when change makes commitment unreasonable; it calls certain things sacred in a desacralized world; it requires uniformity of a world where creativity and individuality are actively pursued ... In short, religious life is faced with its own relevancy crisis.

In the same survey, a young Jesuit from Quebec explained his attitude to religious obedience thus:

> Young Jesuits are involved in the democratic movement and feel very alien to the hierarchical system of authority. They see authority as a service and consider it self-evident that decisions should be made by all those concerned in carrying them out.

Religious obedience no longer has the same meaning today,

even among those in the highest positions of responsibility. The former Archbishop of Bombay, Mgr Thomas Roberts, a Jesuit known for his outspoken unorthodox opinions at the Council and elsewhere, had this to say just before his death about what St Ignatius called 'obedience of the intellect':

> 'It is because I learned this kind of obedience, because I am a son of God and not a slave, that I have called into question several things which are usually taken for granted. The so-called "artificial" means of contraception, for example. To ask such questions is more than a right, it is a duty: the strict duty of Christian obedience, which must be rational ...'[3]

One can also mention Fr Arrupe's own attitude towards the 'civil disobedience' of Daniel Berrigan, an American Jesuit pacifist. Along with other Catholic pacifists, Berrigan had been imprisoned for having destroyed military files and sprayed documents with animal blood in a protest against the war in Vietnam. During his 1971 tour of the United States, the General made a point of visiting Daniel Berrigan in prison and issued the following statement:

> I am well aware that public opinion – in the Society, the Catholic community and the country – regarding Fr Berrigan's ideas and actions is divided, sometimes bitterly and passionately. My decision to visit him in prison should be seen not as a mark of approval, but simply as an expression of my concern as superior for all members of the Society of Jesus.

But one can easily become entangled in nearly insoluble conflicts. In fact contraception, mentioned by the late Archbishop of Bombay, became a subject of contention among Jesuits in 1968, less, however, because of the contents of the encyclical *Humanae vitae* itself, which condemned artificial contraception, than about the fourth vow: loyalty to the Pope. Some used this vow to argue that Jesuits could not question the encyclical's cogency, at least not in public – such was the position of the magazine *America*, for instance. Another Jesuit magazine, *Orientierung*, published in Zürich, Switzerland, riposted that the attitude of every Catholic must be based on truth and conscience. *Orientierung* cited a letter sent to all the major superiors throughout the world by Fr Correia-Alfonso, Secretary of the Society of Jesus, who wrote: 'The kind of obedience called for by the Father General is active, intelligent, and open to further research.'

However, several Jesuits interpreted the fourth vow so broadly – stating for example that in serving the Church one may be called upon to criticize the Pope – that early in 1972 Fr Arrupe made an appeal for all members of the order to show greater loyalty to the Pope. As he remarked: 'Criticising authority, either in private or in public, is an easy way of getting attention.'

But Jesuits are not only inclined to criticize others; they are also capable of ruthless self-criticism. They have kept up the practice of exchanging experiences, started in the seventeenth century by the French Jesuits in New France (now Canada), in their 'relations' – long letters which were sent to their brothers in Europe. Modern duplicating processes have produced a proliferation of newsletters of all kinds, sometimes in several languages, that are circulated around the world, like those of *Promotio justitiae*, the magazine of the Jesuit Social Institute in Rome.

In one issue, Alex MacDonald, an Australian Jesuit, reflects on his somewhat unusual job. Hours: 10 pm to 4 or 5 am; place of work: Melbourne; occupation: sitting in sleazy bars and night shelters around St Kilda's; specialization: listening to the problems of prostitutes and drug addicts. Alex has learnt a lot from all his listening:

> We are afraid of powerless people. They make us realize that
> we have power over the lives of others, over theirs perhaps.
> We are filled with power. What terrifies us is that we soon lust
> after power. I remember, one evening in one of our shelters for
> the homeless, I lost my temper with one of the inmates, so that
> we finished up by screaming our heads off. As a parting shot,
> I took advantage of my position of power and asked him to
> leave . . . .

The abuse of power – an ever-present temptation – leads us to indulge in lording it over others, even on excellent pretexts. It is quite another thing to have the strength to give power to the least-privileged members of our society. This can have untold repercussions. On 28 July 1982, Mgr Francisco Claver, a Jesuit bishop at the head of the Malaybalay prelacy

in the southern Philippines, addressed 400 American fellow
Jesuits. He spoke from experience. An active group of Catholic
Filipinos was involved in the opposition to the Marcos regime
which had imposed martial law, 'a euphemism for what is usually called dictatorship and its version of reform. It was forced
on us, with the aim of transforming us into "a new society".
The idea was that we would accept and say "amen" to all
the grandiose projects dreamt up for our greater good by one
man, together with his ideology, his discipline, his decrees and
everything else.' A vain hope. Because those who recover the
power that has been confiscated from them, 'decide for themselves what it means for them and how to make use of it'.

The Jesuits in the Philippines have an impressive pastoral
organization including schools, the mass media, work with
tribal minorities and a training programme for the laity. It was
not long before conflict with the regime erupted. Mgr Claver
explained that

> The government and the military tried to infiltrate our
> groups – and also the Communists ... Their efforts failed, and
> they now use intimidation and harassment. All this convinces
> us that we are on the right track. But it also raises a disturbing
> fact: that the Church has power and is feared.

The bishop asked his fellow bishops to examine their consciences carefully. The attempt to equate justice and faith
is not free from risk. Evangelization in the name of social
justice can easily become 'pure politics', and the struggle
to put things right a simple desire for revenge. All power is
ambiguous. Francisco Claver gave this warning:

> The black Pope, the Pope's shock troops, the kind of
> intellectual training we receive, our institutions, the enormous
> variety of our undertakings, our numbers – put these all
> together, and you have an idea of the power wielded by our
> 'little Society'!

Problems such as this example from Asia and those spelt out
by Fr Arrupe have in fact been present throughout the history of the Jesuits – which partly explains the constant battles
they have fought. However, the twentieth century has proved
a watershed. The scope of Jesuit 'power' is no longer a consequence of Rome's strategy but a result of battles and conflicts

relating to the aspirations of minorities and local communities; it now plays a leading role in social confrontation rather than in major ecclesial debates; it no longer stands for European centralism but is found in new centres of cultural and theological development, such as the Far East, Latin America and the United States.

Although by 1962 the Society of Jesus had reached its peak in terms of numbers, having quadrupled in less than a century, that period of growth was nevertheless an extremely difficult period. As anticlericalism released its hold, the First World War broke out. At the height of the debate over Modernism, the first attempts at social, theological and biblical open-mindedness within the Church were stifled by antagonism and suspicion.

Pius X, who was Pope from 1903 to 1914, had inherited the pontifical absolutism resulting from Vatican I. The 1906 encyclical *Vehementer nos*, while protesting against the French law separating Church and State, set the tone of the period: 'The pastoral body alone possesses the right and the authority necessary for the promotion and guidance of all members towards society's ends. As for the multitude, they have no right other than to let themselves be led and obediently follow their shepherds.' On 16 June 1883, the first edition of the French daily newspaper *La Croix* heralded the mood at the turn of the century. This new paper, declared its editorial, will be 'Catholic, exclusively Catholic, Apostolic and Roman ... Vile news-sheets find their way into every garret and cottage – therefore a cheap, Catholic paper is needed to combat this widespread evil.'

This militant Catholicism, authoritarian at the top, clerical in construction, but fundamentally devout, entered the twentieth century with a superabundant religious personnel: in 1901, there were some 56,000 secular priests in France, 30,200 monks and 130,000 nuns in 16,000 communities. Whatever its shortcomings, the French Church produced a veritable cultural explosion. Through the works of such writers as Péguy, Claudel, Mauriac, Bloy, Bernanos, Maritain and Mounier, French Catholic literature gained worldwide recognition.

At the same time, Western colonialism was at its peak, bringing missionaries in its wake. The White Fathers in

Africa, the Foreign Missions in Indochina, the Lazarist Vincent Lebbe (1895–1940) in China: in the eyes of the missionaries, the Church's influence was not to be separated from the 'civilizing' influence of the mother country. As for spirituality, edifying thoughts were all that was demanded.

If this militant Catholicism was coming to terms with the modern world, it was not exempt from verbose intolerance and doctrinal pettiness. Léon Bloy railed against the 'pontificating bourgeoisie', Bernanos berated the frightened bigots and Mounier, founder of the magazine *Esprit*, deplored the decadence of a certain type of Christianity which had reached a stage of 'malign debility'. He condemned the timorous soul-searching of bigoted, petit-bourgeois and Jansenist Catholicism in his *Affrontement chrétien* (1944). Elsewhere, however, he did not hide his admiration for such instigators of genuine renewal as Cardijn and Guérin, the priests behind Catholic Action and the working-class Christian youth movement JOC (Jeunesse ouvri-ère chrétienne), and Frs Lagrange, de Grandmaison and Lebre-ton, who were responsible for theological and biblical research.

Liturgical reform was also taking place in the great Benedictine abbeys, as Dom Lefebvre's well-known *Missel des fidèles* testifies. The ecumenical movement also took root in various innovations after the First World War, such as the 'Malines Conversations' organized between 1921 and 1926 by Cardinal Mercier and the Anglican Lord Halifax. Fr Yves Congar's early writings and the work accomplished by Dom Baudouin and the monks at Amay represented attempts to bridge the gap between Rome and the other Christian churches.

To oversimplify, it could be said that Catholicism in the first half of the twentieth century was poised between two worlds. On the one hand, the experience of the previous century, pious and generous but authoritarian and individualistic; on the other, the aspirations of the modern world, attracted by the potential riches of science and by cultural effervescence and faced with the challenge of totalitarian systems. Mounier was certainly inspired when he wrote the first editorial of *Esprit* in the form of a manifesto aimed boldly at 'bringing about a new Renaissance'.

Catholicism has rarely been so productive, after a period on the defensive, as during the period from the beginning of the century to Vatican II. Caught up in this whirl, the Jesuits occupied an important place, even if they were not always the driving force. They focused their energies on old people's homes, youth movements like the Eucharistic Crusade, workers' missions, theological research and teaching. Their network of secondary schools and universities spread rapidly through many countries, particularly in those, like the United States, where freedom was greater than in France.

Urgency was in the air. The Jesuit Fr Albert Valensin (1873–1944) wrote in his diary in 1926 of the excitement felt throughout the order: 'The world is in need of moral and intellectual leadership. Men with drive and sound practical sense, who are capable of becoming leaders, must rise up.' A dangerous proposition, although pronounced innocently enough: before long the 'leaders' would rise up, and too many people, in their eagerness for guides to lead them out of the international morass, would be unable to detect and denounce their perverse seduction before it was too late. However, while the West was bracing itself to withstand the shock of 1939, the Society was quietly reviewing the way it saw its commitment to the world. Some remarkable people, concerned particularly with social matters, deserve special mention.

Born in the north of France, Henri-Joseph Leroy entered the Society of Jesus in 1867. After the publication in 1891 of Leo XIII's encyclical *Rerum novarum*, on the conditions of workers, he seized the occasion to preach on issues which were very controversial at the time: social justice, poverty and the dechristianization of working-class communities. Catholics were divided and needed to be brought together, instructed and organized.

Henri-Joseph Leroy sought out collaborators, raised support and explained his method. He wanted to produce a doctrinal work, distributed in pamphlet form, that was both accessible and essentially meaningful. The first issue appeared in January 1903 – Action Populaire was born. At a time when everything else seemed to be collapsing, Catholicism was being brought back to life. Fr Leroy's work was encouraged in Rome *mezzo forte*. The General's assistant prescribed prudence: 'Avoid allowing the work to become political.' The beginnings were promising. At the end of one year Action

Populaire had sold 60,000 pamphlets, known as the 'yellow papers'.

Gustave Desbuquois, one of Fr Leroy's young colleagues, showed such enthusiasm for Action Populaire that he was made director in 1905 and remained there for 40 years. Cardinal Liénart was to say of him: 'Without Fr Desbuquois the social movement would certainly never have become what it was.' Like Leroy, Desbuquois came from the north of France. He was born on 14 December 1869 in Roubaix, the fifth child of a family of bakers. A brilliant student, he was thinking of reading law or the sciences when a retreat made him abruptly change course, and at twenty he entered the Jesuits. Almost all of his training, like that of his companions, took place abroad – in the Netherlands and Belgium. His studies were arduous and he remembered his teachers with mixed feelings. It was in Enghien, Belgium, that he met Henri-Joseph Leroy for the first time.

As head of Action Populaire, Fr Desbuquois played a leading role not only in the development of that institution but also in the social conscience of a large proportion of French Catholics. In 1912, he designated, in no uncertain terms, the 'two brute forces' which went against the Church's social doctrine: 'materialistic socialism and pagan plutocracy'. Desbuquois was not afraid of denouncing 'corrupt wealth, the fruit of usury and speculation to the detriment of human labour, the employer's as well as the worker's'. To the Jesuits gathered in Enghien he made remarks that, even today, would not be considered trite: 'Every priest should be social-minded and trade-union-minded.' This brought cries of protest. In spite of very moderate articles in *Etudes* in 1912 on 'Catholic social action', Fr Desbuquois was violently criticized by traditionalists who saw the very idea of a trade union as a threat to liberalism and property rights.

However the director of Action Populaire was far from preaching class struggle. His views, inspired by 'principles of justice and of class unity', were by no means intended to undermine employers' rights. But some Catholic employers, supported by Pius X's pro-liberal theses, denounced this as treason: 'the right of authority and command' is threatened by 'so-called Christian democracy'. Had not Pius X stated, in a letter to the French episcopate in 1910 condemning Marc Sangnier's publication *Le Sillon*: 'Society cannot be built up if the Church does not lay down the foundations and oversee the work'? Fr Desbuquois was reproached both for advocating collective forms of action, thus endangering the employer's sole authority, and for accepting interdenominational trade unions in defiance of the sole authority of the Church. According to the enemies of Action Populaire, by becoming trade-unionist, social action displayed tacit hostility to employers; true Christian principles, on the contrary, taught workers not to demand ever higher salaries but to 'stay in their own subordinate position, on pain of social anarchy'. In other words, socialist ideas had illicitly taken root in the doctrine of the Action Populaire Jesuits. An unforgivable sin.

Cardinal Luçon, Archbishop of Rheims, warned Fr Desbuquois: 'You are known to us only by your enemies.' To the enterprising director of Action Populaire, who was managing to ride out the storm, kind souls advised patience. 'The time [for trade unionism] is not yet ripe.' Eventually resistance and patience bore fruit. Whereas Leo XIII had called on the Catholics of France to 'rally round' the Republican cause, Action Populaire and Fr Desbuquois were to contribute towards getting the Church to support the social movement. Although this early spadework failed to achieve a truly active movement, it nevertheless developed consciences and opened up Christian understanding of economic, social and political issues.

From its base in Vanves, just outside Paris, Action Populaire continued the work undertaken by Frs Leroy and Desbuquois. The institution published two magazines, the *Cahiers d'Action religieuse et sociale* and *Projet*, organized meetings and lectures, and ran a social-studies programme at the Catholic Institute in Paris. What is more, it had many imitators within the Society of Jesus. In 1965, before the 31st General Congregation which was to elect Fr Pedro Arrupe as General, the order had no less than 23 'Centres for Action and Social Research' throughout the world, mostly set up between 1950 and 1960. Eleven of them were in Latin America, five in Europe, two in Africa, two in Asia. The three others were in the USA, Australia and Jamaica.

The way opened by these pioneers did not simply lead to the setting up of social centres and intellectual stimulation, even if Jesuits have a predilection for transforming society through such means. The Second World War was to change, once again, the Society's apostolic projects. The Jesuits, like so many other Christians, were not content to stand on the sidelines. They went straight into the fray and, for many, the ordeal was a revelation. Among them was a certain Henri Perrin, whose 'itinerary'⁴ was remarkable and yet also representative of a dramatic stage in the evolution of the Society of Jesus and the Church.

In October 1940, Perrin, already a priest, joined the Jesuit novitiate which had been evacuated to Cazères-sur-Adour in the south-west of France. He was 26, and came from the north-east, where he had suffered poverty from an early age – his father having died in 1916. He had been with the army in Sedan at the beginning of the German invasion in May of that year, and in 1943 he was one of the first voluntary – and clan-destine – chaplains to leave with the young conscript workers sent to Germany by the STO (Service du travail obligatoire). Unmasked, imprisoned then repatriated, Henri Perrin first withdrew to the Action Populaire centre. But his experience in Germany among the workers had affected him permanently.

> The contact of those thousands of men, whose everyday life I used to share so intimately, has left a heartache that nothing can relieve. I now come across their fellows daily in the crowds filling the shops, buses and trains, crowds to whom I feel so close but for whom I have once more become an outsider.

An outsider! Henri Perrin could not resign himself to being one. At the end of 1946, he announced his decision to 'take up the life of a worker'. The project, which had been maturing since his return from Germany in 1944, filled him with both joy and apprehension:

> I do not feel that easy, and I am disturbed by the thought that I am giving my twenty years' studying, travelling, training and experience entirely to the working class, that I have decided to live among them, at their rhythm, in perfect unison with them.

Fr Perrin wanted to make the leap. Not only 'to help others to act', but to act directly at grass-roots level, by breaking off all ties with the protected milieu of ecclesiastical and clerical institutions. To live, finally, without defences or protection. The war had brought priests, monks and nuns out of their ghettoes and Perrin had no desire to return.

Negotiations, procedures and delays had to be endured, mistrust dispelled. But he was no longer alone. Early in 1948, he joined two Jesuits who were already settled in the XIIIth arrondissement of Paris, in the parish of Notre-Dame-de-la-Gare, where the parish priest, Maurice Deluze, was a true apostle. Two other Jesuits, Maurice Husson and Jean Lacan – a relative of the psychoanalyst Jacques Lacan – joined the group. Jean Lacan stayed there for fifteen years before moving to Ivry-Port, where he died in 1982 after fighting constant battles for the working classes. As early as 1944, he had been the first signatory of a letter sent to the French provincials by ten Jesuits anxious to motivate their order:

As the Society was once at the forefront of the cultural movement of the Renaissance, should it not now be at the forefront of the working-class movement? Can it not now find a formula to plunge its priests in among the workers just as it set up colleges to Christianize humanism?

The first test of the new 'formula' was the Notre-Dame-de-la-Gare group. Perrin got a job in a plastics factory as a caster, then a turner. The firm was not aware that he was a priest. Although longing to tell, he held his tongue. He became involved in the trade union movement and changed jobs several times. At the end of the first year the results were modest: 'We are not very sure where we are going. We have left the world of security for one of insecurity where the quest will be long.'

The first national meeting of French worker-priests was held on 7 May 1949. Less than two months later, the Holy Office issued a decree condemning Catholics for joining or collaborating with Communist parties. The publication of the document unleashed a huge press campaign. Above all, it unsettled the worker-priests and the militants gathered round them. The summer passed in endless discussions as to what attitude to adopt. While Roman suspicions intensified, the demands of the mission became clearer:

Awareness of being a commmunity detached from the
ecclesiastical world of the Church in a Christian country.
Awareness of being a community that is always attached to the
poorest of this world. With the need to make a clean break.
Not belonging first and foremost to the clergy, the Catholic
world, or a religious order, but instead to the working-class
world, in all its suffering.

This note of Henri Perrin's, dated January 1950, is of paramount importance in understanding the drama that was brewing. A few weeks later he wrote to the Christian Democrat (MRP) deputy in his area to make him aware of the conflict which, all over France, led workers to demand higher salaries. 'In this strike', he wrote, 'I blame the employers.' The priest had not only chosen a different way of living in the world, he had also chosen his camp. The Society of Jesus hesitated to back him fully. Soon Henri Perrin was forced to leave both the order and Paris, where his presence was considered inopportune in such turbulent times. In June 1951, the Holy See demanded an annual report on each worker-priest and banned any increase in their numbers.

Perrin signed up on the building site of the dam at Notre-Dame-de-Briançon. In 1953 events came to a head. The seminary of the Mission de France, in Limoges, was closed on 6 September. On the 23rd, the nuncio conveyed to 26 bishops and religious superiors instructions from Rome concerning worker-priests. Cardinals Liénart, Feltin and Gerlier hastened to Rome to defend their cause. It was a waste of time and effort. After a second visit to the Vatican in November that year, the cardinals were forced to pass on the orders in a laconic declaration: 'After ten years' existence, the worker-priest experiment, such as it has evolved to date, cannot be maintained in its present form.'

To all intents and purposes, this was the death sentence. On 28 December the Society of Jesus recalled its worker-priests. Although no longer a Jesuit, Henri Perrin wrote a bitter letter in February 1954:

I remember with sadness Father General's letter in 1949,
designating the industrial world as the objective for the
Society's evangelization. It rings as a mockery when one
sees the results. The mountain gave birth to a mouse. The
bourgeoisie still has the order's live forces at their disposal. We

are retreating further into our ivory tower and into a foolish anti-Communism.[5]

On 27 October the same year, Henri Perrin was killed outright in an unexplained motor-cycle accident. On 26 October 1956, another Jesuit worker-priest, Joseph de Lorgeril, died after a lingering two-year agony. Cardinal Feltin wrote this of him to one of his friends:

> He had really achieved what we had hoped to see from all those who devoted themselves to the worker-priest movement. The decisions that were taken about that form of evangelization undoubtedly affected him greatly, and one can even say that they killed him.

The crisis affecting the worker-priest experiment was not the Church's only trauma, but was one of the most dramatic revelations of the changes to come. Those involved attempted to negotiate a gradual change of mentality, but the institution feared a violent clash of wills. Its abrupt intervention to bring the experiment to an end merely precipitated the crisis, at the cost of great human suffering. The Society of Jesus gave way, but did not give in. In December 1953, *Etudes* published a conciliatory article signed by Fr Jean Villain, who had been one of those to back the Notre-Dame-de-la-Gare venture. In accordance with the Roman criticism, the author stressed that if Pius XII had intervened with 'such authority', it was because he had been 'worried, and justifiably worried, about the worker-priests'. However, he finishes on a firm, optimistic note, bordering on a challenge: 'More than ever, it is time for worker-priests.'

History has partly confirmed his prediction. There were 50 French Jesuits in the working-class mission in 1990, twenty of whom were actual worker-priests – the others being either retired or involved in various associations doing social work or health care. Belgium has some ten members in the field, including the Jesuits working with down-and-outs. In August 1989, 90 European Jesuits in the working-class mission met at La Baume, near Aix-en-Provence. There are about 150 in the whole of western Europe. The main problem, according to an Italian Jesuit working in a timber co-operative, is:

> 'to be truly with the working classes, to live their life even in

politics and unions. Every one of us has discovered that politics
are necessary to change things (...). It is a question of making
the Church understand the dramatic situation the worker is in.
In the south of Italy the Church does nothing – it is in league
with the big landowners – and the parish priest is always
one of the richest men in the village.'

Now restored to favour, the worker-priests and Jesuits
engaged in the social apostolate had long remained 'misunder-
stood prophets'. This expression, applied to Pierre Teilhard
de Chardin in 1970 in a book by Fr Ouince, is a reasonable
comparison between the Jesuit scientist and the working-class
missionaries.

The Society of Jesus, which produced a host of researchers
and teachers from the very beginning, has never retreated
from the outposts of science in spite of the risks. Teilhard
de Chardin is no doubt the most outstanding example this
century, but he exemplifies the guiding rule that runs
through the Society's history: enlarge thought and action so
that they may become passageways from man to God, and
there carry out God's plan for mankind. 'You have struggled
enough so that Man might be deified', prayed Teilhard. 'It is
now my turn to force open the gates of the Spirit. Let me
through.'

Pierre Teilhard de Chardin died in New York on 10 April
1955, on Easter Sunday – an appropriate day for someone
whose whole life had been devoted to the pursuit of the
Absolute. Right from his early childhood in Auvergne, where
he was born on 1 May 1881, he was obsessed by the Tangible
and the Definitive, and by the appeal of matter and the universe. 'If I have always loved Nature, in my childhood and
ever since, completely and with growing conviction, I can say
that it was not as a scientist, but as a believer.'

Brought up by a pious mother, Pierre was educated at the
Jesuit school of Notre-Dame-de-Mongré, in Villefranche-sur-
Saône. There he was 'unbelievably good' in the blunt words
of one of his teachers, Henri Brémond, who was also later
to make a name for himself. The bright pupil had nonetheless already experienced real internal crises. Having made
a ploughshare into his 'iron god', he was to discover before
he had reached the age of ten that iron rusts. The search for

'consistency' was to turn into an uncompromising religious quest. At eighteen Teilhard entered the novitiate of the Society of Jesus at Aix-en-Provence. His decision was motivated by a desire for perfection. Despite his attraction to science, he considered giving it up. Luckily, however, he was dissuaded from doing so by his novice master. After studying literature in Laval and philosophy in Jersey, he was sent to Egypt to teach physics and chemistry at the school of the Holy Family in Cairo. In the desert one day he faced temptation: '... Matter was there and was calling me. To me, in my turn, as to all the sons of man, she repeated the words heard by each generation. She appealed to me so that, giving myself wholeheartedly to her, I would adore her.'

Faith was stronger. Or rather it was always to be a composite part of his explorations of matter and history. Back in Europe, Teilhard started the four-year theology course in preparation for the priesthood. He was ordained in 1911, and the following year met Marcellin Boule who asked him to go and work with him in the natural history museum in Paris. A career in palae-ontology was opening up for him when the war brought his research to a temporary halt. Teilhard joined the army in 1915 as a stretcher-bearer, second class. He stayed at the front until the end of the war and was a corporal at the time of his demo-bilization in 1919.

In spite of the horrors of war, this period was to bring his thinking to maturity. Between 1916 and 1919, he wrote some twenty essays in which he described his vision of the world. 'It seems that the front is not only the firing line, the flashpoint between warring peoples, but also the crest of the wave that is carrying the world towards its new destiny.' The war was also for Teilhard a 'baptism into reality'. It gave him the chance to define his position as a believer and a Jesuit. 'How to be as Christian as possible while being more human than anyone else.'

After the war, Teilhard was able to go back to his studies, and obtained his science doctorate in 1922. He was immedi-ately made president of the Geological Society of France, and the rector of the Catholic Institute of Paris offered him some geology lectures. Meanwhile, a manuscript on 'original sin' that he had submitted to his superiors already gave them cause for concern. He was advised to 'work for Christ without talking about him', the first time he was condemned to a cruel silence that was to last, with a few rare exceptions, until his death.

The 'note on original sin' got as far as Rome and the timing could not have been worse. The Modernist controversy was barely over and the mere word 'evolution' made the Curia tremble. Teilhard left the teaching profession that he had so recently taken up, and this sudden freedom turned him into an explorer. In 1926, he left France for Tianjin, which he had first visited in 1923, and supervised the excavations of Choukoutien. By 1931 he was able to maintain with Abbé Breuil that Sinanthropus was a *homo faber*, a stone-cutter who used fire. In 1931–32, he took part in the Chinese expedition organized by Citroën, the 'Croisière jaune'. One major book came out of that period, *Le Milieu divin*, written in 1927. Teilhard had believed that his work would be published quickly, but it was not in fact printed until after his death. For many years clandestine copies of his book were surreptitiously circulated, particularly among young Jesuit theologians, and Teilhard's reputation grew – to his misfortune.

In the midst of his explorations, Teilhard began writing his master work in 1939 – *Le Phénomène humain* (The phenomenon of man). Life emerged from the cosmos, 'hominized' to give birth to the 'noösphere', the zone of reflective thought, the last stage of evolution. But life continues to progress. Humanity rises through an increasingly complex socialization that directs it towards its centre of convergence, the 'Omega point'.

After a brief stay in Paris in 1939, Fr Teilhard returned to China for what he expected to be a short time, but the war kept him there for seven years. Back in Paris again, where he was laid low by his first heart attack in May 1947, he could not fail to notice that his opponents had not disarmed during his absence. He spent a month in Rome in the autumn of 1948 and there met the Father General, Jean-Baptiste Janssens, whose authorization he required to publish *The Phenomenon of Man* and to submit his candidature for a Chair at the famous Collège de France.

The General's objections and those of the Holy Office are revealed in the notes that Fr Teilhard made in a few simple exercise books, parts of which have been published. On 8 October he wrote: 'Conversation with Fr General: "Employ better educational methods ... My essays are vague ... Beware of neo-humanism being simply a fashion ... Evolution, yes – but only in moderation."' In spite of the General's fatherly reception, the two requests were turned down. Moreover Pius XII's encyclical *Humani generis* in 1950 was aimed in part at Teilhard's opinions, though without actually naming him. But an official commentary in *Osservatore romano* openly attacked the scholarly Jesuit, by then the *bête noire* of conservative philosophers and theologians.

Meanwhile, however, there were Jesuit colleagues who remained friends with Teilhard and supported him discreetly, such as the future Cardinal de Lubac, who was himself under suspicion at the time. One of the most faithful Jesuits was Fr Pierre Leroy, and Teilhard wrote to him from New York, where he had lived from 1951 onwards, just six weeks before his death:

> How curious it is that, worried as I am, and about so many
> points, I do not feel the slightest bit concerned by all this
> opposition, but rather encouraged or at least excited by it.
> Such resistance stimulates me, because I feel so very sure
> of expressing what is, basically, in the thoughts and hearts
> of us all.

Teilhard was not mistaken. The posthumous success of his works confirmed the need that was making itself felt in a large section of the Church. His books are today sold in their hundreds of thousands. Furthermore, his philosophy permeates certain texts of Vatican II, in particular the Pastoral Constitution on the Church in the Modern World. John Paul II himself, in his first encyclical, describes Christ as being the 'centre of history and the cosmos', thus using 'Teilhardian' language that would have greatly disturbed the censors in the 1950s. As for Fr Janssens's successor, Fr Arrupe, he is perfectly explicit: Fr Teilhard's conceptions are 'in keeping with a concern that has always been fundamental to the Society of Jesus, driving it to daring apostolic ventures, such as that of Fr Ricci in China, to mention just one. A major concern for us that we try to convey by our presence in various places where the Church has up until now been too often absent.' Without a doubt, Teilhard de Chardin has been one of the prime movers of ecclesiastical evolution in the last few decades.

To Teilhard's name can be added a long line of writers, theologians, researchers in all fields, often hidden away in obscure laboratories, who all followed the same inspiration: the Church can take its chances in the world and make its message credible only by overcoming the remnants of Jansenism and distrust of the progress and regression that are always possible in the human condition. The spirituality of the Society of Jesus is inherently optimistic, since it calls for a positive confrontation of society's values. The spiritual writer Fr Varillon (1905–78) turned this attitude into a motto which sums up the Jesuit commitment: 'One hand on the beauty of the world. One hand on the suffering of man. And two feet firmly on the task in hand.'[6] To guard against a disembodied 'pious' interpretation, he added: 'To turn people away from taking an interest in earthly matters is what I call spiritual slaughter.'

A tireless lecturer, a great connoisseur and admirer of Claudel, François Varillon always retained a sense of the task in hand. He was behind the proposal made in 1941 to Fr Gaston Fessard (1897–1978) to write a tract against the dangers of Nazism and collaboration. The 'tract' became a 50-page manuscript, *France, prends garde de perdre ton âme* (France, beware of losing your soul). Printed in two versions, one in Lyons and the other in Salon-de-Provence, the brochure became the first of the *Cahiers du Témoignage catholique* (Catholic witness) immediately renamed *Témoignage chrétien* at the request of a Protestant friend and member of the Resistance, Roland de Pury. These journals played a major role in the 'revival of conscience' of Christians in France under the German occupation. Truth, held captive in the midst of cowardice and fear, finally managed to surface. *Témoignage chrétien* became the weapon of unarmed, but effective, power. Moreover it restored the honour that had been lost by a large proportion of Catholics.

After the war, the Society went on with its work on more peaceful fronts. Although intellectual wrangling continued, the proliferation of new undertakings, linked to the regular growth in numbers, presaged a less turbulent future. When Vatican II opened in October 1962, 52 Jesuit bishops were present in the vast nave of St Peter's. The numbers are surprising for an order whose rule frowns on episcopal respon- sibilities, but the Society of Jesus is also the largest missionary institution in the Church. Of its members, 6,700 live and work in mission territories, hence the number of appoint- ments to the hierarchy. There arrived in Rome, therefore, American Jesuit bishops from Alaska and British Honduras (later Belize), a former Polish deportee who was Bishop of Lusaka, Frenchmen from Chad, Belgians from the Congo, Indians, Indonesians, and Cardinal Augustin Bea, a German biblical scholar and pioneer of the ecumenical movement. The Society also sent numerous eminent specialists, such as Karl Rahner, John Courtney Murray and Henri de Lubac. After so many painful experiences, the whole order thus gave the impression of solidity and strength never before equalled in its history.

The Belgian Jesuit General Jean-Baptiste Janssens died on 5 October 1964. The 31st General Congregation was convened on 5 May 1965 to elect his successor. At its opening Fr Maurice Giuliani, a Frenchman, addressed the 224 delegates thus: 'We need a General who can keep the Society in contact with the world to which salvation must be brought.' Fifty-seven-year- old Fr Pedro Arrupe, Provincial of Japan, where he had spent the greater part of his life, was elected on the third ballot. He was convinced that some of the Society's apostolic methods were no longer appropriate to the modern world.

Immediately after his election he spelt out the priorities: atheism, Marxism, ecumenism, social and international justice, cultural evolution in Africa, the Eastern countries and the West. Theological, philosophical and scientific research and reviews should deal with these issues and find solutions for them within the modern ideological context. Teaching methods should be modernized to make use of social com- munication systems like the radio and television. His speech ended on a forthright note: 'The adaptation must cover struc- tures, acts, men and mentalities. Not an easy operation! Let us think of that transformation which in the world of industry is called "reconversion".'

The terms were clear. The turning point had arrived and the programme was drawn up. Now to work! The General Congregation, following its usual custom, had not only to elect a leader. On the agenda, beside the new General's remarks, there was a pile of 2,000 'postulates' (petitions and propositions) sent in by Jesuits from all over the world who, also, were longing for a new lease of life.

The Congregation adjourned in July 1965, waiting until the end of the Council. The second session of the Congregation opened on 6 September 1966. The proceedings resulted in 42 decrees which had required no less than 1,427 votes before being finally adopted. Focusing on the renewal of spiritual life, new demands of obedience and the requirements of modern evangelization, they produced great effervescence in the Jesuit ranks. Training was radically restructured. Studies were to be a real preparation for the apostolic life and to correspond to the needs of the present. Theology was to be founded on a detailed study of Holy Scripture. Present-day issues, especially social ones, were to be dealt with more thoroughly. This training was aimed at those fields of evangelization which are particularly urgent today: higher education (science, research and technology), the world of work and professional organizations, international institutions, geographical zones of rapid development, where Christian ideas clash with opposing ideologies, the 'new pagans' in traditionally Christian countries. Finally Paul VI himself entrusted the Society with a specific mission, which he defined in a speech given before the election of the new General: 'fight atheism with might and main.'

Obedience was of major concern at the time of the 31st General Congregation. The delegates were aware of this and, in the light of a 'keener sense of personal freedom and responsibility', they asked for authority to be exercised in a spirit of service and dialogue. Obedience was not to go against the dignity of man, but rather to reinforce it by contributing to healthy personal development. Everyone, superiors and subordinates, must take part in the drawing up of decisions, and this implied discussion, collaboration, and a sense of community.

The 31st General Congregation finished in some confusion. The day before the end, 16 November 1966, the fathers were received by Paul VI in the Sistine Chapel. The setting was impressive, the Pope solemn, his tone grave, with a severity that disturbed many of his listeners who believed that a serious 'reappraisal of life' had been carried out.

> Do you, sons of Ignatius, soldiers of the Society of Jesus, want to be today, tomorrow and always what you have been since your foundation (...)? This question which we are putting to you would have no *raison d'être* if it were not for the rumours that have come to our ears concerning your Society (...), about which we cannot hide our surprise and, in some cases, our sorrow.

The Pope then added reassurances that were as clear as the bitterness of his remonstration. However, the press seized on the incident: 'A blow to the Society of Jesus.' This was taken up by Bruno Ribes in the January 1967 issue of *Etudes* in an article entitled 'A Jesuit revolution?' It left a persistent doubt hanging over the nature of the relations between the Holy See and the Society, even if, at the time that the delegates of the 31st General Congregation dispersed, any assessment seemed premature. Temporarily dispelling anxiety, Fr Arrupe found comfort in St Paul's words: 'Finally, brethren, we wish you all joy. Perfect your lives ... keep peace among yourselves, and the God of love and peace will be with you.'

While the delegates of the 'little' society of Ignatius made their way to the airport to fly off to the four corners of the earth, the General was alone. In a small chapel, near his office where he would later set up a photo of the world, the General was kneeling on the floor, deep in prayer. There, in the silent chapel, he began laying the plans of the Society's 'major strategies'. In particular those that concern what is still one of the order's principal spheres of influence: education.

THE CLOSING OF THE COLLEGES

Many Jesuits consider that the privileged action
of the Church towards youth no longer depends
on possessing one's own teaching establish-
ments but on the influence of chaplains, teachers
and educators in institutions run by others.

EDMOND VANDERMEERSCH SJ

The first seven Jesuits who, on 15 August 1534 in Montmartre, decided to consecrate their lives to the service of God and the Church did not wish to set any limit or particular objective to their promise. They were true sons of that Renaissance which pushed back the frontiers of the known world and reopened European culture to its non-Christian roots in Rome and Greece. The renewal of the Church called for an identical religious movement, a repudiation of anything that might stand in the way of men's freedom of action: there was to be no benefice of clergy, no Divine Office, no monastic life, no parish ministry; nothing that could impede their action by permanent commitments.

And yet, 25 years later, these seven companions had become several hundred in an order called the 'Society of Jesus' and their reputation was based on the most stable and organized of institutions: the colleges. In 1559, on the death of their founder, they were responsible for 42 establishments, 163 in 1579, 333 in 1608, 517 in 1626, 714 in 1710. But, as Fr Bernard Basset notes,

> Teaching, for Jesuits, was never an end in itself. They entered
> the field in the early years of the Counter-Reformation,
> when Catholic education was in a parlous position after
> the medieval structures had collapsed. Because they saw
> education as a powerful means for restoring the Catholic faith
> in Europe, the Jesuits founded and developed their colleges
> wholeheartedly The Jesuit *Ratio Studiorum* was an amalgam of
> pedagogic methods that the early Jesuits found to work. Their
> methods were reached by trial and error over many years.
> Though they themselves were all scholastically trained, in
> the traditions of the medieval schoolmen, yet, when it came
> to the rising generation, they deliberately chose a humanist
> approach. Drama, music, sundials, fireworks, geography, the

pagan classics were used without any disguise, to fashion Christian men.[7]

The English province ran colleges on the continent (St Omer, Ghent, Watten, Liège, and others) to teach schoolboys and train its own members. In 1693, of the 327 members of the province, 119 worked in England, 155 manned the Continental colleges, 40 were scattered across Europe, ten staffed the mission in Maryland, and the rest were in the more distant mission fields. After the return of the English Jesuits to their native country, and the re-establishment of the Society in 1815, efforts were concentrated on the province's famous public school Stonyhurst (founded in 1593) and the other colleges it soon opened throughout the world. By 1905, the English Jesuits administered large colleges in many places: Mount St Mary's (1842), Liverpool (1842), Glasgow (1859), Beaumont (1861), Preston (1865), Grahamstown (South Africa) (1876), Malta (1877), Georgetown (Guyana) (1880), Wimbledon (1893), Stamford Hill (1894), Bulawayo (Zimbabwe) (1896) and Leeds (1905).

At the same time, 'Continental' Jesuit teaching methods were being criticized. In 1880, the *Pall Mall Gazette* published a hostile account by an anonymous Jesuit author. He had the French educational crisis in mind, but, says Fr Basset, his assessment of the virtues and deficiencies of the Jesuit system 'was almost certainly read with care by the Victorian Jesuits, among them Gerard Manley Hopkins and other distinguished converts to the Society: Christie, Newman's companion at Littlemore; Coleridge, son of a famous judge; Hathaway, former dean of Worcester College; Walford, one-time housemaster at Eton and George Kingdon, a graduate from Cambridge, a convert well ahead of Newman's day'.

The writer accused the Jesuits of stifling any independence of spirit in their boys, and of dismissing those whom they could not curb. They were charged with too much supervision, with encouraging boys to tell tales about each other, with reducing all their students to a standard type. He does praise the Jesuits, however, for their undoubted skill as teachers and for taking trouble with the less intelligent pupils, adding 'they have a real talent for developing a boy's aptitudes'.

Whatever the truth in these remarks, in France the Society

was engaged in a bitter struggle to 're-Christianize' the sons
of the bourgeoisie. After the French Revolution and the
restoration of the Society, one of the major concerns of the
Jesuits in France was to provide Christian teaching within
a society that was steeped in Voltairean anticlericalism and
revolutionary atheism. Unable to open up establishments
again until 1850, the Jesuits taught in small seminaries that
catered for students other than future priests. With the passing
of Falloux's law[8] in 1850, Jesuit colleges multiplied. By the time
they were first banned, in 1880, there were 30 colleges, where
815 Jesuits taught 10,822 pupils. These figures take on their
real significance when placed in the schools context of the
time. In 1890 there were 17,503 students in France: in other
words the colleges catered for 62 per cent of the student
population. It is interesting to note that in 1880 there was 1
Jesuit for 13 pupils and that a hundred years later the ratio
had dropped to 1 for 58.

Did this increase in the number of colleges, which continued
into the 1870s, contradict the initial conception of the Society
by its founders? It is plausible. Or at least, if one can speak
of deviation, it is only because of the excessive importance
given by some to teaching when the Society had always had
all-embracing apostolic aspirations.

Very soon after its recognition by the Pope, the little group
of 'reformed priests' – known as 'Iniguists' or followers of
Ignatius – attracted men wishing to devote to the service of
the Church a new-found generosity and sense of God brought
about by the *Spiritual Exercises*. At the outset, Ignatius and his
companions only wanted trained theologians, as they were
themselves, to join their group. This elitist practice could not be
continued for two reasons. Firstly, calls for help came from
bishops, princes and towns throughout the Church shaken by
Renaissance humanism and the criticisms of the Reformation.
Help was needed to check heresy in Europe and to convert
the new worlds of Asia and America. For this need alone,
recruiting only theologians would not have provided enough
manpower. At the same time many young people without any
training in theology also sought to enter the Society.

Being a realist, Ignatius set up 'training centres' alongside
the universities. Originally opened for future Jesuits, these

centres soon accepted other young men eager for a good Christian and humanist education. They were not themselves teaching establishments but provided board and lodging and educational training and supervision for the students who were taught in the neighbouring universities. The training was based on practical work and 'repetitions' supervised by some of the more advanced Jesuit students – the 'assistants'. Such was their success that Jesuits were asked to set up colleges everywhere. Before long, public and ecclesiastical authorities allowed these colleges to carry out the teaching themselves and to award diplomas.

To satisfy the demand of the students the Society devised a new type of institution and a new form of training. Whereas the medieval university was an open place for lectures and debates between doctors, the Jesuit colleges were to be teaching communities. The students – all non-resident – came to attend lectures and to be coached in work methods. Above all they were subjected to continual assessment. The system was particularly effective because of the strong ties between the Jesuit teachers sharing the same project and formed in the same way.

Along with the change in structure went a change in teaching methods and subjects. The medieval university was arranged around the key subjects of theology and philosophy, with grammar, rhetoric and logic, necessary for understanding texts, being taught in the arts faculty. Law and medicine were considered of minor importance as they led directly to a professional life, rather than to clerical power.

The shock waves produced by the Renaissance came from a rediscovery of profane Latin and Greek literature and a new interest in the ancient Near Eastern languages, giving access to non-Latin Christian traditions. Consequently the arts faculties changed their role: they became non-ecclesiastical sources of knowledge where a whole population came to quench its thirst for things modern. Language skills, and the social power they accorded, became cultural objective number one. Latin and Greek would no longer be learnt for the sake of studying ecclesiastical texts and making a clerical career, but in order to master contemporary thought: following society's example, studies were to be laicized. As in Greek sculpture, man became the measure of everything: thus modern humanism was born.

Many public bodies wished to give their youth a humanist education – the key to social success. But there was no question of their founding universities which entailed doctrinal, and therefore ecclesiastical, supervision. They were not interested in theology, or even philosophy, still steeped as they were in scholasticism. The Jesuit education was exactly what they were looking for. In most cases there was no theology, just the subjects most in demand: grammar, rhetoric, logic and the great classical authors.

Why should the Jesuits – whose main aim had been rebuilding the Church weakened by Renaissance modernism and the Reformation – undertake this task? Ignatius and his companions recognized that Christianity, as a universal model for society, belonged to the past. Each baptized person must discover for himself Christianity and the type of Christian life God expects him to lead. Such was the radical message of the *Spiritual Exercises*, at odds with the traditional thinking according to which embracing Christianity necessarily implied entering a Christian community – a convent, monastery or parish.

It is difficult for us today to realize what a revolution the *Exercises* represented for the people of his time, familiar only with medieval spirituality, based on the writings of the cloistered mystics (St Bernard, Eckhart, Ruysbroeck, Julian of Norwich) or, more often, on the crude representations of heaven and hell painted on church walls or acted out in mystery plays. St Ignatius, on the other hand, wrote a practical manual of spirituality: a series of directives for examining one's conscience, praying, making basic choices for one's life, and meditating. It does not dwell on doctrine or theology, but offers a pragmatic and systematic outline of the Christian life. The aim of the exercise is to discern traces of God's action – Ignatius called it 'the Spirit of God' – in creation and human action.

The method is based on the powerful motive of human desire, but diverted from worldly things and channelled towards intellectual and spiritual exercises. It is a kind of rational psychological technique, which consists in examining one's life in every detail, in the light of Christ's exemplary life, 'relived' and 'experienced' in a physical way. It was really a premonition of psychoanalysis. When he first read the *Exercises*, the French psychologist Roland Barthes, amazed by this insistence on detail and 'book-keeping mentality', observed that 'Ignatius wishes to turn the retreat-maker into a neurotic, in order to reinforce his obsessive tendencies'.

This psychological approach to Ignatius has been taken a good deal further by W. W. Meissner, both Jesuit and Professor of Psychoanalysis at Boston College, in his recent book.[9] Examining Ignatius's ascetic tactic of *agere contra* (acting against his evil impulses), Dr Meissner writes:

> In psychoanalytical terms there are certain risks in the general approach of rooting out inordinate attachments and vices by practising the opposing virtue. An attempt to regulate libidinal desires by the mechanics of *agere contra* would seem to repress or suppress such impulses and rule them out of court – at least out of the court of conscious access. (. . .) – In the cave of Manresa, Inigo set about a program of fasts, sleepless nights, vigils, penitential practices like flagellation and inflicting pain – standard practices in the lore of ascetic spirituality – as punitive attacks on the body as the seat and source of physical desire and pleasure.

How effective were such practices? asks Meissner. In his view,

> We have reason to wonder. The techniques he proposes in the *Exercises* for implementing the *agere contra* have an obsessional quality. Repeated, frequent and detailed examinations of conscience are recommended. We are reminded of Inigo's own scrupulous torments, and the fact that these obsessional practices remained a primary feature of his spiritual teaching and activity to the end of his life. (...) Ignatius was motivated in large part by guilt. From the postconversion perspective, there was much to be guilty about: his libidinous desires and amorous adventures; his flamboyant aggression that kept sword and dagger at hand for any adventure.

Meissner's verdict is uncompromising:

> The terms of Freud's equation relating internal and external aggression seem to bear themselves out in the pilgrim's [Ignatius's] turning of his immense aggression against himself. The outcome was an overwhelming sense of guilt and the sadistic, destructive assault of the superego – reflected particularly in his pathological scrupulosity, his intensely self-punitive ascetic practices and especially his suicidal impulses.

Are there, then, any redeeming features?

One might be tempted to say that this was essentially masochism, in which Ignatius's sadistic and destructive impulses had been transformed into a punitive and self-inducing attack on himself. Undoubtedly, this transformation of instinctual derivatives was part of the picture. However, we must also consider that his ascetic effort took place in the context of a highly specific value system and in relation to a powerful and newly-formed ego ideal. In addition, Inigo de Loyola was a child of the Catholic culture of sixteenth-century Spain, both in his role as sword-swinging, amorous courtier and hidalgo, and in his role as penitential ascetic.

However one explains the inspiration of the *Exercises*, no-one can deny their potency. In Fr Basset's analysis,

This extraordinary spiritual method should not be disregarded in a true assessment of Jesuit influence. Ignatius, when he devised his scheme, was himself a layman, a recent convert, victim of scruples and fears. Far from pooh-poohing mental distress, he expected it and made allowance for it, starting his Exercises with certain basic lessons for the right ordering of one's life. (. . .) In more recent times, the spread of retreats in schools, the use of the word for quiet week-ends in the country, may have diluted the strength of the Ignatian cure. The Ignatian *Exercises*, properly performed for thirty days – even for eight days – prove an unusual and adventurous experience.[10]

To cite one example among many: John Henry Newman re-counts in his *Apologia pro vita sua* how, in the last troubled period before his conversion to Catholicism, he made the *Exercises*:

What I can speak of with greater confidence is the effect produced on me a little later by studying the *Exercises* of St Ignatius. For here again, in a matter consisting in the purest and most direct acts of religion – in the intercourse between God and the soul, during a season of recollection, of repentance, of good resolution, of inquiry into vocation – the soul was *sola cum solo*; there was no cloud interposed between the creature and the Object of his faith and love.

By his individualistic approach to God, *sola cum solo*, Ignatius was the first of the 'moderns': he bridges the gap between the

Middle Ages and the Age of Enlightenment. He was a humanist, calling his followers to holiness without leaving the world, and it was logical that the Jesuits' strategy should follow the humanist movement, however ambiguous that might be. Moreover, by setting up colleges in all big towns, they quickly became its promoters. Thus they were in direct contact with those who best typified the modern age, and were able to offer to convert to Christianity not their intellectual universe but their personal faculties: will, freedom and intelligence. The essence of the *Exercises*.

By so doing the Jesuits hoped to propose an equivalent of the Protestants' 'private judgement' in the interpretation of Scripture. The Reformation was not a refusal of Christianity but of a certain authoritarian hold exercised by the Church in order to confiscate individual religious practice. The personalized Christianity of the *Exercises* makes sense only if it leads the person making the retreat to serve others. So it is with the colleges. Training the young is not everything. The college, as an institution, must be at the service of the community that it has founded.

The Jesuit colleges were designed to be centres of influence for all sociocultural activities rather than mere teaching establishments. Besides the teachers, the college housed groups of Jesuits called upon to carry out a wider ministry: personalized Christian guidance through the *Spiritual Exercises*; the teaching of the catechism through sermons and public lessons, and popular missions to bring people back to the faith. Gradually, these activities took precedence over the teaching proper.

From 1556 to 1710, the number of colleges continued to increase but less than the Jesuits' other activities. In Europe alone, in 1556, 42 colleges represented 92 per cent of all Jesuit establishments; in 1579, 144 colleges represented 77 per cent; in 1608, 293 colleges represented 71 per cent; in 1626, 444 colleges represented 64 per cent; in 1710, 612 colleges represented 52 per cent. Furthermore, even the Jesuit teachers had to devote some of their time to apostolic duties other than teaching. Ignatius had sensed the danger of installing his men in institutions with assured income and patronage. He would not allow professed members to 'live off' the colleges by residing in them. This is a sign that, for him, teaching was just one way among many to serve a wider apostolic plan. The Society's place was out in the world, in freedom and evangelical poverty, in search of all those who await the Good News.

Nevertheless teaching was to become a compulsory assignment during the training of young Jesuits. Since they were educated to a high academic standard, they were required – while gaining this knowledge – to share it with the underprivileged. Pedagogical interest: the only true knowledge is that which one can impart to others. Ascetic interest: the 'regent' (assistant or tutor) served both the teacher and the pupils by helping the latter understand the thinking of the former.

The strategy of allowing oneself to be carried along by a cultural movement to accompany men in their spiritual search and offer them personal conversion is a risky undertaking: a humanism closed to all transcendency may well contaminate apostles rather than bring them closer to others. The Jesuits did not escape unscathed. Especially once the humanism of the Renaissance no longer inspired the renewal of a society in search of itself, but became simply the cultural background of a self-satisfied century. The Jesuit colleges reached their peak as places of evangelization and enlightenment of a progressive society in the seventeenth century. This was particularly so in France, which was at that time, by its population and power, the first nation of continental Europe, where it held a leading position, a quasi-monopoly, in the Christian and cultural field. Louis XIV's century was the golden age of French mysticism. The martyrs of New France lived and worked in Jesuit colleges before leaving to evangelize the New World.

And the New World occupies a special place in the history of the Jesuits. Today, there are 4,745 Jesuits in Canada and the United States, or approximately 20 per cent of the total membership of the Society and the greatest single continental contingent. At first sight, this 'special relationship' between Jesuits and the Americans may seem surprising. Surely the founding fathers were trying to escape the religious intolerance and theological squabbling associated with Jesuit casuistry? And yet the direct spiritual approach and methodical teaching methods of the Jesuits obviously struck a chord with the political pragmatism and no-nonsense creed of the American success story. There was an unexpected harmony between Ignatian spirituality and American realism.

And it should not be forgotten that 'young' countries, like the United States, had little idea of the Society's murky past: the Jesuits could start out with a clean slate. We have seen how, in Canada, Jean de Brébeuf and his companions underwent incredible hardship, often ending in torture and death, to convert the Iroquois Indians, and some of the French Jesuits travelled as far as the Mississippi and Louisiana. It was a hard and haphazard business: when the Society was suppressed in 1773, there were only 23 missionaries in the United States.

It was after the American War of Independence (1775–83) that the American Jesuits came into their own. Their strength lay in having accompanied the social promotion of the Catholic immigrants. In the eighteenth century the Jesuits were few in number – this was in proportion to the small number of Catholics: 30,000 in 1789 – and they led a very precarious life after the suppression of the Society. As a footnote to Jesuit history, it is interesting to note that, in 1788, thirteen ex-Jesuits in Maryland, including the future bishop John Carroll, drew up a petition asking to be attached to the Jesuits in Russia: as we have seen, the Society of Jesus was never suppressed in the Russian Empire, where several Polish Jesuit houses had been placed under the protection of Catherine the Great after the partition of Poland in 1771.

When John Carroll became the first American bishop (by democratic election, what is more) the Society no longer existed. When it was restored in 1814, Carroll thought seriously of resigning his bishopric to rejoin the order, but felt obliged to consider the interests of the fledgeling American Church. While he was busy setting up the hierarchy, the Jesuits were nurturing the faith of the immigrant population, largely Irish and Italian, in a generally hostile environment, by opening Sunday schools, colleges and universities. Today, Catholics make up over 30 per cent of the population, and half of the Catholic universities are in the hands of the Jesuits. Arriving in the United States two centuries after the creation of the Society, they opted directly for higher education, opening universities in preference to high schools.

But there is a reverse side to the coin. Those whom the Jesuits helped up the social ladder are tempted to close the door to the lower echelons of society; the Polish or the Irish who sent their children to college now dislike them mixing with Blacks or Hispanics, yet, as we have seen, the latter make up more than 40 per cent of practising Catholics. They speak Spanish and do not yet feel truly American. They are even despised in their own Church, and their integration is one of the Society's main tasks in America.

The Black problem is even more urgent. On learning that there are more Blacks in prison than in higher education, one realizes just how urgent. On the other hand, the ethnic group with the highest percentage of its children in higher education is the Irish. More than 50 per cent of young people of Irish origin are at college or university. Even Jewish children are not so well placed. It is this new educated Catholic middle class that the Society of Jesus has to convert to its new message of racial justice and peace.

And the drop in Jesuit vocations poses a dilemma to the Society. As the President of Georgetown University told me,

'The overall population of the Society has declined by about a third since its peak in the mid-1960s. In the United States, for instance, this results in drastically smaller and, in some cases, more aged Jesuit communities in high schools and universities. How can the Society respond to new apostolic challenges, thus encouraging recruitment among the young, while at the same time caring for the old and honouring its previous apostolic commitments?'

Back in Europe, the eighteenth century marked the decline of Jesuit colleges and, some historians would say, of the Society itself, fighting a losing battle against the Age of Enlightenment. In France, Jesuits, without themselves avoiding the temptations of worldliness, opposed the philosophers engaged in the Encyclopedist movement. Born of the Renaissance and its humanist ideals – which they had Christianized – the colleges were helpless when confronted with the new ideas which would sweep away not only the *Ancien Régime*, but the religious attitudes that went with it. There are no Jesuit saints in the eighteenth century.

In the nineteenth century, the Society was restored rather than reinvented. It remained loyal to the Church of the *Syllabus*, which condemned the movement of secularization, socialism and human rights. It taught the sons of the landed gentry, pious and royalist, and the sons of the reigning bourgeoisie – often Voltairean – who hoped, thanks to these old-style but reputed pedagogues, to acquire a social legitimacy that would enable them to enter high society.

The Society's aims remained apostolic: it hoped to re-Christianize the ruling class, and through it the whole of society. And by the beginning of the twentieth century it had managed to convert the elite. But mentalities had changed since the Revolution: individual liberty and free speech put the citizen at the centre of things, not a titled elite. More important, the working class was a force to be reckoned with, and the Church had lost the working class. This explains the conservatism of the colleges between 1850 and 1950: like the majority of their pupils, the Jesuits were ultramontane from a religious point of view, and politically Royalist. Instead of swimming with the stream, as they had during the Renaissance, they were struggling against the tide. The Catholic Church as a whole appeared as a besieged citadel, a ghetto threatened by the lay, republican society. And the Jesuits stood out as the staunchest defenders of the papacy.

Little wonder that the French Jesuits were forbidden to teach in 1880, and exiled once more in 1900. They opened colleges abroad, where they received the sons of the old nobility, rather as the English old Catholic landed families (the Petres, the Plowdens, the Poles, the Poultons, the Cliffords, the Arundels, the Molyneux, the Cliftons, the Staffords, the Vaughans, the Talbots, the Scarisbricks, the Mainwarings, the Mores) had sent their sons abroad in recusant times.

Many things changed in France after the Second World War. Building restrictions and a drop in vocations led the Jesuit superiors to transfer a dozen colleges to the diocesan clergy. At the same time, rethinking the causes of the decline in Christianity guided the ever-fewer Jesuits towards other fields:

the labour movement and the commitment of worker-priests, overseas missions, aid for the Third World, human sciences and chaplaincies for students whose numbers increased four-fold between 1950 and 1970. Young Jesuits spontaneously gave themselves to those tasks that they felt corresponded to the Ignatian ideal of a Christian presence in the sociocultural movements that moulded society.

On other continents – where vocations increased until 1965 – the Society's investment in teaching continued to grow proportionally, especially in higher education, in Asia and the USA. But the new awareness that followed the Council, and which was sharpened by a drop in vocations and many departures, in all parts of the world, prompted a reappraisal of an apostolic strategy that was based on traditional educational lines instead of supporting the demand for widely varying forms of inculturation. Faithful to Ignatius's apostolic intuitions, rediscovered through fresh historical analysis, the Jesuits discovered that the demanding business of running educational establishments scarcely ever served the purpose of evangelization, whilst it wore men down spiritually.

It is surely more important to announce the Gospel in the context of the social and cultural impetus that drives each man and each social group forward. After the Council, and under the inspiration of their new General, Pedro Arrupe, the Jesuits began to re-evaluate their corporate commitments worldwide. Arrupe's predecessor, Fr Janssens, had given directives mainly concerning the colleges themselves or the life within them. Fr Arrupe's attention was directed more towards the various needs of the world in relation to the organization of colleges and other educational establishments. In a letter to French Jesuits in 1965, he stressed the fact that the Society's schools had to become aware of the evolution in the Church and the surrounding human community, with all its psychological, social and cultural changes. In other words, the emphasis Paul VI placed on justice in the encyclical *Populorum progressio* and in his letter to Cardinal Roy, on social justice, had to be reflected in the content and style of education.

These reappraisals produced highly critical reports, particu-larly from Third World countries. In India, according to a 1972 statement, 'the Church appears to be a proselytizing agent, with its vast network of schools, colleges and hospitals, and completely self-confident'. In Latin America, 'the Jesuits are seen as conservatives in the service of the rich and powerful. We often counsel the people in power without questioning the values of that elite (. . .). Our schools can and must become instruments of freedom, development and social change.'

Decisions followed. In 1965, in Quebec, the Jesuits kept only two secondary schools out of six. One was handed over to lay people, two were integrated into the public system and one was closed. In 1971 it was the turn of the famous Patria College in Mexico City to be closed. New educational objectives were set for all Jesuits in Latin America: 'Equal opportunities and sharing of real educational advantages; elimination of illiteracy, parity of education in town and country; education of workforces for the common good without favouring one social class over another, education encompassing all the authentic values of each national community' (Oaxtepec document, 1971).

In 1973, in Valencia (Spain), at the international congress of Jesuit old boys, Fr Arrupe repeated these objectives firmly and precisely. His lecture, with the revealing title 'Train men to serve others', had great repercussions and a few unexpected results – the president of the Spanish old boys' association immediately handed in his resignation.

On some continents, educational institutions that differed greatly from the traditional colleges had already been set up. One such was the Fe y Alegría movement, started in 1945 by a Venezuelan Jesuit, which developed a network of semi-vocational schools in Latin American countries. Another, started by French Jesuits in Abidjan, Côte d'Ivoire, offered correspondence courses in agriculture. Schools remained a major preoccupation for many Jesuits, however, who worked hard to free them from over-academic tendencies and to satisfy new educational needs by using modern technology, such as audio-visual methods, computers, and the like.

For the Jesuits of the 1990s, school education has once again become, as in 1550, a simple means, not an end. The end is the announcement of the Gospel in the most suitable way for the needs of the time and place. These needs have changed, however. Schools now have much less influence. The aims of education have become more functional and technical. Modern society allows young people so much freedom that the future adult's education takes place through the media, group activities, sport and collective leisure pursuits, as much as, if not more than, through school and university. These considerations, added to an appreciable drop in vocations and pressing demands from other sectors within the Church and society, have persuaded Jesuits to modify the proportion and manner of their commitment to education.

This is evident worldwide. In 1973, some 10,000 Jesuits out of a total of 29,500 were involved in either full-time or part-time education. They taught 1,150,000 people in 607 universities and schools in 60 countries; that is, 337,000 pupils in primary, 343,000 in secondary, 398,000 in higher and 81,000 in adult education, plus 163,000 in the 337 Fe y Alegría centres. The number of pupils has increased steadily, both before and since 1973. World statistics at the end of the 1980s showed 3,000,000 students in 1,300 teaching establishments, including 200 universities. Conversely the number of Jesuits working in this field has been declining. In 1968 there were 11,600: roughly a third of the total number of the Society. Five years later there were just 10,000. Given the drop in numbers in nearly all provinces, it would be mathematically impossible to replace the entire 10,000 as they retired or were moved to other tasks.

Globally speaking, then, the Society is now much less involved in teaching activities than before, especially in Western, secularized countries, where vocations have dropped sharply. But it cannot be inferred from this that there has been a deliberate policy by the Jesuits to abandon their schools. It is rather a question of redistribution of manpower on a rational basis. This was made clear by Fr Peter-Hans Kolvenbach himself. On 7 June 1989, at the first General Assembly of Jesuit Higher Education in the USA, held at Georgetown University, Washington, the General spoke of the place of education among the Society's priorities, a hard-line speech which dotted all the *i*s and crossed all the *t*s in contradicting the theory of total disengagement mentioned above.

Some Jesuits are undecided and question the Society's apostolic commitment to higher education. The Society asserts that the service of the faith and the promotion of justice are the *forma omnium* (touchstone) which must be present as a priority in all our different forms of apostolate. But, this shift in our priorities is by no means an invitation to question the value of education as such. In spite of false interpretations, Decree No. 4 calls on the contrary for an intensification of our teaching apostolate!

There is no ambiguity here. It is not education that is called into question, but the way in which it should be integrated in the apostolic effort defined by the 32nd General Congregation. As Fr Kolvenbach continued,

> Instead of seeing the promotion of justice in the name of the Gospel as a threat to the educational sector, this apostolic priority we have received from the Church must be considered a pressing invitation to re-evaluate our universities and colleges.

These establishments are required to retain their 'Jesuit identity', which the General defined in the following terms:

> The Ignatian vision of the world is a vision which embraces the whole world, confronting sin, whether personal or collective, but stressing that the love of God is more powerful than evil or man's weakness. It is an altruistic vision which stresses the absolute need for discernment and allows a generous place for intelligence and feeling in the formation of superiors.

Recalling that 'the social, cultural and educational context has changed beyond recall during the last three decades', Fr Kolvenbach then outlined a number of guidelines for Jesuit teachers, as well as for 'the numerous laymen devoted to their task'. Firstly, 'No aspect of education is neutral, not even pure science. All teaching transmits values, values which can serve to promote justice.' Secondly, an 'interdisciplinary approach' must be encouraged in order to tackle 'the key questions facing men and women on the threshold of the twenty-first century. What discipline can claim alone to provide collective solutions to such precise questions as those posed by genetic research, takeover bids, the defining of human life – from beginning to end – urbanization and the housing crisis, poverty, illiteracy, progress in medical and military techniques, human rights, the environment and artificial intelligence?'

Thirdly, those engaged in the Society's teaching apostolate should 'take the initiative to collaborate with the Jesuits working full time for the direct promotion of justice'. Fourthly, since Jesuits belong to an international apostolic order, they should help 'train men and women in the service of others throughout the world'. Fifthly, this mission of world evangelization 'implies close collaboration with the Church's hierarchy, even when such collaboration seems to raise difficulties'. And sixthly, since this mission is 'closely linked to our preferential option for the poor (...), Jesuit education should be available to the underprivileged, but not exclusively'.

Finally – and bearing directly on the subject of this book – Fr Kolvenbach stated: 'I want to make one thing clear: the Jesuit community in the university does not wish to exercise power, but it should exercise its authority. Its role is to guarantee the transmission of Gospel values to the student body, since this is the distinctive mark of a Jesuit education.' A distinctive mark perhaps, but one which had been somewhat lost sight of over the centuries; Jesuit colleges have been valued more for their discipline and scholastic superiority than for their evangelical spirit.

Fr Kolvenbach returned to this theme in 1993, at an International Workshop on Ignatian Pedagogy held near Rome. He stressed once more that 'From its origins in the sixteenth century, Jesuit education has been dedicated to the development and transmission of a genuine Christian humanism.' And, after quoting Charles Dickens: 'It was the best of times, it was the worst of times, it was the spring of hope, it was the winter of despair', he concluded on an optimistic note:

> I am personally greatly encouraged by what I sense as a growing desire on the part of many in countries around the globe to pursue more vigorously the ends of Jesuit education which, if properly understood, will lead our students to unity, not fragmentation; to faith, not cynicism; to respect for life, not the raping of our planet; to responsible action based on moral judgement, not to timorous retreat or reckless attack.

NOTES

1 Emile Rideau, 'Les ordres religieux actifs', article on St Ignatius and the Society of Jesus in *Les Grands Ordres Religieux*, vol. III (Flammarion, 1980), pp. 676–7.

2 In 1980, 95 per cent of the 800 (70 Jesuit) worker-priests in France were union members as opposed to an average membership of only 25 per cent of the total workforce.

3 Mgr Roberts was also known for his biting wit. He recounts how he was pursued by a pious woman, on the ship to India, who wanted to kiss his episcopal ring. Exasperated, he proffered his left buttock to the astounded lady, saying: 'By all means! I always carry it in my hip pocket.'

4 *Itinéraire d'Henri Perrin* (Editions du Seuil, 1958).

5 H. Perrin is referring to General J.-B. Janssens's instruction of 10 October 1949, on the social apostolate of the Society of Jesus.

6 François Varillon, *Beauté du monde et souffrance des hommes* (Editions du Centurion, 1980).

7 Bernard Basset SJ, *The English Jesuits, from Campion to Martindale* (London, Burns and Oates, 1967).

8 Count Frédéric de Falloux was a French politician responsible for the law permitting private education.

9 W. W. Meissner SJ, MD, *Ignatius of Loyola: The Psychology of a Saint* (Yale University Press, 1992).

10 *The English Jesuits*.

PART III

A CHURCH WITHIN THE CHURCH?

1

Black Pope versus white

A MAN WITH A DESTINY: PEDRO ARRUPE

> *Take Christ out of my life and everything would*
> *fall apart, like a body from which the skeleton,*
> *the heart and the head had been removed.*
> PEDRO ARRUPE

> *Time and again, our origins, our studies and our*
> *backgrounds 'shield' us from poverty, and even*
> *from the worries of everyday life. We have access*
> *to certain powers that are denied to others.*
> 32ND GENERAL CONGREGATION

The principle of 'subsidiarity', by which the superior must not do what the subordinate is capable of carrying out, was particularly applied in the Society after Father Arrupe's election. Devoid of all authoritarianism, he ruled the Society by example, placing complete trust in his colleagues. It is obviously a more demanding form of command than coercion, but also more evangelical. The drawbacks, if any, of Father Arrupe's method came from his 'incorrigible optimism' – his own words – in regard to the future of the world, the Church and young people. In short, he believed in 'Providence'. In 1981, the French Provincial described Fr Arrupe thus:

No dogmatism mars his thinking, which remains open
to the grace of God that acts through the complexity of
temperaments and situations. He respects institutions, as
does anyone who is aware that the decisions he takes will
affect the destiny of others; but he seeks, and always finds,

a way of reaching each individual to show him the path to freedom.[1]

Freedom is indeed the key word for understanding the personality of the man largely responsible for the change of course taken by the Society in the mid-1960s. But what is more dangerous than respect for freedom? Not everyone, understandably, appreciated the General's backing of his colleagues in all circumstances, even when they had made mistakes. His refusal to resort to the use of authority and power never faltered. The last three Popes reproached him mainly for just this: they called him 'weak' because his style of authority differed from theirs. To understand what was behind the long quarrel between 'black Pope' and 'white Pope', it is necessary to start by describing Pedro Arrupe, that 'little man parachuted to the head of the Society of Jesus in 1965', to borrow his own words again.

His character is certainly relevant to our theme: the 'power' exerted by the Jesuits could not but change with the arrival of Fr Arrupe on the scene. In the past it was identified with legitimate authority (that of the Pope or the king), but now it took the guise of a counter-force to the ruling power, questioning the established order rather than taking control of it. The shift in style was slow, uncertain, never quite universal, but it finished by making its way into almost the whole body of the Society. Fr Arrupe's strength was that of the (seemingly) weak, of the unarmed; a spiritual strength even more formidable than brute force.

The 27th successor to Ignatius of Loyola was born in Bilbao on 14 November 1907 into a staunchly Catholic family: 'A truly holy mother, an exemplary father, closely united brothers and sisters; in short, a warm and happy family background.'[2] Pedro was the youngest, and the only boy, of five children. Their architect father, Marcelino Arrupe, became one of the founders of the Catholic newspaper *La Gaceta del Norte*, out of religious conviction.

When he was ten, Pedro Arrupe's mother died. After his primary and secondary education in his native town, he went to Madrid to study medicine. He was eighteen when he lost his father too. While devoting himself 'ardently' to his studies, he and some friends joined the St Vincent de Paul movement, then rapidly developing in Madrid. Every day the students visited impoverished families on the outskirts of the town. The future Jesuit General, on his own admission, discovered an entirely new world; this experience greatly affected his subsequent decisions. For the first time in his life, Pedro Arrupe came into contact with poverty and children who ate only once a day. A spectre that was to haunt him:

> It was thus that there took root in me a growing desire to help others and the determination to assist not only all those poor people we met on those visits, but many others . . .[3]

As a young man, Pedro Arrupe was neither lukewarm nor colourless. He loved the theatre, music and the opera. Preferring scientific works to literature, he quickly obtained his diplomas in anatomy and therapeutics. Out of curiosity when visiting Lourdes in February 1926, he got permission to attend the tests carried out by the Medical Board officially set up to examine claims of miraculous cures. At medical school, the staff and students used to speak of the 'hoaxes' of Lourdes. But for Pedro it was, one might say, a literal *coup de grâce*. So impressed was he by the atmosphere in Lourdes that he decided to enter the Society of Jesus. On 15 January 1927 he stepped over the threshold of the novitiate in Loyola.

Bilbao, Madrid, Lourdes, Loyola: the journey was just beginning. Chance would soon shape the international nature of Arrupe's life. From his very first days as a novice he had a clear vision of a missionary vocation in Japan. However, in February 1932, the Spanish Republican Government ordered the dissolution of the Jesuits. Arrupe was exiled to Belgium, the Netherlands and the United States to continue his studies in philosophy and theology. In 1938, after two laconic replies from Fr General Ledochowski, asking him to be patient and to test his missionary vocation still further, he finally received the much-awaited letter: 'After having examined your request before the Lord and having discussed it with your Provincial, I intend sending you to the Japanese mission.'[4]

The young priest's career could well have followed a very different path. Pedro Arrupe was asked to take part in an international congress on eugenics which was held in Vienna in 1936. He made two speeches that apparently drew the attention of several world-famous experts. Ordained priest on 30 July the same year, he set off for the States with the idea of specializing in psychiatry. He was received somewhat coldly by the New York Provincial: 'Psychiatry? No, no. All the Jesuits who want to study psychiatry need to see a psychiatrist themselves!'[5]

Pedro Arrupe was far from unbalanced. Order, counter-order? He toed the line and waited. While in the USA he carried out his 'third year' or tertianship, the final period of study and reflection before making one's solemn vows in the Society. It was there, in Cleveland, that he received Fr Ledochowski's letter giving him permission to go to Japan, fulfilling the desire that medicine and psychiatry had almost made him forget. Pedro Arrupe spent his last three months in America visiting Spanish-speaking prisoners in a New York penitentiary.

Prison life, moreover, was to become familiar to Pedro Arrupe from the inside also. Newly arrived in Japan, 21 hours from Tokyo by train, he was in an isolated outpost when Japan declared war. Coming from the USA and speaking very little Japanese, Arrupe was suspected of spying and imprisoned. He spent a month in a cell in Yamaguchi.

> I spent days and nights in the cold of December, entirely alone, without a bed or a table, or anything (...). I learnt a lot during that period: the value of silence, of solitude, of severe poverty, of the interior dialogue with 'the guest of my soul'. I think it was the most instructive month of my life.[6]

An even more brutal experience was in store for him. In 1942, Pedro Arrupe was made novice master at Nagatsuka, four miles from Hiroshima. On 6 August 1945, he witnessed the explosion of the first atomic bomb used in warfare.

At five o'clock that morning, an American B-29 plane flew over the town. A routine flight. The inhabitants had nicknamed it the 'American Mail'. It had passed overhead every day since the beginning of the air raids but had dropped only one shell. Hiroshima was a quiet town, spared by the war. Seven fifty-five: a fresh alert. The sirens warned of an approaching enemy aircraft. Nothing to worry about. Eight ten: the sirens' wailing stopped and the roads started to stir again; life, barely disrupted by the alarms, carried on as usual. Five minutes later, said Fr Arrupe,

> a gigantic flare, like a magnesium flash, suddenly leapt into the sky. I was in my office with another Jesuit. The sight made me leap from my chair and run to the window. At that instant, a sort of dull continuous roaring reached our ears. It sounded more like the roar of a waterfall than the sudden explosion of a bomb. The house shook. The windows shattered into a thousand pieces, the doors and windows were torn off their hinges and the sliding partitions typical of Japanese houses, made of reeds and dried mud, broke up as though they had been struck by a giant hand.[7]

The monster's hand had turned everything upside-down. And yet, in the house, the 35 Jesuits were unharmed. At just a few miles from the epicentre no-one was even injured. Astounded to find no sign of a crater caused by the mysterious bomb, the priests climbed a nearby hill from where there was a good view of Hiroshima. But the town was no more. All that they could see was a burning plain.

What on earth was this new invention of human madness? Like all the other witnesses of this tragedy, Pedro Arrupe had no inkling of the terrifying truth. His immediate reaction was in keeping with his personality: he first went to the half-destroyed chapel and then set about transforming the novitiate into a makeshift hospital. All the members of the household followed their superior's lead. Arrupe, the ex-medical student, summoned up his half-forgotten knowledge while collecting the contents of the medicine chest: 'a little iodine, a few aspirins, citric acid and bicarbonate of soda'. Against the effects of the atom bomb.

A crowd of refugees, with burnt, disfigured and mutilated bodies, was already trying to make its way, sometimes on hands and knees, towards the Jesuits' home. Everyone told the same story: 'I saw a bright light, then heard a terrible explosion ... and that's all. Nothing else happened to me.' Nothing else. In actual fact, their tissues were badly burned by atomic radiation. Tiny blisters formed on the skin; four or five hours later they became running sores. In some cases the after-effects appeared very much later. Hiroshima is still licking its wounds today.

On that terrible day of 6 August, heavy rain, brought on by
the bombing, started to fall on the smouldering town. Pedro
Arrupe and a few companions decided to make their way to
another Jesuit house in the middle of Hiroshima. The sights
were beyond belief. Thousands of bodies cut to pieces, a child
dying between white-hot beams, and from all around came the
unbearable screams of the injured. Arrupe's little group took
five hours to reach the five Jesuits who lived in the town.
Amazingly, although they were all injured, not one was fatally
so. The walk back to the novitiate – turned hospital – took a
painful seven hours. During one involuntary rest the group
heard the faint murmuring of someone dying. They searched
under the ruins of a building, but without success. Suddenly
one of the Jesuits called out: 'There he is, father! We're walking
on him.'[8]

During the following weeks Pedro Arrupe became a surgeon,
operated with rough and ready equipment, confronted disgust,
fear, failure and death. He seemed able to withstand the
onslaughts of the apocalypse without flinching. His keenest
emotion was felt many years later in Colombia when he saw
an American film on the events of 6 August 1945. He was unable
to go on watching and had to leave the cinema.

He found it much more difficult to remain detached on
a spiritual plane. The day after the explosion he celebrated
Mass at five in the morning, before helping the sick and
burying the dead. The chapel was full of bodies stretched
out on the floor. In that suffering congregation there was
not a single Christian. *Dominus vobiscum.* How could one
pronounce those words in such a place? Could God really be
with men in that cataclysm? Pedro Arrupe was unable to
move; he stood, with his arms raised, as though paralysed,
gazing at that terrible human tragedy. But the Mass continued.
By celebrating Mass under such Dantean conditions Pedro
Arrupe was close to Teilhard de Chardin. He clung to his
faith in Christ. 'Remove Christ from my life and everything
would collapse – like a body from which the skeleton, heart
and head have been taken out', Fr Arrupe would say over 35
years later.[9]

The ordeal of Hiroshima did not shake Pedro Arrupe's
determination. He stayed on in Japan and became the Jesuit

Provincial in 1954. It was in this capacity that he was called to Rome to elect Fr Janssens's successor at the time of the 31st General Congregation. Fr Arrupe was virtually unknown in Europe when he was elected General of the Society of Jesus on 22 May 1965. Wide circles of Jesuits and the public at large discovered a friendly, jovial man, who was always ready to talk to the sensation-hungry press, and to laugh and joke.

The new General liked to listen, discover new subjects, encourage initiative. His pet hates were lukewarmness and empty verbosity. 'The world (...) is swamped with words and speeches. It wants facts.' It was not feigned unity or an artificial sense of obedience that Arrupe demanded from his priests, but rather a way of behaving that displayed total belief in the Gospel, warm affection and availability.

'Jesuits hate hero worship', Fr Arrupe told his colleague Jean-Claude Dietsch when explaining his style of command. The General started by rearranging the austere building of the *Curia generalis* (the Jesuit Curia in Rome), to make it as gay and as informal as possible. Setting up a bar within the walls of the grim Jesuit headquarters and putting small tables in the refectory, with no special place for the General, may be mere details but they are significant. Dialogue, consultation and information characterized the human aspect of the Arrupe style. Although authority remained centralized it became more and more identified with discussion. Four assistant generals elected by the General Congregation; twelve regional assistants representing every corner of the world; and fifteen bureaus and secretariats make up the central administration. Every year the Curia receives some 17,000 letters which the General obviously cannot read personally. All the mail nonetheless reaches the General's desk in the form of summaries prepared by the assistants and secretarial staff. Moreover a crucial rule allows every Jesuit to write to the General in person. Any such letters will arrive on his desk in their unopened envelopes.

A climate of confidence based on personal relations, pointed out Fr Arrupe, is not only a basis for power in the Society but also 'the most dynamic force for government'. The main element of Pedro Arrupe's 'politics' was to encourage initiative without stifling sensitivity, within a global vision of the needs of the Church and the world. This led him to travel around frequently to judge emergencies for himself, to decide which works and charities to promote and how to help bring projects to a successful conclusion. When the 32nd General Congregation opened in 1975, the General already knew personally over 200 of the 236 delegates who arrived in Rome.

Arrupe's method was also demanding. One day the General wanted to meet the new director – a young inexperienced priest – of one of the Society's institutions, and suggested an appointment in Rome. The date coincided with a wedding that had been booked for some weeks. The priest was not prepared to change the arrangements, even to obey the General. He promptly informed Rome. The reply came back immediately: your ceremony finishes at such a time, so it is possible to get to the airport, catch a plane and still be with me at the time stated. The young priest was there on time.

Thus modern technology can serve obedience; as it also does fraternity. The Jesuits have always been a little nostalgic for the days of the first companions, who were ever ready to meet, discuss and plan the future. When dispersed throughout the world, it is more difficult to form close ties, but air travel does help. Pedro Arrupe built up quite a reputation as a globetrotter, even if he did try, with some irony, to play down the number of his trips: 'In comparison with my colleagues in other religious orders, I think I must be, of all the members of the Union of Superiors, the one who travels the least.'[10] All the same, he managed to clock up an impressive number of air miles per year.

In 1968, for example, he went to Austria early in February, visiting Vienna and Innsbruck. He gave a talk to former pupils, met two-thirds of the Austrian Jesuits and attended receptions given by civil and religious authorities. April: off to Brazil, where he spent a whole month travelling around the country. Hours of talks with communities, question and answer sessions, daily sermons. The Society of Jesus Yearbook paid tribute to the airlines, which 'kept perfectly to schedule and enabled the General to get from one part of that enormous country to another in a minimum of time'.

Back from Brazil on 15 May, the General was off to Yugoslavia next on 10 June. Zagreb, Maribor, Ljubljana, Split, Dubrovnik and Belgrade. Here Fr Arrupe spoke in German, there in

English peppered with a few Italo-Hispanic expressions; else-where again he used French and gave a sermon in Latin. During a university meeting the students questioned him and told him of their wishes and what they expected from the Society: 'We need more priests for our group.' Fr Arrupe quickly retorted: 'Fine, but give us some novices.' At that time, there were nearly 300 Jesuits in the two Provinces of Croatia and Slo-venia.[11] The year was not over yet: on 22 August the General took off for Colombia to attend the Eucharistic Congress and the Medellín Conference, which was to have a decisive effect on the future of the whole Church in Latin America. Various meetings were arranged to fit in with his commitments so that he could encounter some of the 694 Jesuits working in that country.[12]

Between journeys, work continued in Rome. In November 1967, always attentive to world events, the General wrote a letter on racial problems, which didn't pass unnoticed, to the Jesuits in the United States:

> The bloody race riots that recently took place in the United
> States are a tragic warning of the danger that threatens this
> country, unless effective measures are taken, rapidly and in
> good faith, to suppress social injustice and blatant poverty.

The victims of racism are clearly identified: the Mexicans in the South West, Puerto Ricans in New York and Chicago, Indians in the reserves in the West, agricultural workers and, of course, the large Black minority.

Fr Arrupe does not hide the failings of his order: 'Our social services for the Blacks are not what they ought to be.' A few exceptions, such as John Lafarge and John Marko, saved the order's reputation, 'but, during the last few decades (. . .), the Society has increasingly tended to identify itself with the middle classes, i.e. with only one sector of the population'. Each Jesuit was asked to examine his conscience carefully.

> Too many Jesuits are cut off from the lifestyle of the poor,
> and therefore of the majority of Blacks ... We have not yet
> fully understood that, since it is at the service of the whole of
> humanity, the Society is especially at the service of Christ's
> poor.

At the time this hard-hitting letter was written, there were more than 8,000 American Jesuits,[13] divided into ten Provinces,

each running several schools and universities. The General did
not underestimate the very considerable influence of this vast
teaching organization. It must be used, he said, for conferences and debates on free access for all, regardless of race or
colour, to housing, work, social advancement, hygienic conditions, urban development and, naturally, for the integration
of qualified Blacks on the teaching and administrative staff of
Jesuit institutions.

Several months later, on 14 April 1968, Fr Arrupe sent another
letter, this time addressed to all members of the Society. It
dealt with internal problems relating to 'poverty, work and
communal life'. The scale of values, the use and distribution
of goods could not remain such as they were at the time of
Ignatius. How could one remain faithful to the original spirit
and still have large teaching establishments? How was one to
invest in scientific research, earn a living in secular jobs, run
magazines, set up training centres and put life into communities without giving in to the temptation of financial gain, to
profitability for its own sake? Furthermore, inequalities arose
between communities and between members of a community,
because of differences in salary. Fr Arrupe stressed the principle of sharing goods completely, without which the spirit of
poverty is devoid of substance: 'No superior in the Society can
tolerate the practice of private property.'

On 8 September 1973, the cry rang out: 'Action stations!'
The General convened the 32nd General Congregation. On
that occasion, Fr Arrupe asked all Jesuits to reflect on the
demands made by new apostolic needs in the midst of a
rapidly changing Church and world and consider how to attain
better 'spiritual, intellectual and structural' conditions, capable
of meeting future challenges.

The General's decision was neither unexpected nor a mere
whim. Since 1970, the need for a new, carefully prepared General Congregation had been making itself felt in nearly all the
provinces. 'Adaptation', the Society's great principle, needed
to find a common voice. History waits for no man, and the
Jesuits, in this case, are not prepared to lag behind. More
often than not, they prefer to be one step ahead. The German
Jesuit theologian Karl Rahner remarked several months before
the meeting opened that the Church's metamorphosis 'came

about suddenly, with all the abnormalities and the dangers of indispensable mutations that have to "catch up" too quickly'. Such a process was necessary, however, if the Church did not want to remain a rural, petit-bourgeois institution, typical of ancient Europe, with an ever diminishing membership. This transformation equally affected the Society of Jesus. The only difficulty, once that fact was accepted, was that the future was uncharted territory; there were no 'fine Ordnance Survey maps, with all the roads clearly marked', said Rahner drily.

New pathways had therefore to be found. The 32nd General Congregation was opened on 3 December 1974, with this in mind. Having gathered 237 participants representing the 68 Provinces and 22 Vice-provinces of the Society of Jesus, it sat until 7 March 1975. Its originality was to stress repeatedly the link between evangelization and the advancement of justice, service to the Church and service to man. Not simply an artificial or tactical link, but a real, indissoluble one. The delegates were convinced that Christian hope 'is not an opium, but a driving force towards a firm and realistic commitment to change the world and, in so doing, call attention to the other world'. Christian salvation and human liberation coincide, making the world a better place to live in.

The 32nd General Congregation's fourth decree, 'the service of faith and the promotion of justice', defined the new fundamental criteria for Jesuit action. Its drafting was extremely difficult and time-consuming, but it remains today the essential text of reference for its definition of the Society's style, approach and priorities. Jesuits must feel and show solidarity with all those who are victims of injustice in any form. This solidarity is not easy because

> our origins, our studies and our backgrounds often 'shield' us from poverty, and even from the worries of everyday life. We have access to certain forms of power that are denied to others.

The power brought by education, relations and security. To act on the structures of society constitutes an 'apostolic objective' because it affects men's normal everyday life, the only one that really matters.

> We must therefore work to change the attitudes and opinions that breed injustice and sustain the structures of oppression.

Drafted by several commissions, revised and adopted by the members of the 32nd General Congregation, Decree 4 nonetheless reflects one of the major aspects of Fr Arrupe's thinking. The Society's originality, he had told the congress of former Jesuit pupils in April 1973, 'is not the spirit of [the Council of] Trent but fidelity to God's historic call which, at that particular time, invited the Society to adopt that spirit'. The same attitude is required today of Jesuits in the face of violence and political and social oppression. Their behaviour must constantly combine 'personal conversion and structural reform':

> If it is necessary to fight our evil tendencies and the consequences of sin, why should we not also fight those 'institutional' sins that affect us all through social structures? There is no serious theological reason for making a differentiation.

Decree 4 did not remain merely theoretical. It was behind the Society's engagement in the struggles and conflicts in Latin America and in the resistance to the Marcos regime in the Philippines; but it also inspired the reappraisal of Jesuit commitment to the privileged classes. The study of economics, politics and social science has become an essential part of the training of young members in the Society. Action and lucidity are inseparable:

> The commitment to the promotion of justice and to solidarity with the voiceless and powerless, demanded by our faith in Jesus Christ and our mission to announce the Gospel, should incite us to inform ourselves thoroughly about the problems they encounter, then to recognize and assume our responsibility in tackling their social situation.

This decree about the Jesuit mission today, combining service of faith and promotion of justice, was followed by a decree on 'inculturation'. The commission detailed to study this theme had first coined the term 'indigenization'. The neologism finally adopted, 'inculturation', is hardly more elegant but does convey rather better a process that the Society has long been experimenting with: how does one implant the Gospel tradition and Christian dogma into each culture, without destroying it? How does one become a Christian without being excluded from one's own culture? Decree 5, on 'inculturation of the Faith', is the shortest of the 32nd General Congregation. All it does, practically, is to call to mind the Society of Jesus's missionary endeavours – let us not forget people like Ricci and Nobili – and ask of the General that 'this work [of inculturation] be carried out with even greater vigour'.

Fr Arrupe took this mandate very seriously. In his eyes, the danger run by the 'Latinized' West was the result of an unawareness of the need for inculturation. The Church takes root in a specific historical context. Christ himself was a Jew and his faith was expressed through the culture of his people. In the sixteenth century, the Church had opted for a particular form of Christian inculturation in the context of the Counter-Reformation, the Renaissance, Roman and Latin predominance in theology and the European conquest of newly-discovered lands overseas. Today, it is necessary to break with the spirit of colonialism and neocolonialism and to abandon the 'cultural imperialism' which the Church finds so difficult to get rid of.

Missionary expansion and the refusal to give undue importance to any given culture began to change attitudes. After the 32nd General Congregation, Pedro Arrupe was convinced that no cultural value 'could be ignored or destroyed: each one must be valued and accepted'.[14] This outlook and method were quite novel: 'It is a matter of giving up our superiority complex and monopoly of forms of expression.'[15] Europe no longer stamps the whole world with its trademark. The centres of gravity have shifted. Moreover, according to Fr Arrupe, 'it is enforced uniformity, not variety, that creates divisions'.[16] Even if these divisions do not lead to violent confrontation, they give rise to formidable tensions, difficult to cope with, such as pluralist demands in the face of centralist tendencies, national sensitivity against Latin tradition, a clash between ancient civilizations and 'the over-Westernized, paternalistic and complacent presentation' of the Catholic faith and, finally, tension between bold experiments and the patience required to avoid splitting the Church. Inculturation is the guiding principle which allows each culture to express itself within the Church, to voice the same faith in a different way.

The Society showed a significant change in strategy here. Inculturation is to contemporary evangelization what the 'conversion of the elite' was to previous centuries. In an Easter message that he sent to all Jesuits in 1978, Fr Arrupe maintained that inculturation was more than a theoretical knowledge of new ways of thinking or the discovery of traditional cultures, it was 'the experiential assimilation of the lifestyle of the groups with which they were working, such as drop-outs, immigrants, inhabitants of inner city areas, intellectuals, students and artists'. According to him, many Jesuits, especially those in the developed countries, are not aware of 'the gulf separating faith and culture' among the young. This was another field of exploration where calculated risks must be taken to reduce the gap between evangelization and society.

Pedro Arrupe was thinking particularly of the Society's new ventures. On 3 December 1973, in spite of his reservations about the order, Paul VI had acknowledged that

> Everywhere in the Church, in the most advanced and difficult
> fields of action, at the crossroads of different ideologies, in
> those social sectors where man's most pressing needs confront
> the permanent message of the Gospel – there Jesuits have
> been, and always will be found ...

This Good Conduct medal could only encourage the General to lead his troops to the battle front. There were so many perils to face, such as the problems of atheism and Marxism, and confrontation with Islam.

During the Bishops' Synod on the family, held in Rome in 1980, Fr Arrupe spoke about drugs rather than theoretical problems affecting family stability. Several months earlier, at Christmas 1979, he had sent telegrams to some twenty Major Superiors to ask what could be done to help refugees. Arrupe was deeply distressed by the plight of the boat people and could not remain inactive. With the encouragement of the Society he founded the Jesuit Refugee Service. Later he decided that material aid was not enough. It was necessary, he said, to go to the root of the problem. 'The Society's special grace is to invest its manpower in the fields of theology, philosophy and sociology, to study the tragic examples of misunderstandings within societies ...'[17]

The path taken by Fr Arrupe before involving his Society in the Refugee Service is typical of him. In 1979, a meeting was arranged at the Society's General Curia. Taking part were not only members of the order but also Robert McNamara, manager of the World Bank, Aurelio Peccei, founder of the Club of Rome, and many other leading figures. McNamara pointed out that 15,000 people were dying of starvation every day. He told Fr Arrupe that although solutions existed they were obstructed by the selfishness of countries. It was the same situation for refugees, whose numbers at the time were estimated at 16 million. The logical conclusion drawn by Arrupe went as follows: the Society's tradition and its Constitutions required it to work for the propagation of the faith, certainly, but also for the reconciliation of enemies. Collating political analysis and the aims of the Society convinced Fr Arrupe that it was necessary to act. Not only had the refugee problem not been solved but the situation was getting worse: 'We cannot accept this state of affairs', he concluded. Furthermore, Decree 4 of the 32nd General Congregation on the service of faith and the promotion of justice gave him the legal backing he needed. The decision was made:

> Our option for the poor leads us to the refugees, who
> are the least privileged of all . . . We must be ready to go
> anywhere . . . We often talk of 'insertion' – here is an excellent
> opportunity to put it into practice!

The General allowed nothing to stand in his way. Had not the provinces already drawn up their apostolic plans? The Society's distinctive feature is mobility, not advance planning. Shortage of men? Look for volunteers and they will be found. And they were. Funding? 'Money and management are already in place thanks to the various organizations.' The Jesuit Refugee Service now works closely with the United Nations High Commission for Refugees. Operations have been mounted in Ethiopia, Zaïre, Chad, Zambia, Zimbabwe, Indonesia, Hong Kong and in several camps in Thailand. And, more recently in Somalia, Rwanda, Haiti, Cuba . . .

Fr Arrupe was to spend his last day's work as Jesuit General in Bangkok. That was 6 August 1981. On his way back from a visit to the Philippines, he had stopped off to see for himself the work the priests were doing among the refugees of that region. Some fifteen Jesuits were present at the meeting. The General did not simply encourage their undertaking, he repeated his position on the Society's place in the Church and society:

> I beg you to realize that when the Society enters a new field, the first reaction is one of mistrust! The Society is feared everywhere. 'These Jesuits are cunning so-and-sos!' people think. 'And so powerful!' But, as I remarked the other day at the Ateneo in Manila: we are not as bad as people say, but neither are we as good as others think! No, we are ordinary people – ordinary in the sense that we are not geniuses. There are perhaps geniuses in the Society, but they are few and far between! It was said of old that the great strength of the Society lay in its well-trained mediocrity ... According to the thinking of St Ignatius, excellence is not intellectual excellence, although it can be. But our true excellence is our self-sacrifice. That, in my opinion, is what is paramount.

Fr Arrupe then called on his listeners to pray intensely: 'We have so many meetings and reunions but we do not pray enough.' 'What I am telling you are things I wish to stress', he added, saying that his message was 'perhaps my swan song for the Society'.

A remarkable premonition. Once the meeting was over Pedro Arrupe flew back to Rome. On arrival at Fiumicino airport, on the morning of 7 August 1981, he had a stroke causing paralysis on one side and an almost total loss of speech. The tireless traveller was from then on condemned to an armchair in a small room in the Curia infirmary. On 10 August, in accordance with the Society's constitution, he appointed Fr Vincent O'Keefe as vicar-general to stand in for him during his illness or until the election of a new General.

Two months later, on 6 October, the Society's 'Consult' (council), composed of the General's Assistants and Fr O'Keefe, was in session when the porter received a telephone call from the Secretariat of State to say that Cardinal Casaroli would arrive at midday with a message from the Pope for Fr Arrupe. The Secretary of State did not ask to see any other member of the Society. Nonetheless, Fr O'Keefe met the cardinal and accompanied him to the patient's room. There Mgr Casaroli asked the vicar-general to leave. The visit lasted just a few minutes.

Then, without saying a word, the Cardinal was escorted to the exit. When Vincent O'Keefe returned to Fr Arrupe's room he found the Pope's letter lying on a small table. The General was crying.

NOTES

1 *Pedro Arrupe: L'espérance ne trompe pas* (Paris, 1981), with an introduction by Fr Henri Madelin.
2 Ibid.
3 Ibid.
4 Quoted in *Pedro Arrupe, itinéraire d'un Jésuite* (Paris, 1982).
5 Ibid. The provincial's reply is reminiscent of Samuel Goldwyn's famous retort on learning that one of his actresses wanted to consult a psychoanalyst: 'Anyone who wants to see a psychiatrist should have his head examined.'
6 *Itinéraire d'un Jésuite.*
7 *Ibid.*
8 *Ibid.*
9 *Ibid.*
10 *L'espérance ne trompe pas.*
11 By 1994, this number had dropped to 255.
12 By 1994, this number had dropped to 382.
13 By 1994, this number had dropped to 4,261.
14 *L'espérance ne trompe pas.*
15 Ibid.
16 Ibid.
17 Ibid.

2

Conflict with the papacy

It is not likely that the Pope would persecute the Society, which is very much his own and is devoted to his service, although in itself such a thing is possible.

IGNATIUS OF LOYOLA

In his letter of 6 October 1981, John Paul II informed the Jesuit General of his decision to appoint a 'personal representative' to the Society. The person chosen was Fr Paolo Dezza, an 80-year-old Italian Jesuit and a confidant of the Pope. Another Italian Jesuit was appointed as 'assistant delegate' – 53-year-old Fr Giuseppe Pittau, a former rector of Sophia University in Tokyo, then Provincial of Japan. The two men were to be principally responsible for preparing the General Congregation.

Even if, in theory, Fr Arrupe retained all the prerogatives of his office, the Pope's unexpected intervention indicated a scathing repudiation of his policies. How else interpret the dismissal of Vincent O'Keefe, who had been chosen by his peers with the General's approval to run the Society during Arrupe's illness, and his replacement by a man entirely devoted to the Pope?

That infringement of the internal rules of the Society left no further place for doubt: John Paul II was indicating his intention of taking control of the Society of Jesus by closely supervising the election of Fr Arrupe's successor. And while his gesture lacked elegance, he knew that he could count on unwavering fidelity from the General and his assistants. The 'fourth vow' would hold.

In spite of this famous vow, by which Jesuits making their

solemn profession of faith put themselves more especially at the Pope's service – or perhaps precisely because of it – relations between the Society of Jesus and the Holy See have in fact often been far from calm. This vow does not imply a promise of blind obedience to the Pope, but a total commitment to the service of the universal Church. After the three traditional vows of poverty, chastity and obedience, the professed Jesuit adds: 'In addition, I vow special obedience to the Supreme Pontiff with regard to missions.' The strict object of the vow is extremely limited and very rarely called upon since it is reserved for any special mission assigned by the Pope. However, one should not underestimate the importance, in the initial vocation of Ignatius and his colleagues, of their decision to be at the disposal of the Vicar of Christ, regarding missions. On the other hand, Popes have often overstepped their rights in considering the Society as an instrument of their policies, or even as a private army, dedicated to their person.

It was not the first time, then, that a Pope had intervened in the internal government of the Society. As already mentioned, during Ignatius's life, Paul IV wanted to reimpose a sung, choral office[1] and to abolish life tenure for the General. Later, Pius V continued to call for the re-establishment of the choral office. As for Sixtus V, he wanted the Society to drop the name 'Jesus', 'blind obedience' and 'account of conscience' to be abolished, and certain requirements of poverty to be reduced. But it was clearly Clement XIV who went furthest of all, by purely and simply abolishing the order itself.

'A thousand complaints have been lodged against these religious, who were denounced to our predecessors Paul IV, Pius V and Sixtus V by many, including several princes', wrote Clement XIV in his papal brief *Dominus ac Redemptor*. 'All our predecessors have been greatly distressed', he went on, recalling the fruitless efforts of Innocent XI, Innocent XIII and Benedict XIV, who deplored 'so many disputes, upheavals, and such horrible turmoils'. There was only trouble, dissension, 'very dangerous' sedition, 'and even scandals which led to hate and enmity among the faithful'. The kings of France, Spain, Portugal and the Two Sicilies had found themselves 'forced' to banish Jesuits from their kingdoms, insisted Clement XIV, explaining that it was the

kings who, with a view to appeasement, had asked for
the order to be abolished, as had many bishops and many
leading dignitaries. This was why, wrote the Pope: 'After
mature examination of the facts at our disposal, invoking
the fullness of our apostolic power, we hereby suppress
and abolish the Society of Jesus. We cancel and annul each
and every one of its offices, functions and administrations,
houses, schools, colleges, retreats, hospices, statutes, customs,
decrees, Constitutions, even those that have been confirmed
and approved . . .'

By signing that death warrant on 21 July 1773, Clement XIV
was bowing to the pressure of the kings of Portugal, Spain
and France: at the conclave that had elected him, representatives of the Bourbon dynasties had insisted that the *papabili*
promise, once elected, to abolish the Society of Jesus. That
not very glorious episode for the papacy would be harshly
judged by posterity. Here, for example, is what the English
Catholic historian Christopher Hollis has to say in his history
of the Jesuits:

> Sometimes, to defend Clement XIV, it is claimed that he did
> not accuse the Jesuits in his Brief *Dominus ac Redemptor*. He
> merely says that others, throughout history, have brought
> accusations against the Society. This is true, but he repeats the
> accusations as though he believed them. His major complaint
> is that, wherever Jesuits are to be found, disorder reigns.
> There is not the slightest allusion to the fact that the Jesuits
> were attacked for having defended the papacy ceaselessly for
> two centuries. A Pope might at least have had the honesty to
> mention it.
>   The Brief is written in a particularly unpleasant, snivelling
> and obsequious style. (. . .) As Cardinal Antonelli, Prefect
> of Propaganda, would say subsequently to Pius VI who
> questioned him after the death of his predecessor: 'The final
> judgement and the execution of the Brief broke every law.
> The Brief is founded on nothing but accusations easily refuted
> and shameful slanders. The Brief contradicts itself (. . .) and
> contradicts and annuls, as far as it can, many bulls and
> Constitutions signed by the Holy See, received and recognized
> by the whole Church, without giving a motive. These reasons
> are sufficient to prove that the Brief is null and void.' It is not
> easy to find an excuse for Clement XIV's behaviour for, if the

accusations were groundless, his condemnation was even more unjustifiable. His conduct was unworthy, as everyone agrees. In our own century, Pius XI deplored this 'painful chapter of history'! As for Jesuit historians, they have always been loth to criticize a pope, even one such as Clement XIV, on account of their fidelity to the papacy.[2]

In his book *The English Jesuits*, already quoted, the Jesuit Bernard Basset writes dispassionately:

> In the very magnitude of its destruction, the suppression of the Society of Jesus stands unique. In 1750, the Society had numbered 22,589 members, divided into 42 provinces, with 669 colleges, 61 novitiates, 335 residences and 273 mission stations. Whatever the charges brought against their stewardship, the Jesuits could look back with pride to a massive achievement, and this they certainly did. (...) The destruction of the Paraguay Reductions alone caused untold suffering and confusion, opening the road for a greedy colonialism that the missionaries had successfully opposed. That there had been faults in the Jesuit machine, no Jesuit need deny. The Order may have grown too great, too powerful, too monopolistic and, in an unexpected way, too conservative.
>
> One may pity Pope Clement XIV, placed as he was in an impossible position and tied by the promises and commitments of his early years. A heterogeneous army of rivals united against the Order: the French *Parlements*, traditionally hostile to the Jesuits, the Encyclopedists, bitter against religion, the Jansenists, the Regalists, the colonial exploiters and a clique of curial money-grubbers, out for immediate gain.

Forty-one years later, when the Society was reinstated by Pius VII, it once again proved to be entirely devoted to the papacy. It was only in this century, and after Vatican II and the Society's 32nd General Congregation, that one finds divergences between the Society, whose desire for reform was personified in its General, Pedro Arrupe, and the Holy See, represented by the three postconciliar Popes: Paul VI, John Paul I and John Paul II.

A quite minor incident concerning the internal running of the Society triggered off a spate of sensational headlines in the press at the time of the 32nd General Congregation: 'Pope's commandos up in arms', 'Pope silences Jesuits', 'Pope forbids

Jesuits to speak'. What was behind this Jesuit 'revolution'? The affair would hardly bear mentioning if it had not helped to sour relations between Jesuits and the Holy See for quite a long time.

Vatican II had asked that the status of members of religious orders be renewed and that clerics and non-priests be placed on an equal footing, with the same rights and obligations. The Society has three degrees of membership: *temporal coadjutors*, taking vows of poverty, chastity and obedience, but who are not priests; *spiritual coadjutors*, who are priests; and lastly *professed priests* who are allowed to take, as well as the usual three vows, that of obedience to the Supreme Pontiff. These divisions have existed since the time of Ignatius, when the founder was forbidden to have more than 60 fully professed priests in his order. Since hundreds of applicants were coming forward and Ignatius did not want to refuse any of them, his stratagem was to limit admission to profession to the required number, accepting the others as temporal and spiritual 'assistants' (*coadjutors*). The stratagem became an established custom. Although the limit of 60 was abandoned, the practice continued: governing posts are filled by fully professed priests only.

However, this system of categories runs counter to modern feelings. Anyone joining the Society of Jesus has generally no intention of remaining in an inferior kind of position. Furthermore, criteria laid down for choosing priests to be accepted for professing the four vows have laid greater and greater importance on academic success. Admission to profession depends on a final examination in theology and all university results obtained over the years.

Even if more spiritual criteria are now used to appoint professed priests, many Jesuits, during the last few decades, have been uncomfortable about the offensive aspect of the inequality caused by degrees. Besides, legally, every Jesuit is bound by obedience to the Pope, owing to the special bond between the Society of Jesus and the Holy See.

Prior to the 32nd General Congregation, the majority of provinces had come out in favour of the abolition of distinction according to degree. As early as November 1974, Fr Arrupe had notified Paul VI of this fact. In his opening address to the Congregation, on 3 December 1974, the Pope

warned the members against any change which might modify
what he considered an integral part of the Society. What is
more, the tone of Paul VI's speech betrayed his profound displeasure with this tinkering with the order's rules:

> Why are you questioning everything? A deep state of
> uncertainty has arisen in your ranks, worse still, a certain
> fundamental questioning of your very identity ... What has
> happened to your desire to collaborate in the Pope's mission
> with confidence? Are the clouds that we saw in the sky in
> 1966, even if they were somewhat dispersed by the 31st
> General Congregation, still casting shadows over the Society?

The warning was clear, and a letter dated the same day from
the Secretary of State, Cardinal Jean Villot, went into greater
detail: as regards the proposal to extend the fourth vow to all
members of the order of Jesuits, even non-priests, 'the Supreme
Pontiff informs you that, after careful consideration, such an
innovation appears to present serious difficulties that render
the necessary approval of the Holy See impossible'. In plainer
words: the Pope asks the Jesuits not to discuss the abolition
of degrees and, should they persist, he will not give them his
approval.

The 32nd General Congregation, believing that the Pope had
not forbidden it to air its views, returned to the attack. After
a memorable landslide vote (228 for, 8 against), it was decided
that the question of degrees could be dealt with. On 22 January
1975, in a fresh vote, the delegates decided that they should
once again inform the Pope of their opinion in favour of the
suppression of degrees. But Paul VI held that, in doing so,
the Congregation had acted against his wishes. In a handwritten letter sent to Fr Arrupe on 15 February, he maintained
his position: 'No innovation whatsoever can be allowed with
regard to the fourth vow.' The discussion was finally over. The
Congregation surrendered.

'Though we are not unconditional "papists"', said Fr Arrupe,
'Jesuits owe loyalty and obedience to the Pope.'[3] Had the
Society been guilty, by opposing Paul VI's wishes, of rebelling
against his sovereignty and breaking the ties which formed
the essence of the order since the time of Ignatius? Fr Arrupe
thought not. He calmly referred to Paul VI's speeches during

the 32nd General Congregation: 'There was no (. . .) excessive remark or overstepping of authority, but rather paternal concern; their acceptance by the whole of the Society is, for me, a proof of its health.'[4]

Fr Arrupe had one last audience with Paul VI on 18 May 1978. The main subject raised was the preparation of the Conference of the Latin American Episcopal Council which was to be held in Puebla, Mexico, in October of that year.[5] The atmosphere, said to be friendly, seemed to have removed the thunder clouds which had loomed since 1966.

But, on 6 August, Paul VI died in Castelgandolfo. John Paul I succeeded him on 26 August, and an audience was planned for 30 September between the new Pope and the assembly of 'procurators' (delegates of the Society who decide on the appropriateness or not of calling a General Congregation). On the morning of 29 September, an astonished world learnt of the Pope's death.

Less than forty-eight hours after his election, John Paul I had sent a polite handwritten note to Fr Arrupe thanking him for the Society's good wishes. However, during his brief 33-day reign as Pope, Luciani had prepared another document – the talk he was to give the procurators on 30 September. The contents of that speech, which were finally revealed on 8 December, with the agreement of John Paul II, who was elected on 16 October, displayed a certain harshness. John Paul I recalled that his predecessor, Paul VI, 'had so loved, had prayed, done and suffered so much for the Society of Jesus'. He then went on to recommendations that are barely disguised reprimands:

> Do not allow Jesuit teaching and publications to become a source of confusion and disorientation . . . This naturally presupposes that a sound and solid doctrine be taught in the institutions and universities training young Jesuits.

John Paul I did not have time to explain more fully what he really thought or what he reproached them with. It is now known that at the time of Paul VI, many bishops, and especially apostolic nuncios, complained bitterly about the Society's publications, which they found too outspoken, not to say irreverent, with regard to the Roman magisterium and local authorities.

Among other things, they reproached Fr Arrupe for not 'keeping his troops under control'. This criticism was ill-founded. On 13 and 14 January 1974, at the request of the General himself, the editors of the main European Jesuit journals met just outside Rome. In the words of one of the participants:

> We had gone with mixed feelings: what could the General
> have against us on behalf of the Holy See and the bishops?
> No doubt he had a few misgivings about us, for instance
> that we did not have enough respect for the thinking of the
> Pope and the Roman Curia (. . .). We understood perfectly that
> the General did not doubt our fidelity to the Church when he
> recommended that quality to us, but that he was asking us to
> deepen it further.[6]

Whereas Paul VI and John Paul I had merely expressed their 'surprise' and 'sorrow' and requested that matters be corrected, John Paul II went into action. Regretting the 'deplorable deficiencies' that he detected in the Jesuits, he could not trust those in charge of the Society to make the desired changes. With remarkable humility, and feeling no doubt disavowed by the Pope's words, Fr Arrupe decided to resign and leave to his successor the job of putting the situation to rights. Having told the provincials of his intention, he then informed John Paul II, out of simple courtesy. To everyone's surprise the Pope asked the General to postpone his resignation so as to allow more time to prepare the General Congregation that would elect his successor.

After Fr Arrupe's cerebral thrombosis on 7 August 1981, leaving him unable to govern, came the second dramatic event mentioned earlier – the Pope's letter of 6 October appointing Fr Dezza as personal delegate.

Thus, by two successive authoritarian acts, the Pope intervened in the running of the Society, not shrinking from disregarding the *Constitutions*. It was the first time in the order's history that a Pope had acted directly in such a manner. There was the well-known occasion, for example, when the French government asked Clement XIII in 1761 to appoint a special Jesuit vicar-general for France, who would be more or less independent of the General; the Pope had refused outright with this famous reply: *Sint ut sunt aut non sint* (Let them [the Jesuits] be what they are or let them not be).

Public opinion found it hard to understand the replacement, without any explanation, of Fr Vincent O'Keefe, an American who was particularly well qualified to follow the line laid down by the last General Congregation, by an 80-year-old Italian. Fr Dezza, an intelligent conservative, was John Paul II's confidant. He was highly regarded by the Vatican for having been the private confessor of the last four Popes. However, this did not prevent sharp initial reactions from within the Society. In the 1983 official bulletin for Jesuits in France one reads: 'This decision, interpreted, rightly or wrongly, as a repudiation of Fr Arrupe and of the 32nd General Congregation, aroused intense emotion throughout the Society.'

The Canadian Provincials, both English- and French-speaking, pointed out, somewhat sarcastically, that the Pope, coming as he did from Eastern Europe, was not very conversant with the democratic methods current in the Society. They more or less hinted that, within the ideological system under which the young Wojtyla had grown up, his 'personal delegate' would be called a 'commissar' ... In the English weekly *The Tablet* a Jesuit described the Pope's move as a 'brutal insult' against one of the holiest and best loved Generals since St Ignatius. And a group of eighteen West German Jesuits, including the distinguished theologian Karl Rahner, sent a letter of protest to the Pope in which one reads:

> Even after having prayed and meditated, it is not easy for us to recognize 'the hand of God' in this administrative measure, for our faith and the experience of history has taught us that not even the highest authority in the Church is free from error.

An allusion to Clement XIV, perhaps?

A rather more moderate tone was adopted by the French Provincial. In a letter to the superiors Fr Madelin wrote of 'our faith being put to the test' and acknowledged that

> it is impossible to hide that what is now happening to us lies
> outside the normal course of the law that governs us. Does
> not that law allow Generals to resign, communities to express
> themselves through provincial and general congregations
> and the General to appoint a vicar-general in the case of the

temporary incapacity of the head of the Society?

The French Jesuit bulletin mentioned earlier explained the background to John Paul II's intervention. Having recalled that the only Jesuits the Pope knew well were Polish ones, who worked closely with the diocesan clergy in the parishes, and with whom, in Cracow, he had been on excellent terms, it gave a chronological account of the dealings that Cardinal Wojtyla had had with the leaders of the Society since becoming Pope.

Just before the conclave in October 1978, the General asked Cardinal Villot for a copy of the speech John Paul I was to have made on 30 September to the Congregation of Procurators, made up of 80 Jesuits elected from all the Society's provinces. The cardinal replied that it was not for him to agree to that request, but that the decision should be made by the next Pope or the college of cardinals. The General insisted that the college consider the matter. Thus it was that for two days the Society was discussed. While many cardinals spoke in its favour, many alluded to the difficulties they had with the Jesuits in several countries.[7] It was the first time, according to Fr Pittau, the assistant delegate, that Cardinal Wojtyla had had such an experience, and he was made uneasy by it; this was confirmed after his election, during his first audiences with bishops.

In the months following his election, the Pope met Fr Arrupe only twice, and very briefly. Then came the attempt against the Pope's life on 13 May 1981, and the General's illness. What do the writers of the French bulletin have to say on the subject?

The general opinion is that there was a lack of communication between the Vatican and the Society. John Paul II confined himself to the warnings given by his predecessors. When he received complaints from some Church official about the Society's members or institutions (for it is a well-known rule that one talks more readily about what is wrong than what is right), he had the impression that the Jesuits were taking no notice of those warnings. On his side, Fr Arrupe had intervened forcefully each time that a reproach was made. But he had done so according to the Society's own code of government – which is paternal and personal – without making his admonitions and sanctions public, so that the Vatican, ignorant of the fact and with a touch of bad faith on the part of certain avowed opponents of the Society, could be justified in suspecting a widespread laxity.

To return to Fr Madelin's letter, in which he advised his subordinates to keep a low profile, he wrote to the superiors:

> The period we are now entering is rather delicate. The Society, with its characteristic failings and qualities, should not seek to justify itself. Furthermore, it should resist the suggestions of those who would like to set it up as a rival 'Church' to the true Church. (...) The Society, I am firmly convinced, will be judged, in the eyes of a large number of people, on the quality of its 'discretion' in the face of what is happening to it, on the manner in which it gets through this present ordeal and on the strength of unity which it is capable of showing.

The example of adult obedience, reasoned but loyal, given by that letter seemed to have been followed by the majority of Jesuit leaders throughout the world: proof indeed that the legendary 'Jesuit obedience' still functioned. Here, moreover, is what Fr Pittau told French Jesuits after the crisis:

> These last few months have been a time of quite deep spiritual experience for the Society. The Pope's intervention was an exceptional act. The appointment of a delegate and a delegate's assistant is without precedent in the 450 years' history of the Society. I can say with pride that the Jesuits accepted the Holy Father's intervention very well. There was talk of Jesuit resignations, of provincials and superiors refusing to serve under this extraordinary government. Nothing of the like has happened. I know, because I read all the letters that arrive from the whole world: there has been no request to leave the Society that has been brought about by the Holy Father's intervention. No provincial superior has resigned from his post ...
>   This naturally does not mean that everyone welcomed the Pope's interference. Many were affected deeply by it and wondered about the reason for that intervention, others saw it as an occasion for a deeper reflection on our apostolate and our vocation, but basically the attitudes expressed have been the reactions of filial obedience, of Ignatian obedience. Having read all those letters, I can truthfully say that the Jesuits' behaviour

has been dictated by faith and the spirit of obedience, but also by a deep desire and hope that the government of the Society will return without delay to its normal functioning and that the General Congregation and the election of the General can take place as quickly as possible.

John Paul II himself seemed to have been impressed by this flawless show of obedience. At the end of 1981, he visited Fr Arrupe at the Jesuit General Curia. The General greeted the Pope with the words: 'Holy Father, I renew to you my pledge of obedience, and the obedience of the whole Society of Jesus.' To which the Pope replied: 'Father General, sustain me with your prayers and your suffering.' And John Paul II added for the benefit of the assembled community: 'As I have been edified for many weeks by the Society, so am I edified by today's meeting.'

In November that same year, Fr Dezza decided that he would bring together all the Provincials of the order in the Villa Cavalletti, near Frascati, on 23 February 1982, to take stock of the Society's situation and to communicate to them the Pope's wishes for the future. This meeting took place in complete freedom. According to Fr Madelin:

It was invaluable to hear what each judged best to say, without fear and with that freedom that comes from the Spirit of God. We were not in a Parliament, nor in a soviet where everything is prepared beforehand, nor in a hazy atmosphere where reality is forgotten, nor under the influence of organized pressure groups.

True, no doubt. But the aim of the exercise was above all to acquaint the Provincials with the Pope's grievances. They were all received in audience by the Pope at the Vatican on 27 February. Echoing Fr Madelin's remarks, the Pope began by saying:

The undoubtedly singular and exceptional situation called for an intervention, an 'ordeal', which – I say this with great feeling – has been received by the members of the order with the true spirit of Ignatius.

The Pope then listed the tasks traditionally entrusted to the Society since its foundation – the renewal of Christian life, the

242   *The Jesuits*

Spiritual Exercises, the spreading of true doctrine, education of the young, the training of clergy, theological research and, of course, the missions. Here John Paul II gave three examples: St Francis Xavier (for his missionary zeal), the Paraguay Reductions (human development and a fairer social life), and Matteo Ricci (inculturation). Defining the Jesuits' new mission, he stated:

> The Church today expects the Society to contribute effectively
> to the implementation of Vatican II (...) to help the whole
> Church to move forward along the broad path laid out by the
> Council, and to convince those who are unfortunately tempted
> to stray down the progressive or conservative byways to return
> to the true path. (...)

How was this to be done? The Pope asked the Jesuits to adapt the 'different forms of traditional apostolate which still today retain their full value' and to take an even more active interest in those enterprises that Vatican II promoted in particular: ecumenism, greater dialogue with non-Christian religions, and the problem of atheism. He next laid stress on the promotion of justice, which is 'an integral part of evangelization'. However, he also chose to repeat what he had said in 1980 in Rio de Janeiro, on the sacerdotal way to promote justice, in a service 'that was not that of a doctor, a social worker, a politician or a trades union leader'. And the two conditions for carrying out this mission? Firstly, 'sound, extended training of future apostles of the Society' – intellectual and spiritual training, through the *Exercises*. Secondly, 'sound, pure doctrine'. The Pope elaborated here on the special bond between the Society and the Roman pontiff, the college of bishops and the departments of the Roman Curia.

Thus John Paul II extended the scope of the fourth vow to cover not only the Pope but all the structures of the Universal Church: Pope, Roman Curia and bishops. In other words, Jesuits were to collaborate with all the hierarchical and institutional authorities and not contest or compete with them.

Before letting it be understood – the carrot after the stick – that it

> will be possible this year to convene the General Congregation
> which will not only give the Society a new General, in

accordance with the wishes expressed some time ago by the venerable Fr Arrupe, but also communicate to the whole Society new enthusiasm for carrying out its mission, with renewed vigour, in line with the hopes of the Church and the world,

John Paul II had adopted Paul VI's judgement, made in 1974 at the 32nd General Congregation:

> Your Society is, as it were, a test of the vitality of the Church across the centuries; it forms a sort of crossroads where the difficulties, the temptations, the efforts and the enterprises, the durability and the success of the whole Church meet in a very significant way.

Is there not a contradiction, however, in wanting the Society to be at the crossroads of the tensions between the Church and the world, with all the innovation, audacity and adaptability that this implies, and at the same time to be considered as a model of rigid orthodoxy and military obedience? Can one ask pioneers to conform completely with common rule, or those sent to outposts to avoid taking risks?

The task that John Paul II asigned to the Jesuits can be summed up in the phrase: 'the implementation of Vatican II'. Everyone – or nearly everyone – is in favour of the Council, but which one? For a start, the event itself was very ambiguous, since the texts voted by the Council Fathers were the result of long arduous discussions and confrontations, accompanied by countless amendments, and bear traces of the continuous compromise between an open-minded majority and a conservative minority. Also, the Council was considered by some – including the present Pope – as a goal, a point of arrival, a pastoral achievement rather than a doctrinal one, which must be made known and implemented, but which we must not go beyond, at the risk of 'betraying' it; and by others – including the superiors of the Society of Jesus appointed by Fr Arrupe – it was considered as a starting point, already out of date since it had taken place 25 years before, but creating a spirit and climate of open-mindedness that would allow and stimulate further innovations and inventions.

In his address of 27 February 1982, John Paul II had chosen a middle-of-the-road interpretation of the Council, thus avoiding the pitfalls of a progressive or conservative reading of the event. In a document entitled 'Directives for carrying out the wishes of the Holy Father', sent to all the Jesuits by Fr Dezza on 25 March, a month after the Provincials' reunion, the 'orders' appear even more restrictive than those set out by the Pope. In another letter to the whole Society, sent on 9 December 1982, the Pope's personal delegate again laid emphasis on fidelity to the Pope and the bishops:

> The Supreme Pontiff and the bishops are the visible signs of the love and presence of Christ among his people. They have a special mission to accomplish for the good of the people of God. The Ignatian charism incites us to show them total loyalty, composed of love and sympathy: in a word, we must identify ourselves with them. This love and spirit of service should especially prevent us from criticizing them, out of a sense of intellectual, moral or theological superiority or a prophetic charism. It is certainly not in keeping with the Society's spirit to oppose the Church's authority as though we were placed above it.

And, with regard to the implementation of the Council, Fr Dezza added: 'The Society must carry out this task, as a whole, by the active collaboration of all. We must overcome our individualism (...), even if that means giving up our own opinions and inclinations.'

Even counting on Ignatian obedience, one wonders how long intelligent men, however devoted they may be, might be expected to renounce their own opinions and inclinations in the interest of a central, external authority. Here, for example, is what was written on the subject in 1977 by the late French Jesuit Michel de Certeau, in an article entitled 'The end of the post-conciliar period':

> The term 'Church', in the singular, contrasts with the ever more diversified and contradictory practices and beliefs among Catholics. These differences proliferate as post-conciliar activity, based on a utopia which stimulated people for a long time, runs out of steam. They grow in number or simply reappear in a landscape where, like the setting sun, the reformist and unitarian myth created by Vatican II (1962–65), sinks gently out of sight.
> These practices and beliefs, masked by Catholic or Evangelical

credentials, are no longer controlled and even less established by Roman authority. The fact is no doubt not so new. Christianity in the first centuries and in the Early Middle Ages consisted of highly differentiated and often very autonomous 'Churches'. But local authorities imposed their law. After the process of centralization that accelerated in the nineteenth century and during the first half of the twentieth, an explosion occurred everywhere, even if the administrative machinery remained in place. It all happened as though the immense ecclesiastical body left the different parts that composed it to their own devices. The fragments born of earlier religious periods were formerly stratified and integrated into a whole; today they are growing apart. Christian movements used once to be united; what is left of them, sizeable or minute, flourishing or declining, appears today to be drifting out of orbit. Each follows its own particular trajectory, under the influence of local, national and international forces which escape from the control of a centre.

If Michel de Certeau appears too much on the 'fringe' to represent the Society of Jesus – although his analysis seems judicious to me – let us summon another witness, the leading German Jesuit theologian Karl Rahner, who died in 1984. I met him at his home in Munich – a simple room in the Jesuit faculty in Kaulbachstrasse. Undoubtedly one of the most influential theologians this century – he was born in 1904 – Karl Rahner wrote a thesis, in collaboration with the philosopher Martin Heidegger, on 'knowledge according to St Thomas Aquinas', which he published in 1939 under the title *Geist im Welt* (Spirit in the world). The author of over 3,000 articles, his best known books are *Theological Investigations, Mission and Grace, Questions for the Church, A New Interpretation of the Faith* and *Foundations of Christian Faith*. In a survey carried out just before his death among 554 North American theologians from 71 different denominations, Rahner was put in third place, after Paul Tillich and Thomas Aquinas, as having had the greatest influence on their thinking.

At 80 years old this little white-haired man in big horn-rimmed glasses was disarmingly young at heart and modest. Without the slightest Teutonic pedantry, he did not take himself at all seriously and loved telling stories, his eyes twinkling mischievously behind his thick bifocals. One story he told me was of a private audience he once had with John Paul II. 'I did a lot of talking', he said, 'and the Pope did a lot of listening, without saying anything. Well, I know what I think but I still do not know what the Pope thinks! Moreover', he added pensively, 'I have never been invited to have breakfast with him as some people have' – he mentioned the names of Hans Urs von Balthasar and André Frossard – 'and he didn't even have a photographer there to take the traditional official photo with the Pope.' A short pause. 'It was probably because I was wearing a tie instead of a dog-collar!'

Faced with the problem raised by Michel de Certeau of the disintegration and fragmentation of the Church, Rahner suggested two solutions. On the one hand, he reckoned that the Church was likely to decrease greatly in number:

> 'It is not obvious that Christianity must enjoy a massive presence. It is possible that Providence needs only a small proportion of humanity to belong to the Church, which will perhaps be formed by a small group who will bear witness to the possibility of salvation.'

But, on the other hand, he was convinced that we were moving towards a 'world Church'. As he explained,

> 'The adoption of the vernacular in the liturgy by the Council is the forerunner of a world Church within which individual Churches will exist independently, in their own cultural spheres, and no longer as European exports.'

Such inculturation must be far-reaching, according to Rahner.

> 'Does the sexual and marital moral code for the Masai in East Africa have to be that of Western Christianity? Why should an African tribal chief not live like the patriarch Abraham?'

Among his most urgent preoccupations, however, he mentioned the progress of ecumenism. He had had enough of 'fine speeches' and 'new theological commissions', and complained that 'Rome never makes concrete suggestions for reconciliation between Christians'.

> 'The Holy See could adopt more flexible ecclesial structures than at present, more accommodating, for example, concerning

mixed marriages. As regards infallibility – the main obstacle for Protestants – I have suggested before that Rome should declare that, in the future, it will make no infallible declaration without first consulting, not only all the Catholic bishops, but also the Protestants. Vatican I did not define the conditions for *ex cathedra* pronouncements and the question remains open.'

In the field of theology, without sharing the extreme positions of Hans Küng on papal infallibility and ecumenism, Karl Rahner found the Church's magisterium too heavy-handed and suspicious.

'The immutability of dogma is invoked far too readily, without allowing for the great scope for progress within present definitions. I have made a case, for example, for a recognition of Protestant ministries, but the time is not yet ripe. Even the International Theological Commission no longer serves any useful purpose, since it is under the thumb of the ex-Holy Office; that is why I resigned from it.'

What did Karl Rahner think about the future of the Society of Jesus?

'Should the Society try to behave like the "monolith" that it has appeared to be in the eyes of many, then it would only represent a bygone age, and could no longer be of genuine help to the Church. That it must refuse to parrot a new form of modernism, spurious and stupid, goes without saying. But it is not so easy to say what that means. Those who claim to know with precision are more often than not dyed-in-the-wool conservatives. To anticipate an unknown future (that is indeed our destiny, however uncomfortable it may be!), cannot be achieved with detailed maps, where all the paths are clearly marked out in advance. An order that behaved in that fashion, as if everything were crystal clear and had simply to be defended doggedly, would be more suspect in my eyes than the Society in its present situation, where certitude is neither easy nor transparent.'

This last remark of Rahner's expresses clearly the uncertitude in which the Jesuits find themselves: they must 'anticipate an unknown future'. This is also relevant to the subject at hand: the present 'power' of the Jesuits. As Rahner admitted, and in spite of papal reprimands, there is no question of returning to the 'monolithic army' of the past. Neither the falling numbers, nor the new democratic spirit born of the Council would allow it.

After the Council of Trent the task was clear: the territory lost to the Protestant reformers had to be regained, while at the same time the corruption undermining the Catholic Church had to be fought. In a word – Counter-Reformation. One sometimes has the impression that, in the face of the uncontrollable forces of decentralization and secularization released by Vatican II, John Paul II dreams of carrying out a new Counter-Reformation – or rather, a restoration – to minimize what he considers to be the 'damage' caused by the Council. He advocates a 'second evangelization' of Europe so that it 'becomes Christian again', and he seems disappointed that the Jesuits are not rushing forward to the front lines. Hence his interest in Opus Dei, which seems to be the reincarnation of the old-style Society of Jesus, or at least of its less attractive qualities: elitism, secretiveness, conservatism.

How, then, are relations between the Holy See and the Society likely to develop? At the end of the 33rd General Congregation, on 25 October 1983, the Society adopted a twenty-page resolution on its mission in the world today. Describing that congregation as a 'time of grace', which had been marked by 'the voluntary resignation of Pedro Arrupe who, unceasingly during eighteen years, had left his imprint on the Society's apostolate and inspired its spiritual life' and by the 'fortunate election of Peter-Hans Kolvenbach', the Jesuits make amends right at the beginning of the document by stating: 'We are aware that recently, in certain circumstances, our fidelity has not been perfect, and that this has even caused concern to the Church's pastors.'

One can interpret as another gesture of 'reconciliation' with the Holy See, the new General's choice as 'general adviser' – in addition to the four Assistants elected by the Congregation – of Fr Giuseppe Pittau, John Paul II's assistant delegate. Having given these tokens of obedience, the Jesuits were that much freer to avoid compromise on the essentials. They stated, in the introduction to their final document, that they had been able to 'verify, make more explicit and confirm the orientation decided by the last two General Congregations, in the light of the Church's teaching'. They had therefore given up the idea of fresh soul-searching. 'We believe', they wrote, 'that we are in greater need, today, of putting into practice what we have received than producing lengthy declarations or new decrees.'

NOTES

1 Traditionally, in other religious orders, monks and nuns gather at intervals during the day in the choir of the church to sing the liturgical 'hours' (Prime, Sext, None, etc.), composed mainly of the Psalms.
2 Christopher Hollis, *A History of the Jesuits* (London, 1968).
3 *Pedro Arrupe, itinéraire d'un jésuite* (Paris, 1982).
4 Ibid.
5 The Puebla Conference was finally opened on 28 January 1979 in the presence of John Paul II. Its theme was: 'Evangelization in Latin America today and tomorrow'.
6 Personal impressions on the meeting in the Villa Cavalletti, written by Fr Bréchet, editor of *Choisir*, a Swiss Jesuit monthly magazine.
7 It was always the same complaints that came up: in several Third World countries, in particular in Latin America and the Philippines, Jesuits were accused of being 'political activists', since they defended the rights of the poor against the rich and sometimes against the interests of the institutional Church.

3

Power within the Society of Jesus

A RIGID BACKBONE AND GREAT FLEXIBILITY

*The charge of General is to act as the head from
which the necessary impetus descends to achieve
the ends of the Society.*

CONSTITUTION 666

If many Jesuits felt hurt by the Holy See's intervention after
Fr Arrupe's illness, it was not only because it brought into
the open the deterioration of relations between John Paul II
and the Society of Jesus, but also because it contravened the
rules governing the Jesuit order. They could accept an extraordinary decision in the name of obedience, and disregard the
objections of their 'own judgement', but it was the credibility
of the Society's government that was at stake. Were there such
weaknesses in the complex apparatus of power that it could
be erased by a simple pontifical letter?

In retrospect, however, one can see that the structures of the
Society in fact imply a continual tension between the supreme
authority, the Holy See, and individual creativity; between the
centres of decision and personal freedom. The *Spiritual Exercises* produce and shape men – both those who decide and
those who obey – of such incomparable freedom that they are
prepared to give up that freedom. The internal power of the
Society is thus built on a system that constantly combines the
authority of law with personal responsibility. The General's
responsibility is to 'act as the head from which the necessary
impetus descends to achieve the ends of the Society' (*Constitutions*). This downward movement goes from the General to
the Provincials and to the local superiors, but its objective is

to stimulate the desire of each Jesuit to use his talents and his energy to serve the Church.

The reconciliation of the decisions of the General and the other superiors, on the one hand, and the desires or wishes of the subordinates, on the other, is achieved by means of a much decried practice. The Society is, however, the only religious congregation that can legally impose the 'account of conscience', also called the 'opening of conscience', according to which the Jesuit opens his heart completely to his superior about his problems, his projects, his moral dilemmas and his spiritual life – including the most intimate aspects that in other religious orders are revealed only in confession.

The system has been criticized by the Society's opponents, who have regarded it as the principal instrument of an order whose hold over its members is such that they even surrender their consciences, becoming formidable combatants, like soldiers who go to war without weighing up the rights and wrongs of the fight. The 'account of conscience', maintain the Jesuits, is rather a dialogue of 'apostolic discernment'. It is based on the encounter of two wills searching for the best decision, for the individual and for the whole body of the Society, when a problem arises.

The 'account of conscience' is widely replaced, these days, by community discussions. Although these cannot solve intimate problems, in difficult cases where discretion is involved, they do allow a re-evaluation of tasks, the choosing or dropping of jobs involving the whole community, and the practical organization of the household. This system works at all levels in the Society. The Provincial is not moving pawns on a chessboard. The General is not an absolute monarch. He himself often has to give an account of his government to the Pope or the local hierarchy.

The Jesuits' essential goal, through either the 'account of conscience' or community discussions, is – according to the Ignatian expression – to 'be in harmony with the Church' (*sentire cum Ecclesia*). Jesuit organization must be conditioned by this sense of awareness of the Church's needs and this obviously implies unconditional submission by the Society to the Pope.

Such submission is both a surrender of power and a way
of organizing it. The Jesuits never have the last word, as can
be seen in their final compliance with the measures taken by
John Paul II in the early 1980s. But this 'abandonment' must
not be confused with resignation: as long as all arguments
have not been exhausted, as long as there is still a chance of
dialogue and new avenues to explore, a Jesuit will not consider
himself beaten. 'Submission' must take place only when it can
be lived with 'indifference', an Ignatian term designating the
appeasement of one's will by bowing to another's will. Hierarchical relations within the Society are therefore, barring abuse
which is always possible, built upon mutual confidence and
on the significance of the apostolic mission entrusted to the
Jesuits, which form a basis of all its 'strategies'.

The late Fr Louis Beirnaert, a French Jesuit who studied
psychoanalysis with Jacques Lacan, had, up until his death
in 1985, been working on a psychological interpretation of
St Ignatius's writings – somewhat along the same lines as
W. W. Meissner.[1] I asked him how he understood Ignatius's
teaching on blind obedience: *perinde ac cadaver* (like a corpse).
Fr Beirnaert replied that

> 'Taken at its face value this expression is simply scandalous.
> But to understand obedience as Ignatius saw it, and as it is
> practised in the Society, you have to put it into its historical
> context. It all began with a group of companions roaming
> over Europe and preaching the word of God. Having no
> "boss", but only a leader, Ignatius, they soon felt the need for
> internal coherence and decided to appoint a "superior", chosen
> from within their ranks: "one of us". This is why obedience
> in the Society is always paid to one of the companions, who
> represents God and Christ but remains "one of us". Which
> explains why, from its origins, Ignatian obedience was based
> on dialogue between superior and subject, a perpetual ongoing
> exchange, carried out by correspondence when distance made
> personal contact impossible.
> 'You will have observed that in the phrase *perinde ac cadaver*
> and "blind obedience", there is a "corpse", i.e. "death", and
> blindness, i.e. "night". Such terms belong to the mystical
> tradition. And, indeed, I believe that the act of obeying, even
> unto death and in the dark, which every Jesuit can experience

some time in his life, is a fundamental experience. When Ignatius required obedience to one's superior, it is not based on the latter's personal qualities or his better judgement, but simply because he represents God. He is "in the place" of Christ, who cannot lead us into error. This does not mean that the man representing Christ cannot make a mistake. Neither does it mean that the subject has to accept the reasons given by his superior. We can quite well continue to hold our own view, the result of mature reflection, while still obeying "in the dark": that is the spiritual value of this obedience.'

Still unconvinced, I put to him the case of Teilhard de Chardin. If one can accept, at a pinch, that the silence imposed on Teilhard during his lifetime was salutary for him, was it beneficial to the Church and its intellectual honesty?

'A man's work can easily bear fruit after his death. This was the case with Teilhard: he was a man who continued to develop his ideas in private, and yet he obeyed his superiors. He was recognized after his death. Which proves the importance of persevering in one's research without demanding immediate recognition. Your hierarchical superiors can forbid you to teach in a Catholic faculty and to publish your work in Catholic periodicals, but they cannot prevent you from thinking, speaking and writing.'

What about the recent tensions between the Society and the papacy? Hadn't the Jesuits forgotten their fourth vow?

'If the first Jesuits went to Rome to put themselves at the Pope's service, it was because he was in the best position to see the universal needs of the Church. He could send them where they were most needed. Obedience to the Vicar of Christ was accepted with a view to the missions. The recent problems sprang from a conflict between two forms of obedience. If the Pope, who wields authority over the Church and the Society, considers a certain activity to be dangerous he can decide to forbid it, and the "mission" no longer exists. If we do not follow his instructions, we are placing ourselves outside our promised obedience. But such direct interventions as that made by John Paul II in appointing two personal delegates must remain exceptional. Otherwise we would lose our specificity as Jesuits.'

How did Fr Beirnaert react to John Paul II's intervention?

'I bore in mind that our special vow of obedience to the Pope is not made to an individual, with his qualities and faults, but to his function as Vicar of Christ. Obedience is required to the papacy, whoever fulfils the function at a given moment. In this instance, it is true that John Paul II's intervention was contrary to our *Constitutions*. But it would be against the Ignatian spirit simply to judge the man occupying the Chair of Peter and to weigh up the relevance or irrelevance of his decisions. Ignatian obedience, on the contrary, requires us to make abstraction of the human element and to obey the Holy See. At the same time, we have a duty to pursue our work according to our Jesuit vocation, without seeking approbation for our every move.'

This delicate balance between obedience and initiative was well described by Fr John Padberg in his magazine *Studies in the Spirituality of Jesuits*. He first describes the historical context of the papacy as Ignatius knew it:

Almost uninterruptedly up to Paul III, the popes during whose reigns Ignatius lived were examples of worldliness, nepotism, venality and licence, and their examples set the tone for the Roman Curia and the reputation of the Holy See. (...) Suffice it to say that everyone knew that 'everything was for sale in Rome'; in addition, several families were firmly in control of passing on the spoils through nepotism. Through the latter half of the fifteenth and on into the sixteenth century, four families occupied the papal throne nine different times, the clique established by Sixtus IV being the most successful with three pontificates.

Fr Padberg then cites three examples of clear conflicts between Ignatius and the Pope. From the beginning, Ignatius was opposed to Jesuits being made bishops or accepting ecclesiastical honours. He fought hard to prevent Claude Jay from being appointed Bishop of Trieste, Francis Borgia being made a cardinal and Diego Laynez accepting several bishoprics and the cardinalate.

How exceedingly strong was this opposition to accepting a prelacy is clear from a later commentary by Jerome Nadal, one of the closest collaborators of Ignatius, on the section of the Constitutions dealing with the matter: 'Only the Supreme Pontiff can compel the Society in this regard. In

such instances, every manner and means of resisting and
impeding such an intention of the pontiff is to be expended
and exercised, no stone left unturned, lest such a dignity be
imposed. We are not to cease working towards this end or
give up our efforts until we have exhausted every possibility.
This will not be verified until the Apostolic See expressly
obliges us under pain of mortal sin and will obviously brook
no further resistance.'

So much for blind obedience!

What do these examples suggest? Fr Padberg answers his
own question:

> They do not suggest, as one might superficially think, that
> Ignatius said one thing and did another. Rather, they suggest
> that the lived reality of his relationship to the papacy was
> far more complex than we have been accustomed to believe.
> That reality involved a set of values, attitudes and practices in
> continuing interaction. There was gratitude to the Holy See in
> general and, especially personally, to several of the popes, in
> particular Paul III and Julius III, for the support they gave to
> his raw and untried religious order. There was genuine fear
> of what Paul IV might do to the Society. But, with equally
> genuine piety and reverence, the dying Ignatius sent for Paul
> IV's blessing. There was a determination, with both friend and
> foe, to uphold to the very last the distinctive characteristics
> of the Society. There was the use of both prayer to God and
> political persuasion by friends to influence the popes in their
> actions towards the Society.[2]

The Society that is also an all-too-human organization and,
as such, has weaknesses. Its spiritual construction is, consequently, built on strong legal foundations, which ensure the
survival of the order over and above personal deficiencies,
temporary conflicts and the hazards of history. Apart from
the General, elected by the Congregation, it is the Provincials
who run the Society. Their power is extensive: they assign
members to vacant or newly created posts, they appoint some
of the local superiors, they follow the development of the action
undertaken, and ensure a constant link with the hierarchy.
The Provincials are appointed by the General from a list of
three names put forward by the Consult (or Council), of each
Province. No superior, other than the General, is elected.

The Congregation is the supreme authority within the Society. It places its trust in the General but gives him instructions and the mandate to carry out the decrees it has voted. The General is elected for life, but the assistants can ask him to resign. In extreme circumstances they can even force him to. So far, however, the case has never arisen.[3] The Provinces are grouped, by region, into 'assistancies' enjoying a certain amount of autonomy. The principle is always to favour personal relations between individual Jesuits and authority.

Between sessions of the General Congregation, general policy is fixed every three years, alternately by an assembly of Provincials and by the congregation of 'procurators' – delegates elected by the Provinces. For the latter, as for the election of delegates to the General Congregation, the provincial congregations have legal capacity. These congregations, made up of about forty delegates elected by all the members of the Province who have made their final vows, also examine the 'postulates' put forward by the communities or by any single member of the order. The possibility of getting the whole order to discuss a given matter, or even to change course, is thus safeguarded thanks to this decentralization, right down to the individual.

'Electoral campaigns' are forbidden in the Society, and anyone canvassing for power is immediately disqualified. Apart from the office of General, no responsibility is entrusted for life. There is no question of having to put up with an 'impossible' Provincial for more than six years, nor any other superior with an overdeveloped taste for authority. Without being democratic, far from it, the administration of the Society is thus less rigid than has often been said. Its verticality is corrected on every level by the freedom to assert personal desires and by the obligation to monitor the exercise of power.

The balance obtained does not exclude fresh initiatives. Provincial assemblies – at which student Jesuits, but not novices, are present – and congresses for Jesuits engaged in various specialized sectors allow the Society to assess continually the quality or shortcomings of its commitments. The sector-based meetings take place either in Rome or some other venue. Jesuit ecumenical experts, for example, met in Montreal in 1981, following a tradition started during the Council. Eurojess, an association of Jesuits interested in social sciences, organizes a symposium every two years. In 1983, in Ludwigshafen (West Germany), the theme was 'Evangelization and secularization of society in Europe'. European writers of Jesuit journals meet every year to discuss their experiences and exchange ideas.[4]

Opportunities for numerous meetings contribute to form the order's pyramidal structure. Thus the relationship established on an individual basis between the superior and his subordinate is reproduced at a collective level. In spite of inevitable conflicts between the aims of the central authority and the projects at the base, the system is sufficiently flexible to allow, indeed encourage, invention.

Fr Vincent O'Keefe, who was 'assistant' during Fr Arrupe's generalship, spoke willingly about this concern for practising dialogue and collegiality within the Society:

'We work more and more as a team at all levels. Previously, when a new provincial was appointed he was called to Rome for a meeting with the General. Nowadays he comes to Rome to take part in a "colloquium" of superiors. This is what happens: a group of superiors and provincials – including the new one – spend two or three weeks together in our villa near Frascati with specialists in "group dynamics", experts of Ignatian spirituality, lay specialists in management and so on. This permits a real exchange of ideas and work as a group. The new provincial leaves with the impression of having shared a common vision rather than of having been given his marching orders.'

No doubt on account of its organization, the variety of the Society's commitments and the concern for original experiments do not seem to have suffered from the identity crisis diagnosed by Paul VI. This is probably because there is no such thing as a typical Jesuit and, therefore, no collective 'identity' to suffer crises. Asked once to define the Society's 'political line', Peter-Hans Kolvenbach replied: 'There are 23,000 Jesuits, so there are 23,000 political opinions!' The following potted biographies of a few Jesuits, chosen at random, will give some idea of the diversity of the Society.

The Jesuits have always had researchers within their ranks, not only in theology and philosophy, but in all 'secular' branches. Several, especially in France, are involved with human sciences – sociology, psychoanalysis and linguistics.

The Americans, for their part, do not shrink from the latest technologies. Timothy E. Toohig, a nuclear physicist, was a member of the team at the Fermi National Accelerator Laboratory, in Batavia, Illinois. It is over 30 years now since he lived within a Jesuit community. As 'relaxation' after the stresses of the laboratory, he would read theological books, 'those of Rahner, Dulles and Schillebeeckx'. An unusual life?

> Not at all, my life is absolutely in the Jesuit tradition rather than something extraordinary. And science is an aid to humility. The very nature of scientific research, the quest for one tiny piece of the puzzle that forms the structure of the universe prevents an honest man from becoming arrogant.

Jorge Roberto Seobold, now in his sixties, used to divide his time between two apparently incompatible sectors: an inner-city area in Buenos Aires and solar physics. A strange destiny, brought about by the Society's dual attraction for scientific ventures and social commitments. Jorge was an engineer when he entered the Jesuits in 1956. During his novitiate, to gain experience he was sent to work in a foundry as an unskilled labourer. One day, he recounted, the workers came up to him and asked him: 'Padrecito, please don't work so hard, stop for a bit and tell us something about your life and God.' The young student priest realized that social commitment did not mean that one had to 'burn all one's books'.

He returned to his studies, specializing in physics. After his ordination to the priesthood, he joined the National Commission for geoheliophysics as a research scientist; he was later appointed as head of the department for solar physics. He did not, however, move out of the Guadalupe district where he had been living for several years, along with 20,000 Italian immigrants. In 1985, he said:

> I don't believe I have finished my research; I feel that science is intimately bound up with people. It was in this sense that the 'Principle and Foundation' of the *Exercises* became real for me. When I read that all things are made for man and that man is made for God, I interpret 'man' as meaning 'people'.

As for Joseph D. Sheehan, he is a most unusual missionary. He lives in a community of 29 Jesuits serving nineteen small parishes or mission stations among the Oglala Sioux, in South Dakota. Fr Sheehan was once the Provincial of Wisconsin. His Indian 'vocation' arose from a simple idea that often comes to Jesuits who are prisoners of their speciality: the need to live in direct contact with people. Joseph was delighted with his choice, even if it was far from easy, because it taught him something that is rarely suspected by the public at large:

> I live among a people corrupted by their oppression at
> the hands of White men, who settled in their country and
> continue to this day to dominate and exploit them, although
> it is now done rather more subtly than before ... I have never
> seen anywhere a people so deeply wounded by what they
> have had to suffer. The impression of life without hope,
> of unrelieved suffering, tends to affect those working with
> them. I have worked as hard as I could, but I often have the
> impression that it is leading nowhere. I have never felt so
> helpless with my 'ready-made answers' to their problems.

These Jesuit pioneers do not always come up with 'revolutionary' solutions. Before going to join the mission in Chad, Fr Jean Robinne worked among the Portuguese in France for ten years. In September 1978, he took over from a Portuguese priest in the zone of Champigny-Villiers, a dormitory town south-east of Paris, where approximately 15,000 Portuguese live. 'I was overburdened with liturgical duties: five masses in Portuguese every Sunday; 500 children attending catechism; weddings, baptisms ...' A Jesuit's work is not always glamorous! Fr François Yverneau chose to work among immigrant workers, as a packer, on night shift.

> I saw how the Algerians were despised by my French
> companions. It's instinctive: racism is deeply rooted in our
> education and history. I couldn't speak out in public, but I
> tried to give a good example. I made the odd remark to force
> my workmates to question their attitude. But as a trades union
> colleague told me once: 'If we took a stand on that subject,
> we would simply be lynched!'

A Spanish Jesuit, Ismaël Santos, spent thirty years of his life giving sermons, retreats and novenas throughout Spain and then Latin America. On his return he felt uncomfortable: 'Filling in for others with no job of my own did not attract

or satisfy me', he confided to his Provincial, adding that
his heart's desire was to become a country priest. It just
happened that there was a very difficult parish in need
of a priest. No diocesan priest wanted it. The one who
had stayed there the longest had only managed to last
two years. But a Jesuit, perhaps? The provincial's suggestion was immediately taken up by Santos. And he did
not regret it.

In Toronto, Canada's main industrial centre, Fr Doug
McCarthy founded a new type of community in 1973. He
runs The Red House (so called because of its red bricks)
with Louise and her husband Dick, a former Jesuit. They
take in, and care for, ex-prisoners and mentally handi-
capped adults. For the first few weeks, Doug had the
feeling that he had left the Society. Surrounded by his
friends, he declared later: 'The Red House seems to be
built on one of the most essential and most neglected of
human rights: the right to love.' Can this be described as a
'normal Jesuit life'? When Fr Arrupe spoke to the members
of the English-speaking province of Canada in 1973, he
stressed the need to 'Pray and be poor'. The former General's instruction has, at the Red House, become part of
everyday life.

Three Jesuits in Patna, the capital of Bihar in north-
eastern India, have learnt this lesson. They have invented
a new form of ministry in the 'experimental centre' they
opened in 1971. The activities offered are traditional (camps,
retreats, a youth magazine), but the community has opted
for an 'open house'. Everybody is welcome, day or night,
even if this meant that 'we didn't have a moment to
ourselves, for personal meditation or prayer'. Mass is con-
celebrated late in the evening, and it is a lengthy affair.
For the rest, each Jesuit 'spends some time every day
with the Lord, according to his personal convictions and
possibilities'. One of the group says that he is aware
of the suspicion about this flexible lifestyle entertained
by certain superiors, for whom 'it is impossible to be
a good Jesuit without an hour each morning devoted to
meditation or contemplation', but he maintains his point
of view:

For someone who is totally absorbed in the daily life of the
people he is helping, it isn't always easy to find a whole
hour for prayer. But on certain days, he will spend two
hours meditating! The important thing is to be honest with
oneself and to take one's spiritual life seriously.

These thumbnail sketches of a few 'typically atypical' Jesuits
were taken from a document published a few years ago by
the Secretariat of Ignatian Spirituality in Rome, entitled 'How
Jesuits reconcile prayer and work in their lives'. But similar
portraits could be drawn today, wherever Jesuits are to be
found. Leafing through the 1994 Yearbook, published by the
Jesuit Curia, one is still struck by the diversity of the Society's
activities. Here are a few examples:

Fr James Martin writes about his work with the homeless
in East Africa. A member of the Jesuit Refugee Service, he
explains how

in Tigray, northern Ethiopia, we have made a commitment
to the local diocese to help the area to recover from chronic
famine and drought, and offer our services to over 300,000
refugees. In a land devastated by seventeen years of civil
war, we have a team of health workers, experts in water
resources and sanitation programmes, rehabilitation for the
war-wounded, agriculture, women's promotion and small
industries.

To the question as to whether this is religious or social work,
he replies:

With at least fourteen Jesuits full time, and twenty religious
and lay people in the field in Sudan, Kenya, Ethiopia and
Uganda, JRS in East Africa is striving to fulfil the vision of
St Ignatius and Pedro Arrupe in caring for, living with and
loving those in greatest need.

Maharashtra, the third biggest State in India, is a large semi-
arid region with a population of 70 million people, the bulk of
whom depend upon rainfed agriculture and forests for their
sustenance and livelihood. In 1989, a German Jesuit, Fr Herman
Bacher, conceived and launched the Indo-German Watershed
Development Programme, involving the co-operation of village
self-help groups, non-governmental organizations, financial

institutions, government departments etc. The final objective: to enable villagers to develop their own watershed (drainage basin). As Fr Hans Staffner writes,

> The result has been dramatic. Despite a rainfall of only 250 millimetres in 1992, there was sufficient drinking water for the village, grain output has increased by 100 per cent and fish farming has been successfully introduced. More important, caste and class differences have been greatly attenuated and a working friendship established. Ecology has transformed common folk from a silent majority into a dynamic people, capable of improving their own social, political, economic, cultural and spiritual situation.

Many Australian Jesuits are involved in ministry to the country's indigenous peoples, who form two culturally distinct groups: Aboriginal peoples (several hundred different tribes before colonization) and Torres Strait Islander peoples. Fr Brian McCoy writes:

> Our ministry among the Aborigines began in 1882, when Austrian Jesuits travelled from the south of Australia to the Northern Territory. An important focus of our work has been a concern for the training of Aboriginal Church leaders. To date, most of our work has been in urban centres, but over the years we have discerned the need for the Society to be involved with more traditional communities, which provide a kind of 'spiritual heartland' for Aboriginal people. A final and crucial part of our Aboriginal ministry is social analysis. We contributed our research to the Royal Commission into Aboriginal deaths in custody, and some of our members act as lawyers to defend Aboriginal rights.

Fr Frank Brennan is one such Jesuit lawyer, and he recalls:

> I entered the Jesuits in 1975, having studied law and politics. The Provincial asked me to develop my legal skills for the service of the Aboriginal people, who have suffered two centuries of dispossession since the arrival of the British to the Australian continent. As in Canada and the United States, the land rights of our indigenous people have become a very political issue. Some Aborigines think they have suffered too much and gained too little from two centuries of Church people doing good on their behalf. Only through strong and consistent advocacy will they be convinced that the Church

supports them in their struggle for justice, recognition and reconciliation.

One of only eighteen African-American Jesuits in the United States is Fr Eugene Turner.

Of the 4,358 Jesuits in the United States [4,261 in 1994], eighteen are African Americans. The first African-American Jesuit, Patrick Francis Healy, a former slave, entered the Society in 1850, well before the Civil War and Abraham Lincoln's declaration of Independence. He became president of Georgetown College in Washington, which he turned into a university, becoming known as its second founder. Many people did not know that he was black, since his father was Irish and his mother a slave ... Most African-American Jesuits believe that the Society can have a significant influence in addressing the problems of social injustice which African Americans face: 62 per cent of African-American children are born in fatherless households. The homicide rate in the United States for Black males is seven times that of White males. 43 per cent of Blacks live under the poverty line and there are more African-American men between the ages of 17 and 25 in prison than at university.[5]

Fr Lars Reuter writes from Denmark that

Contrary to popular belief there are indeed Catholics in the Nordic countries. Sandwiched between the continent of Europe and the Scandinavian peninsula is the *Regio Daniae,* the Jesuit missionary region of Denmark, which comes under the jurisdiction of the North German Province. The region embraces Iceland and Norway, as well as the Danish dependencies of Greenland and the Faroe Islands. There are two Jesuit bishops: Alfred Jolson, Bishop of Reykjavik (Iceland), and Hans Martensen, whose diocese of Copenhagen (geographically the world's largest) includes Greenland and the Faroes. As in most Western countries, the average age of Danish Jesuits is rising. Luckily, we have men from England, Holland, Hungary, Italy, Poland and, most recently, the United States. Men who, following the Jesuit tradition of inculturation, now regard this 'foreign' country as their home!

On the other side of the world, in Bombay, a Jesuit publishing house, Gujarat Sahitya Prakash, recently published an album of poems, notes and drawings of a fourteen-year-old

Sikh schoolgirl, named Gitanjali after the title of the popular, Nobel prize-winning book of verse by Rabindranath Tagore, the Indian poet-philosopher. It is yet another example of the eclecticism of the Society of Jesus. Fr Parmananda Divarkar explains why the Indian Jesuits are interested in the painfully scribbled writings of a child, who was dying of cancer while studying at a convent school in Bombay:

> She was a lively and popular youngster, full of fun and fond of sports. But at the age of fourteen, her health began to deteriorate, and she soon discovered (nobody knows how) that she was terminally ill. So as not to cause pain to her mother, she decided to keep her secret and face the crisis all by herself. But she was not alone; she was very conscious that God was with her: 'I pray for strength and feel it coming to me, and I know it comes from a higher power.' She manifests a maturity that is rare in the average adult, and seems closer to the wisdom of a sage and the vision of a saint: 'Though I cannot blot out death altogether, I try not to get frightened ... Having to be brave is not easy, nor is it an overnight effect; one has to work on it; it is a gradual process ... I pray to God that he will be with me and give me courage in the face of death. I know he is waiting for me and I am not afraid to face him.' A Christian might say that her dispositions are Christ-like; a Jesuit may even find in them an echo of the *Exercises* of St Ignatius.

These few examples of Jesuit diversity are the result of Fr Arrupe's invitation, spelt out in the 32nd General Congregation, to explore unknown paths and to clear away the dead wood accumulated over the centuries. In this way, innovation can exist alongside the traditional activities of the Society. In fact, many Jesuits are still engaged in giving retreats, serving in parishes, catechetics, preaching, writing or simply counselling others: all classical forms of an apostolate which has never been abandoned.

The network of Jesuit retreat houses remains widespread and varied and, as we saw in the Introduction, there has even been a revival of interest in the *Spiritual Exercises*, with new ways of practising them in one's everyday life. There is also interest in other forms of spirituality: the Charismatic movement has found favour with some Jesuits, especially in France and Belgium, and the Jesuit residence of Bad-Schönbrunn, in central Switzerland, has been experimenting with an adaptation of Zen Buddhism to the Ignatian method. The former Jesuit novitiate of Les Fontaines in Chantilly, north of Paris (a town famous for its horse races and whipped cream), has been turned into a conference centre, whose pastoral setting and library of 600,000 books attracts a large and varied public.

Even Fr Dezza, the Pope's man, admitted in a letter addressed to the whole Society in 1982 that

> the Jesuits are composed of a wide variety of races, cultures and mentalities, not to mention the difference of generation (. . .). To which must be added the different schools of thought which have appeared in the Church following the Council, and which are naturally reflected in the Society.

The famous Jesuit 'mould', whether at intellectual or spiritual level, does not hamper growth of personality or character. The most revolutionary theologian can live side by side with the most hidebound preacher. One Jesuit burns his draft papers in public while another is an army chaplain. A research scientist is often the colleague of a simple teacher. Jesuit communities have been known to include a poet, a psychoanalyst and a television producer, and a worker-priest can hold a degree in philosophy.

And yet, paradoxically, a certain Jesuit identity does exist: all these different men are united by a common tradition and a single passion, a 'family spirit' which allows them to adapt to every situation. This strength is also the Society's weakness. To maintain this unity is a perpetual struggle, and the new generations, often searching for security, hesitate more than before to join an order that seems unsure of its future. Candidates are still prepared to accept the risk, though: in 1993, 600 novices entered the Society, and 562 in 1994. And the variety of their backgrounds also explains the diversity of the order. The problem, as Fr Kolvenbach pointed out, is to discern their motives and weed out the 'social climbers' (particularly in the developing countries) from the truly committed.

The question of the necessity of maintaining, or re-creating, a Jesuit 'model' is hotly debated in the Society. Fr Jan Kerkhofs, a Belgian Jesuit who used to run the Pro Mundi Vita centre in Brussels, known for the excellence of its sociological studies, and who now lectures at the Catholic University of Louvain, is clearly opposed to conformity:

'Polarization exists within the Society, and we already have to live with it. To solve the crisis, we mustn't try to achieve an artificial levelling or normalization, but rather allow the polarization to increase while maintaining communion and encouraging dialogue. For this, total honesty is a prerequisite.'

According to Fr Michel de Certeau too,

'an objective "model" no longer exists, there is only a certain empirical "process". We must accept what I call *ruptures restauratrices* (breaks necessary for renewal): it is necessary to break with the past and, instead of seeking a single solution, undertake a variety of experiences. We must be willing to make mistakes and take the wrong road. We must take risks and open a number of experimental "laboratories".'

But if the model no longer exists, are there any Jesuits left? It is true that, in the past, Jesuits were like chameleons who know how to adopt their background colouring. But at least they knew who they were. Today, many, whether members of the Society or not, wonder about their specific identity. Is Ignatius of Loyola's brilliant intuition still relevant or does it belong to the mentality of a bygone age?

The numerous Jesuits I have questioned in preparing this book have not always given a straight answer. Some of them reduced 'Jesuit specificity' to so little – 'complete availability', 'a great flexibility of action', 'a passionate devotion to St Ignatius for Christ's sake' – that it is scarcely different from that of all Christians. Others stressed Ignatian spirituality, notably the *Spiritual Exercises*. Thus Fr John O'Malley defined the Society as

'a religious order fully dedicated to the help of souls (and bodies) that looks not to some form of social discipline but to inner assimilation of the life-giving truths about our human nature and our relationship with God. This has specificity through the principles and orientation of the *Spiritual Exercises* and through certain developments in our tradition, such as the cultivation of the arts and secular disciplines.'

Fr Leo O'Donovan pursued the same line of thought. Indeed he began by quoting the author of *The First Jesuits*.

'Fr O'Malley gets down to basics by saying that the specificity of the Society is the old ideal of the *imitatio Christi* as this is formulated in the *Spiritual Exercises*, a spiritual document that in turn emphasizes the personal communication each human being receives from God. Most fundamentally, then, the specificity of the Society comes from the spiritual outlook of the *Exercises*: a love for God's creation, a desire to serve and imitate Christ incarnate in creation, a respect for the individually created human person and a respect as well for the manner in which the Creator communicates with each person.

'One historical manifestation of this outlook has been the Society's commitment to education, not just for its own members but for all God's children. As a professional theologian and, now, as a university president, I see the Society's specific contribution to the world of ideas. That is one specific, and very typical, service the Society has provided to the Church, and through the Church, to the whole of this good creation redeemed by Christ. A personal and notable example of this specific service is the career of my old mentor, Karl Rahner.'

Fr Jean-Yves Calvez, then editor of *Etudes*, said: 'We have never really bothered about our specificity, since we don't like to be tied down. Finally, everything boils down to the "discernment" we show in a given situation, deduced from the *Spiritual Exercises*.' And Fr Henri Madelin sees the problem as one of 'visibility' and of pastoral priorities:

'As "Friends of the Lord" we are a community of "life" rather than of "prayer". Fr Kolvenbach has also insisted on the importance of our colleges. In the Lebanon, we have maintained our colleges, and in the United States, there is a Jesuit rector in each high school. In Asia, on the other hand, our work is carried out mainly in parishes and among young people. In Europe, our task is to form the laity, by individual instruction and a return to the *Exercises*. I like to quote Dietrich Bonhoeffer's remark: "We must speak in a secular fashion of religious things, and religiously of secular matters." In a nutshell? We must form people for others.'

Others again stress the need for Jesuits to find a new specific 'strategy'. The French Canadian Jesuit Julien Harvey thinks it is necessary

'to define a new project. This could be twofold. Consisting, on the one hand, in showing the relevance of the *Spiritual Exercises* to the new youth culture (a renewed interest in meditation, Zen Buddhism, the New Age, etc.), and developing, on the other, the "prophetic" wing of the Society, engaged in left-wing causes: sharing the life of the homeless and generally opposing the consumer society.'

All were agreed on one point, however: the external aspects of Jesuit life must change radically. But all did not go as far as Jan Kerkhofs, for whom

'the Society of tomorrow will not be a "religious order" because, in a secularized world, traditional religious – who are "super-Christians" within the Christian community – will no longer have a role to play. The Society of Jesus, whose specificity is to discern the true liberation of man, will open its doors to everyone: men, women, married couples, Protestants . . .'

The Counter-Reformation is dead indeed if a Jesuit suggests letting Protestants in! It is perhaps a rather liberal interpretation of Fr Kolvenbach's definition:

'I would define a Jesuit as a frontiersman, whose task is to bring the Gospel to unknown territories, not in a spirit of conquest but to help people. I prefer agricultural imagery to military metaphors, and I would say that our task is to sow, not necessarily to gather in the harvest.'

Anglo-Saxon Jesuits are perhaps less revolutionary. Fr Robert Murray, who lectures at Heythrop College, in the University of London, defines the specificity of the Society as 'Discipleship of Jesus; building up the *total* People of God in faith and self confidence; Christian humanism; openness to the true values of all peoples'. Fr Edward Yarnold, of Oxford, speaks of 'a close attachment to Jesus Christ, and a consequent missionary thrust. Willingness to be sent by superiors to wherever there is judged to be fruitful work. The recognition of every moment as a challenge to discern, and lovingly do God's will. A breadth of mind which is able to recognize the truth contained in others' opinions.' For Fr Michael Campbell-Johnston, 'the fundamental specificity comes from the *Spiritual Exercises* and the Ignatian spirituality that flows from them. Arrupe was fond of quoting Ignatius's expression *nuestro modo de proceder* ("our way of doing things").' While Fr Vincent O'Keefe describes the Society soberly as 'a group of men who live together as "friends in the Lord" and discern, by reading the "signs of the times", what is for God's greater glory and the good of souls'.

Perhaps the most complete definition, however, was supplied by Fr John Padberg:

'The Society of Jesus is, first of all, at the service of the Gospel. So are all Christians, of course, but it has to be emphasized that Jesuits are first and foremost believing and practising Christians, not some kind of super *savants* or compassionate social workers. The Society is Christian in its Roman Catholic form. This may seem utterly obvious, but one sometimes gets the impression from some of its friends that it would be so much more attractive if it were not Roman Catholic. Not so. Jesuits would not be Jesuits if they were not Catholic.

'The Society is a religious order, not simply an assemblage of well-intentioned people. Rather, it is a group of men committed to each other as a religious order, with the properties, such as the vows characteristic of all orders, and committed to the service of the Gospel, Church and human family. The Society is an active religious order, whose members carry out their vocation of commitment to each other, to others, to the Church and to the Gospel not primarily by contemplative prayer but by active service. That active service is in principle universal. It is not confined to one area, one group of people or type of ministry, but rather is open to any and every kind of service.

'Because the Society is open to a universal service, while at the same time its individual members are obviously not omnicompetent, those members are prepared or "formed" at some length and depth, both in a common spirit and in particular areas of expertise. While these particular areas depend on the needs and circumstances of particular times and places, and on the talents of the members, the common spirit arises especially out of the simultaneously individual experience of making and then living out the *Spiritual*

Exercises, and the shared experience of doing so within the framework of the *Constitutions*. In other words, while the *Exercises* individualize the charism or central characteristics of the Society of Jesus, the *Constitutions* "corporatize" those characteristics of the Jesuit precisely as a member of the Society. In preparing its members, living its life and carrying out its work, the Society relies on decisions that are carried out by a form of centralized governance that is simultaneously directive and personal, because through the practice of discernment it is cognizant of both the individual members and the corporate body.'

Fr Padberg sums up the above in two sentences:

'The Society of Jesus is a religious order of men explicitly Christian and Catholic, which lives out its life as a companionship shaped specifically by the members' individual experience of the *Spiritual Exercises* and by the corporate experience of the *Constitutions*. This dual experience leads individual members to serve God, the Church and humanity, and the Jesuit community to undertake different "missions" or "active apostolic ministries" discerned by its members or confided to it by the Church and at times specifically by the Pope.'

NOTES

1 W. W. Meissner SJ, MD, *Ignatius of Loyola: The Psychology of a Saint* (Yale University Press, 1992).
2 John W. Padberg SJ, 'Ignatius, the Popes and realistic reverence', *Studies in the Spirituality of Jesuits* (May 1993).
3 Fr Arrupe was the first General to have resigned of his own accord.
4 The best-known Jesuit periodicals, throughout the world, are *America* (United States), *The Month* (Great Britain), *Stimmen der Zeit* (Germany), *Etudes* (France), *Civiltà cattolica* (Italy), *Orientierung* (Switzerland) and *Nouvelle Revue Théologique* (Belgium).
5 A Black Jesuit from Chicago, George Murray, was appointed Auxiliary Bishop of Chicago in January 1995.

Conclusion

A RETURN TO THE MINIMA SOCIETAS JESU?

> *And if the Society of Jesus should disappear?*
> *What of it? The Church would survive.*
> ANDRÉ RAVIER (Jesuit historian)

> *If you stay with me, Jesus, even unto death,*
> *I shall be your companion for ever, and neither*
> *the Pope nor Satan can prevent it.*
> A JESUIT, at the time of the suppression (1773)

The time has come to confirm my initial hypothesis. By the recent diversification of their activities, putting the accent on the human sciences, and the shift in their priorities, choosing to help the poor, haven't the Jesuits, far from renouncing their love of power, simply taken over new positions of influence and decision-making? Before examining this possibility in the light of factors that are obviously too complex to admit such a simplistic explanation, it will be useful to recall the historical context which gave birth to the Society of Jesus. A birth which coincided with the Renaissance and the Reformation, two capital events – in many ways contradictory – which shaped the nascent Society. The Jesuits were involved in both and often paid the price of their audacity.

The risk was twofold. The first danger was an excessive engagement in 'worldly' affairs – one can even speak of an early attempt at secularization. St Ignatius's intuition, in refusing to confine himself and his companions to a monastic cloister or to tie them to the liturgical offices that punctuate the working days of contemplative monks, was a belief that the world can be conquered for God through human means, the resources of culture and the riches of nature. But the risk was great (and by no means illusory, as history has shown) of being diverted by these means and of seeking influence, glory and power as an end in themselves; in other words, of replacing faith in God by a purely 'horizontal' humanism. Hence the Jesuits' reputation for intrigue and casuistry. Were they not accused of having coined the phrase 'The end justifies the means'?

The second danger – contrary to the first – was of becoming more papist than the Pope. If the Jesuits were often vilified by kings, presidents and politicians of all shades of colour – so as to be expelled or banished 74 times in the course of their history – it is largely due to their devotion to papal policy, a loyalty rarely recompensed. The most ungrateful of all the Popes, as we have seen, was Clement XIV, who took the cowardly way out by simply abolishing the order.

After the first period of its flamboyant history, when the Society tried to marry the Gospel to humanism, decidedly in advance of its time, by its experiments with inculturation in China and its anti-racism in Latin America, the second period was marked by an equally dangerous alliance with the papacy against Protestants, Republicans, Liberals and Socialists. Increasingly, and right up to the present century, the Society sided with Roman orthodoxy, defending the unchanging tradition of neo-scholastic morality. It became identified with order, unity and indefectible fidelity to the Pope. This is why the change in direction endorsed by the 32nd General Congregation, at the end of 1974, took so many by surprise. Was it possible that the 'progressive' plague had contaminated the Pope's Praetorian Guard?

Observant Jesuit-watchers, however, had seen the premonitory signs. It must be remembered that Fr Arrupe was elected in 1965, at the end of a Council in which the Jesuits had played an important part, especially such theological heavyweights as Karl Rahner, John Courtney Murray, Joseph Jungmann, Henri de Lubac, Jean Daniélou, Augustin Bea, and the like. It was logical therefore that the Society should have been in the forefront of conciliar renewal.

Furthermore, given the high level of intelligence and efficacity of the Jesuits, once the reform movement had got under way it was bound to go far. Whereas other religious communities, less well-structured or simply more divided, hesitated to advance, the Jesuits raced ahead.

This watershed coincided with a rediscovery of the initial intuitions of the *minima Societas Jesu* (small Society of Jesus) dreamt of by Ignatius. If the worldwide membership of the Society is still impressive, the drop in vocations, at least in the West, has necessitated a certain redeployment of troops, leading to the gradual removal of Jesuits from important institutions – universities, colleges, institutes, residences – to give priority to the missions, the founder's first vocation.

The British province is a good example of this. The former provincial, Fr Michael Campbell-Johnston, has returned to his first love, Central America, where he is working with the poor. His successor, Fr James Crampsey, a Scot, admits that dwindling numbers pose a problem to the Society's commitment to education. Even the prestigious public school Stonyhurst has only one Jesuit on the staff, the chaplain. Fr Crampsey explains:

'Since I joined the Jesuits in 1964, the shift has been from schoolteaching to adult education. This is also a result of the renewed interest in spirituality. There is a real thirst for the *Spiritual Exercises* and we have developed a new expanded method, spreading them over nine months, to allow the laity to participate fully.'

Vocations are stabilized at about five a year, but the entrants are older and more experienced. The average age of British Jesuits is a little under 60 years of age. 'If Jesuits are few in number', adds Fr Crampsey, 'they play a leading role in the country's intellectul life.' Fr Jack Mahoney, for example, is an expert on bioethics and, after a skirmish with Cardinal Ratzinger, he moved into a new field. Author of *The Making of Moral Theology*,[1] he now teaches business ethics in the London Business School. Fr Robert Murray, who lectures at Heythrop College, is engaged in writing the 'definitive book' (*sic*) on the prophetic ministry, commissioned seventeen years ago (!), to examine 'how the prophetic charism is discerned and how

utterances which present a *prima facie* claim to be prophetic
are evaluated'. Representing the more conservative faction,
Fr John McDade edits *The Month*.

Can one then conclude that the Society's change of course
was motivated by the desire to 'regain power'? Framed in
such crude terms, the answer is obviously no. It is difficult
to doubt the sincerity of men who announce their intention
to live a more authentically evangelical life by making a 'preferential option for the poor', often at the risk of their lives, as
we have seen in Central America and Africa.

In fact, it is this aspect of self-sacrifice – the exact opposite of
the tarnished image of the Jesuit as *éminence grise* – that attracts
today's candidates to the Society. According to Karl Rahner:

> 'The Society does not attract the attention of the media
> these days on account of its exalted position in the Church,
> or because it still runs a large number of universities and
> produces experts in many fields. Neither is it because, in
> many countries, it has chosen to align itself more markedly
> than in the past with the poor and the oppressed. In my
> experience, it is because in its pastoral, ecclesial and socio-
> political activities it tries modestly, with more or less success,
> to provide disinterested service, through prayer, submission
> to the mystery of God and the serene acceptance of death,
> whatever form it might take, according to the will of Christ
> crucified.'

Without underestimating the attraction of the noble ideal
expressed by the German theologian, it cannot be denied,
however, that many Jesuits, by instinct or choice, choose to
specialize in those advanced fields of research which are vital
for the future of humanity. And even in the social domain, they
are often in the forefront. A cunning ploy? Possibly, but this is
not the only explanation. It is also the result of intellectual curiosity and, above all, the desire to bring the Gospel to all forms of
human activity. This is entirely consonant with Ignatian 'active
contemplation', faith lived in the world according to a fragile
alliance between humanism and the Gospel.

And what does the future hold? First of all, the Jesuits like
to recall, with mock humility, that the Society of Jesus has

not received the promise of eternal life. 'And if the Society of Jesus should disappear?' asks the Jesuit historian André Ravier, answering,

> What of it? The Church would survive. But why speak in hypothetical terms? On different occasions in its history, in certain regions, the Society was suppressed and its members dispersed. (...) Ignatius only founded the Society because, together with his companions Favre, Laynez, Xavier, Borgia, etc., he wished, in answer to Christ's call and with the help of his grace, 'to love and serve the eternal King and universal Lord Jesus Christ'. In founding an order on this premise he was taking an emormous risk: at each moment in its history, the 'value' of the Society of Jesus would only equal the worth of its individual members.

When the order was suppressed in 1773, a Jesuit wrote: 'If you stay with me, Jesus, even unto death, I shall be your companion for ever and neither the Pope nor Satan can prevent it.' And it is the Jesuit's spiritual framework, tempered by the *Spiritual Exercises*, that provides him with the strength to undergo trials, whether they come from the world or the Church itself.

For Karl Rahner, it is because of its unwavering loyalty to Christ that the Society can permit itself

> 'to criticize the Church, and itself, so severely, that it can embark upon unknown journeys; and that it is able to envisage its own history, with its successes and failures, its glorious episodes and pettiness, and even its own annihilation (if this should happen) as a sharing in the destiny of Him whose name it bears, not without pride but with tranquil assurance.'

But, leaving aside these Jesuit clarion calls, what does the future hold for one of the most controversial religious organizations the Church has known? In spite of the recent crisis it has undergone, and in spite of the – temporary? – drop in vocations, it is not likely to disappear in the near future. After the 33rd General Congregation and the election of Fr Kolvenbach, and convened anew for the 34th General Congregation, the largest Catholic religious order is simply at a new turning-point of its chequered history.

First, one must ask what Fr Peter-Hans Kolvenbach has achieved in the decade since his election. Has he given in to the temptation, proffered by a worried papacy, of seeking to regain a certain 'power' – albeit spiritual – by becoming once more the Pope's elite corps and 'strike force'? Or did he have the courage to pursue the open and courageous policy adopted by the previous Congregation in 1975, which defined two priorities: 'the service of faith and promotion of justice' and 'the inculturation of Jesuits in the Third World'?

The second question that comes to mind is: what does the present General Congregation hope to achieve? Are we about to witness a new change of direction? Or even the resignation of Fr Kolvenbach as rumour would have it? In short, what are the major problems facing the Society of Jesus as it approaches the year 2000? I put these questions to a number of influential Jesuits throughout the world, starting with the black Pope himself.

With regard to the first question, some answers were supplied at the end of the Introduction to this book. Peter-Hans Kolvenbach is difficult to pigeonhole as left-wing or right-wing. He is 'elsewhere': neither Roman nor Third World leaning, he is an Orientalist. His studies in history and linguistics have not cut him off from the modern world, however. The long years he spent in Beirut proved him to be an effective and subtle mediator, whose advice and help were sought by all: Christians, whether Latin or Eastern-rite, Catholic or Orthodox, and even Muslims. Having adopted the Armenian rite himself, he rises early to say his long Oriental Mass since he finds the Latin Mass too short. He has no illusions about the too-human aspects of the Church, but he is enough of a diplomat to appease the Roman congregations.

This is where his humour comes in useful. When he was summoned by Cardinal Ratzinger, Prefect of the Congregation for the Doctrine of the Faith (formerly the Holy Office), who complained that ten or so of his Jesuits were giving him cause for concern, Fr Kolvenbach is said to have burst out laughing, saying: 'That's wonderful news! Only ten out of 23,000!' He is above dabbling in curial intrigue, and shows great deference to the Holy See, without giving way on basic principles.

Everyone agrees that relations are more cordial between black and white Popes. Fr Kolvenbach speaks of 'mutual trust', adding ingenuously, 'Our relations are excellent, although (because?) we don't often meet!' More seriously, he explains that 'the communication gap which existed between Fr Arrupe and the Holy See has been breached. It is not to my credit, or on account of my supposed diplomatic talents, but thanks to Fr Dezza. On Arrupe's resignation, the Pope said: "I don't want a repetition of the 32nd Congregation." It was Fr Dezza who persuaded him to allow the election of a new General. I can't pretend that conflicts with the papacy never crop up, but this is not a problem specific to the Jesuits.'

It is true, nonetheless, that Fr Kolvenbach adopted a low profile after his election. He also kept his public declarations to a minimum, in the early years at least. His first 'message' to the whole Society was 23 lines long. After paying tribute to 'the spiritual and apostolic impetus which the Lord gave us through the mediation of Fr Pedro Arrupe', he concluded by saying:

> It is with great faith in the Society that I have taken on this task. The Lord wants to use it to announce the Good News to men of today, in their own language and according to their lifestyle, with a pastoral preference for those who suffer the injustices of this world, and thus to serve the Lord's Church and the Vicar of Christ, Pope John Paul.

This says it all, in very few words: the two priorities defined under Fr Arrupe's generalship, 'faith and justice' and 'inculturation', as well as the service of the Church and the Pope. His second public utterance, a sermon preached on the feast of St Ignatius on 16 September 1983, was 28 lines long. The Kolvenbach era opened with the utmost discretion. But discretion doesn't imply surrender. As we have seen, Fr Kolvenbach not only upheld but even 'reinforced', as he put it, the Arrupe line. Examples include his attitude to the Refugee Service and his understanding of 'Jesuit education'.

When he toured Latin America at the end of 1984 – shortly after the reservations expressed by the Holy See about liberation theology and the 'political commitment' of priests and religious – he stated:

> the real criterion of our evangelical commitment to the poor is not whether we engage in politics or not, for, in a certain sense, we are constantly engaging in politics. It is rather a question of assimilating the following paradox into our lives: only a poor person can get rid of poverty. You can be certain

that no-one will be expelled from the Society solely for having worked with the poor.

Some months later, in March 1985, Fr Kolvenbach addressed a letter to all the Jesuits, presenting a summary of the 1,500 reactions to the 33rd General Congregation, sent in by the regional superiors. The letter is a broad endorsement of the main lines of Fr Arrupe's policy. Stressing the 'unanimous welcome' given by the Society's members to the 'return to normal government', which 'some feared would be difficult if not impossible', Fr Kolvenbach speaks of the need to 'make the most of the spiritual legacy of the last congregations and of Fr Arrupe'.

'After a period of testing and deep suffering which provoked much soul-searching', he continued, 'the 33rd Congregation sends the Society on a mission, once again, to announce the Gospel to non-believers and to those who believe differently, rather than to the faithful of God's Church.' All the missions with which the Pope has entrusted the Society 'require research, experiments and projects which could lead to misunderstandings and even accusations'. According to the General, the authenticity of the mission is guaranteed by 'poverty and discernment'. With regard to poverty, 'several Jesuits would like a more incisive prophetic stand and the announcement of a certain number of concrete measures' designed to make our daily life more compatible with apostolic poverty. Given the cultural diversity and variety of situations, the General asked each Jesuit to react personally.

Admitting that the General Congregation 'has not solved all the theoretical and practical problems, or dispelled all the ambiguity inherent in the promotion of justice through service of the faith', Fr Kolvenbach stressed nonetheless how the liberation theology debate proves that

> the Church is eager to clarify this question, which is the
> object of its apostolic option. (...) The Society's solidarity with
> the poor has a specificity which differentiates it from a political
> party, a trades union or a development organization, because
> this option considers the poor as persons who do not live by
> bread alone.

Repeating that 'the priestly ministry is incompatible with certain social commitments', the General recalled the 'ecclesial dimension' of the Jesuits' apostolate. 'Some of you might imagine that my insistence on this point is a strategic move to ameliorate our relations with the Holy See', added Fr Kolvenbach. 'But everyone must bear in mind that no Jesuit acts alone. We are members of the Church, even if our mission can require initiatives which invite incomprehension.'

The General has been far from inactive. Apart from several other letters to the Society, he has granted a dozen interviews to the press, including the main American dailies. He has also considered setting up a theological commission, which would allow the moral theologians in the Society's different faculties to co-ordinate their research and air delicate questions in the present repressive climate. So far, such a creation has seemed inopportune, lest it appear as a rival to the Vatican's International Theological Commission. Jesuits make do with such existing bodies as the Federation of Catholic Universities, or the Conference of Catholic Theological Institutions, which meets every three years, to exchange their ideas. Fr Kolvenbach does not forbid his theologians from carrying on their research, he merely suggests that they do not seek the official approbation of the Jesuit Curia or of the Holy See, nor give press conferences, but simply publish their work in serious journals.

The General is fully aware that the Society has a responsibility in the moral and ethical domain.

> 'We have to answer people's legitimate questions. It is high
> time, for example, to re-examine the teaching on natural
> law. Or take genetic manipulation, with its ability to split
> embryos, which has been very much in the news recently.
> This raises the fundamental question: if we have the ability
> to do something, does that mean we have the right to do it?
> The prodigious progress of science has simultaneously given
> humanity the capacity to perform technological miracles for
> human benefit and to violate taboos in a way that could
> lead to human self-destruction. We cannot make science
> solely responsible for solving the world's problems or we
> will paradoxically end up achieving the exact opposite.
> Technological progress makes it possible for humanity to
> achieve greater mastery over the universe, but it also increases
> our capacity for destroying the universe.'

A final quotation should set our minds at rest as to whether

Fr Kolvenbach's social conscience is as acute as Fr Arrupe's. In
his address to the participants at the International Workshop
on Ignatian Pedagogy in 1993, he spoke of the social implica-
tions of Christian humanism.

> The root issue is this. What does faith in God mean in the
> face of Bosnia and Sudan, Guatemala and Haiti, Auschwitz
> and Hiroshima, the teeming streets of Calcutta and the broken
> bodies of Tiananmen Square?
>   What is Christian humanism in the face of starving millions
> of men, women and children in Africa? What is Christian
> humanism as we view millions of people uprooted from their
> own countries by persecution and terror, and forced to seek a
> new life in foreign lands? What is Christian humanism when
> we see the homeless that roam our cities and the growing
> underclass who are reduced to permanent hopelessness? (...)
> Late twentieth-century Christian humanism necessarily includes
> social humanism. As such, it shares much with the ideals of
> other faiths in expressing God's love effectively by building a
> just and peaceful kingdom of God on earth.

As for my final question – what are the challenges facing the
Society in the third millennium which the 34th General Congregation placed on its agenda? – I have already quoted Fr
Kolvenbach's reply at the end of the Introduction. I asked him
if he had considered resigning before the end of his mandate,
or whether he respected the tradition of life tenure for Jesuit
Generals.

> 'The Pope's present ill-health is a subject for reflection. Since
> his hip operation he is visibly unwell, his hands shake and
> he seems in pain. Yet he insists on deciding everything,
> overseeing everything. Recently he dealt personally with
> two minor points concerning our General Congregation,
> which could easily have been handled by a subordinate. He
> refuses to delegate his authority, and is already speaking of
> celebrating the third millennium of Christianity.
>   With regard to the Jesuits, St Ignatius laid down the
> principle of life tenure for the General, but even he foresaw,
> in the *Constitutions*, the possibility of a General being
> removed. When a General is elected, no one asks his opinion,
> and in the same way he can be deposed without being
> consulted. His four General Assistants can decide that he is
> no longer capable of running the Society and they simply tell

him: *"Tempus est"* (The time has come). I have no immediate intention of resigning, but I have a problem: bishops are required to tender their resignation at the age of 75. Now if a bishop is deemed unfit to run his diocese after the age of 75, what about running the worldwide Society of Jesus? I shall follow with interest what the cardinals have to say about the resignation of bishops.'

Here is a selection of the other replies I was given concerning the General Congregation and the future of the Society:

Fr Julian Fernandes saw things from his Indian viewpoint.

'I think there should be a reaffirmation of our two basic commitments: our work with the poor and the development of the notion of inculturation. We must present our Indian point of view at this important meeting in Rome where we shall have the chance to review our way of life, here at the centre of the Society. We shall also review the law of the Society (the *Constitutions*), in order to map out our future course of action. We have to find new answers to new problems. We must avoid the temptation of remaining trapped in a given period of the Society's history – such as the privileged Arrupe era – and look ahead. The mass of "consultations" (letters sent from all over the world) can create a climate of change.

'Fr Kolvenbach possesses a different charisma from that of Arrupe. He does not wish to repeat the past, although he does quote his predecessor. He has said that he does not intend to resign, although a procedure exists in theory ... Like bishops who are asked to resign, a General can be asked to step down if he is considered unfit. This happened in the eighteenth century. Of course he is free to raise the question at our Congregation, but the Pope is against changing what he considers the essentials, like the fourth vow or the resignation of the General. He is afraid of our spirit of innovation, of the turmoil that would affect other religious orders if we Jesuits decide to change too much ...'

Fr José-María de Vera, of the Jesuit press office, was more concerned with the mechanics of the operation.

'The "previews commission" (*coetus praevius*), composed of 220 Jesuits, met in Rome in July 1994 to study the voluminous mail received from the Society throughout the world. There are 700 requests from the Provinces to debate certain questions at the Congregation, including: co-operation with the laity; the status of the Jesuit brother; and the international

activities of the Society. Then in September, Fr Kolvenbach
addressed a document (summarizing this mass of letters) to
the whole Society. In October, he attended the Synod of
Bishops, whose theme is the consecrated life.'

With regard to the rumoured resignation of Fr Kolvenbach, Fr
de Vera recalled that the final decision lies with the Pope:

'As a result of the Fourth Vow, it is up to the Holy See
to accept the General's resignation. Fr Arrupe wished to
resign, but the Pope refused. After Arrupe had suffered a
stroke, it was necessary to replace him. The problem of a
General being incapacitated is a real one. Especially now that
people live longer. The time will come when the General's
resignation is accepted as a matter of course, but I don't think
Fr Kolvenbach intends to step down for the time being.'

Fr Michael Czerny is a member of the preparatory team of the
General Congregation. For two-and-a-half years, he has been in
charge of the Jesuit Social Secretariat, created twenty years ago
to advise the General on social matters and to facilitate communication within the Society. Since the 'justice versus faith'
controversy has finally been resolved, a consensus having been
reached over the last twenty years, he sees the Society's task
as having shifted from ideological tension to practical enquiry.
What this means in concrete terms is helping the poor and
the suffering: AIDS patients, refugees, victims of famine and
injustice.

The paradoxes are numerous: the emergence of misery
and delinquency in the affluent West, after the collapse of
Reaganism and Thatcherism, whereas the Third World has seen
the collapse of alternative theories: the co-operative movement,
Marxism, land reform, and so on. This has led to the mirroring
of the First and Third Worlds: they share a tragic similarity.
Jesuits must deepen their commitment and concentrate on the
essentials by shortening their list of priorities.

Although Fr Mark Raper will not be participating *ex officio* in
the Congregation, he intends to put in a word for his refugees:
'I shall be in and out of the office, and shall be able to keep
an eye on the proceedings. To my mind, it is vital that the
23,000 Jesuits realize the importance of the Refugee Service for
the Society. Our work is a profoundly disturbing experience,

and a salutary one ...' Fr Federico Lombardi, another Roman Jesuit, and director of programmes at Vatican Radio, will also be pleading his cause. He will take part as an elected delegate although there will be no *ex officio* representative of Vatican Radio. 'I hope that the Society is aware of Vatican Radio's contribution to the field of social communications', he says modestly, 'and that I can contribute usefully to the debates.'

Among the themes on the agenda, Fr Gianpaolo Salvini, editor of *La Civiltà cattolica*, singles out three:

'Firstly inculturation. In Asia, for example, Christianity is practised by a small minority and Christ is virtually unknown. There are even Jesuits who hold that we can reach God by another route than Christ. This needs discussing . . . Another theme is our collaboration with the laity. This is a necessity, both theologically and practically – to save our institutions. A third problem, and one that worried Fr Arrupe, is the declining number of temporal coadjutors (non-priestly Jesuit brothers). In the *Annuario Pontificio* the Jesuits are described as a clerical order. We must rediscover the vocation of the Jesuit brother. He belongs to the original Ignatian intuition and if he were to disappear something would be lacking ...[2] We should be able to provide a solid Jesuit formation and professional training for someone who doesn't become a priest.'

For him, the major tasks facing the Jesuits in the coming century are:

'the struggle for justice and the evangelization of new cultures. There is no longer *LA civiltà cattolica* (a single Catholic civilization) but several. Today's quarrel is less between science and faith than between culture and faith; it is rather a question of indifference than militant atheism. People have learnt to live without God. They have difficulty in accepting a revealed religion and prefer a "self-service" spirituality.'

Fr Henri Madelin sees the Congregation largely as an exercise in *aggiornamento*:

'We shall draw up new documents, or refer to existing ones, to "spring clean" our legislation: the famous Fourth Decree (on faith and justice) in particular. The Roman synod on evangelization will take place just before, and we shall no doubt translate into Jesuit terms the evangelization of a new world (science, technology, materialism, religious indifference, etc.).

'Western Europe poses a special problem, with its lack of vocations. What does it mean to be a Jesuit today? How can we be "prophetic" in a Church which is tempted to return to its conservative policies? The Congregation will also re-examine its Constitutions with regard to the "degrees" and the rarefaction of Jesuit brothers. Other themes include: co-operation with the laity; evangelization and culture; ecumenism.'

As for the rumour of Fr Kolvenbach's resignation, Fr Madelin is sceptical:

'I think he will maintain a low profile. Perhaps he is preparing a surprise . . . for three years from now? You know very well that the Pope is opposed to such a move. The 31st Congregation maintained the tradition of life tenure, but in the light of longer life spans and the nomination of younger Generals, it has become necessary to allow for the possibility of resignation, either voluntarily or on the advice of his assistants . . .'

Regarding the challenge to the Society of tomorrow, Fr Madelin insists on the religious specificity of the Jesuits.

'Our first task is to be irreproachable as religious. Only then can we branch out to society and the world at large. The Jesuits are tired of politico-religious controversies. They are now seeking to reinforce the religious pole. We are laying a new emphasis on retreats, on the *Spiritual Exercises* (in Great Britain and France). The Society is getting rid of its unwieldy institutions, and this will allow it to find more time for its activities outside of the Society. This is positive in France, where Jesuits teach at the Catholic Institute, engage in research, etc. We must be present in public debate, we must write, speak on radio, appear on television.'

Fr Robert Drinan, Law Professor at Georgetown University Law Center – who is in favour of life tenure for Jesuit Generals – seems concerned above all by the drop in vocations in Western countries:

'Obviously, one of the major problems of the Congregation is to devise ways by which we can increase vocations to the

Jesuit order. It is encouraging to see the number of Jesuits
in Africa, India and elsewhere increasing substantially. A
decline in vocations in the United States is, of course, very
discouraging, but perhaps the Holy Spirit is trying to tell us
something.'

Fr Leo O'Donovan, President of Georgetown University,
points out, first of all, that

'once it gathers, the General Congregation will itself decide
what it considers to be the most pressing problems it must
address.[3] This is its right and history. In anticipation of the
Congregation, however, various commissions have addressed
at least the following: conforming the Society's legislation
to the universal law of the Church, a task made necessary
by the promulgation of a new code of canon law; dealing
with the vocation and the role of the Jesuit brother, a task
made necessary by the drastic decline in the number of Jesuit
brothers, among other reasons.

'Overall, most Jesuits still ask how the Society should live
up honestly to its stated commitment – dating from the 32nd
General Congregation – to have a concern for justice in all
its apostolic endeavours. How, concretely, to make good on its
commitment to live according to a "faith that does justice"? This
is a long-term programme that takes on new forms and makes
new demands as the years pass and political configuration
changes – think, for instance, how different Europe is now
from what it was before 1989 and how many demands for
justice cry out to the world from present-day Africa.'

Fr O'Donovan recalls that the 31st General Congregation
(1965–66) 'provided for the possibility of a General submitting
his resignation for considerations of age or health', and that this
legislation, which he considers to be 'sound', was approved by
the Holy See at that time.

For Fr Joseph Fitzpatrick of Fordham University,

'One major problem facing the Society and the General
Congregation is that of maintaining an adequate Catholic and
Jesuit presence, especially in our colleges and universities.
This raises the question of identifying what it means to be a
Catholic and a Jesuit university at the present time.

'The major tasks of the Society in the coming century will
differ in different places. In the United States, it is a problem

of relating our vast institutional presence to the decline in the
number of Jesuit priests, and to the challenges of education
which will certainly develop in the next century. In South
America, the major task will be one of social justice and the
"preferential option for the poor". This will be very difficult
and at times probably painful. In Africa, it will be the task of
developing Jesuit resources to support the rapid increase in the
number of Catholics throughout the continent, and of assisting
Africans to stabilize their nations, politically and economically.
In Asia, the task will be to relate the Church to the vast
millions of non-Christians who have enjoyed a long and rich
religious tradition.'

Fr Fitzpatrick is in favour of a fixed term for the General:

'It should be generous enough to enable him to accomplish
something and short enough to avoid the risks of serious
illness. I think a period of fifteen years would be reasonable.'

Fr John O'Malley, Professor of Church History at Weston
School of Theology and author of *The First Jesuits*, sees the
need for defining priorities:

'The Society receives many urgent appeals for help and sees
many situations it would like to address. I see two problems
here: first the temptation to ride off in all directions at once,
without setting out some concrete areas where we should
especially direct our energies. These would have to be generic,
since the Society is in such different situations in different parts
of the world. I really think that the special priorities suggested
by John Paul II could well be those areas – "ecumenism, the
deeper study of the relations with non-Christian religions, the
dialogue of the Church with cultures, etc."

'The second problem is that, given the urgent need for
priests in parishes, we might neglect our special call to address
needs beyond "the people in the pews". The latter are the
concern of the diocesan clergy. Among the things that have
made the Society special historically has been its cultivation of
learning beyond the so-called sacred sciences, so that we can be
a real bridge between the Church and culture.'

According to Fr Vincent O'Keefe,

'The principal problem facing the Congregation is: determining
the apostolic priorities for the next century, taking into account
the real needs of the Church and the decrease and "graying"

of Jesuits. For example, can the Society maintain all its present activities, especially in the field of education, or will it have to rethink the ministries it should be involved in?'

Fr John Padberg, director of the Institute of Jesuit Sources in St Louis, is concerned about the transmission of the Jesuit heritage:

'the handing on of the Jesuit ethos, charism and spirit to the lay co-workers of the Society, who will eventually surely be responsible for Jesuit institutions. Faced with this diminution of numbers, the Jesuits will have to decide in what specific works and institutions the Society will continue to invest its manpower.'

As for the coming century, Fr Padberg sees as primordial

'the task of cultivating the imagination to envision new challenges and new opportunities that have not yet even appeared. Intelligence and good will and even, in some cases, heroism are not lacking to the Society.'

Fr Padberg 'doubts very much' that Fr Kolvenbach intends to announce his resignation at the 34th Congregation, adding sternly that

'It would be irresponsible to have allowed the Society to hold provincial congregations, decide on postulates and elect delegates without knowing that one of the central functions of a congregation, the choice of a General, was to take place. On the other hand, I can see the Congregation passing legislation making it easier than it is at present for a General to resign.'

Fr Michael Hurley, an Irish Jesuit, writing for the magazine of the Social Justice Secretariat in Rome, *Promotio Justitiae*, in June 1994, would like to see the revival of a forgotten Jesuit practice: peacemaking.

Reading John O'Malley's *The First Jesuits* I discovered to my surprise that 'reconciling the estranged' (*dissidentium reconciliatio*) is included in the list of ministries given in the 'Formula of the Institute' (. . .). The dissidents in question are feuding groups or factions, and the reconciliation intended is bringing the feuds to an end. O'Malley devotes a three-page section to this special ministry and, very significantly, entitles it 'peacemaking'.

If, as the Congregation approaches, we remind ourselves and
are convinced that 'reconciling the estranged' is a privileged
ministry of the Society, it will clearly apply, without much if
any broadening of its original scope, to Northern Ireland, to
Bosnia, to every place where there is violent fragmentation
along ethnic, national, racial, religious or tribal lines, not
forgetting the polarization in the Church itself. We may go
about it differently from the early Jesuits, but the reconciliation
of feuding, warring factions everywhere must remain a priority
for us. These must surely include couples facing marital
breakdown, Orthodox and Catholics, Protestants and Catholics,
the employed and unemployed, women and men, mother Earth
and her children, Jews and Christians and very many others.

Fr Michael Campbell-Johnston, director of the Pedro Arrupe
Jesuit Development Service in San Salvador, pleads for
boldness and inventiveness. He writes:

'A Spanish Jesuit magazine recently described the main problem
facing the General Congregation as accepting the challenges
of a world in transformation. It goes on to say: "The world
pushes God more and more to one side, injustice is rampant,
horrific socio-economic imbalances abound, modern society
rejects the most basic values. Can a Jesuit ignore this? Can he
in conscience stand aside from these problems? Can he allow
his vocation to confine itself to rearguard actions when the
seriousness of the situation calls him to the front line, however
great the risk?"'

'I would hope that the 34th General Congregation will face
up to this challenge with the boldness and inventiveness that
was such a characteristic of Fr Arrupe, even when under great
pressure from conservatives in the Society and the Vatican. I
was with him during his last few active days as General, in
the Philippines and Thailand. He gave a great talk to some 75
international Jesuits in Manila, the gist of which was: "Be bold,
be adventurous, don't get into a rut, don't be afraid of making
mistakes." I believe the Society needs to rediscover something of
this spirit if it is to confront some of the main problems facing
it and the Church today.'

This Congregation will give the Society of Jesus a new
occasion to reaffirm its commitment to the Second Vatican
Council and to the policy laid down by Pedro Arrupe thirty
years ago and defined by the 32nd General Congregation

twenty years ago in its Fourth Decree on 'the service of faith and promotion of justice'. It will take place towards the end of John Paul II's reign, at a time when the papacy, as conceived by a conservative Polish Pope, has grown strong and centralized at the expense of the national colleges of bishops and the local Churches.

Whoever is chosen as the next Pope – Italian or Third World cardinal, conservative or progressive, pastor or intellectual – he will surely need a strongly motivated Society of Jesus at his service. Among the *papabili* already being mentioned by Vatican-watchers, a name heads the list: that of Cardinal Carlo Maria Martini, Archbishop of Milan (the largest diocese in the world by the number of its priests and laity), 66 years old, and a member of the Society of Jesus. A former Rector of the Gregorian University and of the Biblical Institute in Rome, this brilliant Jesuit, who speaks eleven languages, is a biblical scholar and the author of 40 books on the Scriptures, spirituality and sociology. In an interview he granted *Le Monde* in January 1994, he spoke of the needs of the Church in a very positive way.

'Too many couples think that the Church is not tolerant or comprehensive enough. Too many scientists feel that it puts barriers in the way of their research. If the Church's pronouncements are seen as threats, prohibitions and condemnations this is because we don't make the effort to present the essential Gospel message. What is essential is not the strict observance of a set of rules, but the courage to rediscover one's dignity and freedom. (...) St Paul says that precepts kill. The Church should follow St Paul! No-one is saved by precepts. They are saved by grace and by being given a high ideal to follow. The Church shouldn't worry as to whether its rules are obeyed or not, it should ask whether men are fired with the ideal of the Gospel. A Church which refers to the Gospel is a Church which isn't obsessed by imposing laws and observances, but which offers an ideal to all men.'

Cardinal Martini doesn't rule out the possibility of ordaining married men to the priesthood, 'in certain parts of the world where the crisis is profound, and as an exceptional measure'. This solution already exists, he adds, 'with the conversion of Anglican clergymen and the arrival in Europe of married Catholic priests of the Eastern rite. With time, the question will become less controversial.' The Jesuit cardinal tried to avoid criticizing John Paul II, but when asked what he thought of the harm done to ecumenical relations by the Pope's insistence on a strong Catholic identity, he replied:

'It is true that the institutional Church has proved less permeable to the Council than we had imagined in the sixties; true also that the reaffirmation of our Catholic identity is sometimes badly conceived and badly presented. When I opened our diocesan synod in Milan in November 1993, I stated that we refused to reaffirm our Catholicism, to engage in proselytization or to seek to regain influence. We merely wanted to be ourselves, at the service of society, without harming anyone. I also invited representatives of all the Christian Churches of the region, who were permitted to take part in the discussions.'

To the final question as to whether he still intended to go to live in Jerusalem when he retired, or whether he wouldn't prefer to be buried in the crypt of St Peter's,[4] he replied: 'I should like to end my days in Jerusalem, the Holy City where human history finds its meaning. I should like to be buried there because that is where the tomb of Christ is, nowhere else!'

The Congregation opened therefore at an uncertain time, when Church leaders are tempted to turn the clock back, seeking refuge in the old certainties of a fortress-Church, triumphalistic in its self-satisfaction and relying more on authority and coercion than prophetic and visionary leadership. Will the Society of Jesus have the courage to refuse this temptation and follow the course charted by the visionary Pedro Arrupe and maintained courageously by Peter-Hans Kolvenbach? If so, its 'power' to influence, guide and inspire the coming generations will be more than welcome.

NOTES

1 J. Mahoney, *The Making of Moral Theology* (Oxford, Clarendon Press, 1987).

2 The papal bull *Exponis Vobis* of Paul III (1546) officially established the grade of 'coadjutor' (spiritual and temporal helper) in the Society. The first companions of St Ignatius attracted people who wanted to be associated with them to help carry out the

apostolic activities of the first Jesuits. Among those who wanted to be part of the Society there were both priests and laymen who were accepted as spiritual coadjutors, if they were priests, and temporal coadjutors if they were not ordained. Among the issues the 80 provinces of the Society wish to see discussed at the 34th Congregation is that concerning the vocation and mission of the Jesuit brother in contemporary society. At the death of St Ignatius in 1556, the Jesuit brothers represented 25 per cent of all the Jesuits. This proportion was maintained until around 1920. From that date, a decline in numbers has recently accelerated so that in 1994, the 2,735 Jesuit brothers represented only 11.8 per cent of the 23,179 Jesuits. The 33rd General Congregation (1983) stated: 'The Congregation once again proclaims and affirms the incalculable value of the brothers' vocation, through which the Society develops its mission to the full. The Society needs the brothers, first of all for themselves and then for their labours, for the sake of both its communities and its apostolate.' In the history of the Society of Jesus, five brothers have been canonized and 30 beatified.

3 See Preface, pp. vii–viii.
4 It is in the crypt of St Peter's Basilica, in Rome, that recent Popes are buried.

Index